COLLECTIVE REMEMBERING

INQUIRIES IN SOCIAL CONSTRUCTION

Series editors
Kenneth J. Gergen and John Shotter

This series is designed to facilitate, across discipline and national boundaries, an emergent dialogue within the social sciences which many believe presages a major shift in the western intellectual tradition.

Including among its participants sociologists of science, psychologists, management and communications theorists, cyberneticists, ethnomethodologists, literary theorists, feminists and social historians, it is a dialogue which involves profound challenges to many existing ideas about, for example, the person, selfhood, scientific method and the nature of scientific and everyday knowledge.

It has also given voice to a range of new topics, such as the social construction of personal identities; the role of power in the social making of meanings; rhetoric and narrative in establishing sciences; the centrality of everyday activities; remembering and forgetting as socially constituted activities; reflexivity in method and theorizing. The common thread underlying all these topics is a concern with the processes by which human abilities, experiences, commonsense and scientific knowledge are both *produced in*, and *reproduce*, human communities.

Inquiries in Social Construction affords a vehicle for exploring this new consciousness, the problems raised and the implications for society.

Also in this series

The Social Construction of Lesbianism
Celia Kitzinger

Rhetoric in the Human Sciences
edited by Herbert W. Simons

Texts of Identity
edited by John Shotter and Kenneth J. Gergen

Acknowledgements

The initial idea for this volume grew from a workshop on Collective Memory: Some Issues and Approaches, held at the Communication Department, University of California, San Diego in April 1986 in conjunction with the Laboratory of Comparative Human Cognition (LCHC). The lively intellectual environment of LCHC and Michael Cole's suggestion that such a workshop be organized was crucial to the evolution of this book. The papers from the original meeting were reported in LCHC's *Quarterly Newsletter*, 9(1), 1987. Continuing contact between LCHC and the Discourse and Rhetoric Group (DARG) at Loughborough University of Technology, England broadened the scope of the original workshop. As the project developed scholars from other institutions became involved. The chapters of this volume thus represent the continuing interest in studying remembering as a social activity at Loughborough and San Diego in addition to sampling the work beyond those two institutions.

We gratefully acknowledge all those persons who have patiently contributed to the preparation of this volume: our colleagues and friends at LCHC and of the Department of Communication at the University of California, San Diego; members of DARG and other friends and colleagues within the Departments of Human Sciences and Social Sciences at Loughborough. We should also like to thank all the contributing authors who were so generous of their time and co-operation, and Sue Jones of Sage Publications.

Contents

Chapters 1, 2, editorial matter and arrangement
© David Middleton and Derek Edwards 1990
Preface © Michael Cole 1990
Chapter 3 © Alan Radley 1990
Chapter 4 © Michael Billig 1990
Chapter 5 © Barry Schwartz 1990
Chapter 6 © Michael Schudson 1990
Chapter 7 © John Shotter 1990
Chapter 8 © Yrjö Engeström, Katherine Brown,
Ritva Engeström and Kirsi Koistinen 1990
Chapter 9 © Julian E. Orr 1990
Chapter 10 © Carol A. Padden 1990
Chapter 11 © David Bakhurst 1990

302
Col
1990

First published 1990

SAGE Publications Ltd   SAGE Publications India Pvt Ltd
28 Banner Street   32, M-Block Market
London EC1Y 8QE   Greater Kailash - I
                               New Delhi 110 048

SAGE Publications Inc
2111 West Hillcrest Drive
Newbury Park, California 91320

British Library Cataloguing in Publication Data

Collective remembering. – (Inquiries in social construction series)
  1. Social psychology
  I. Middleton, David   II. Edwards, Derek   III. Series 302

ISBN 0-8039-8234-8
ISBN 0-8039-8235-6 Pbk

Library of Congress catalog card number 89–69831

Typeset by Photoprint, Torquay, Devon
Printed in Great Britain by Billing and Sons, Worcester

COLLECTIVE REMEMBERING

EDITED BY
DAVID MIDDLETON
and DEREK EDWARDS

SAGE Publications
London · Newbury Park · New Delhi

Preface

Michael Cole

Although it is extremely hazardous to undertake the explanation of a single historical event (some would say, impossible), I will invoke the privileged rhetorical status of the preface-writer to suggest why a book on collective memory holds special interest for both the social sciences and society at this particular juncture in human history.

As anyone who has read a newspaper or watched television in the last decade is aware, the problem of collective memory is a familiar and emotion-laden political issue for people throughout the world. When I first accepted the task of writing these remarks, the leadership of the Chinese People's Republic was providing this generation with a televised lesson in the relationship between memory and power. Not only did it deny at first that anyone had been killed in the army's assault on students in Tienanmen Square, the government went so far as to declare it a crime against the state for any Chinese citizen to 'spread rumours' that such killings had occurred. A clearer illustration of George Orwell's syllogism for the ages, 'He who controls the past controls the future; he who controls the present controls the past', could hardly be imagined.

The problem is by no means a new one, nor is it restricted to any one national group. In his brilliant and moving meditation on human nature, *The Book of Laughter and Forgetting*, Milan Kundera reminds us that:

> The bloody massacre in Bangladesh quickly covered over the memory of the Russian invasion of Czechoslovakia, the assassination of Allende drowned out the groans of Bangladesh, the war in the Sinai Desert made people forget Allende, the Cambodian massacre made people forget Sinai, and so on and so forth . . . (p. 7)

Kundera suggests that the problem of socially organized forgetting is particularly acute at present because historical events occur with such rapidity on such a mass scale that they cannot be adequately assimilated into everyday experience. To this we can add the fact that in the modern world, while events halfway around the globe may have a major impact on local life, individuals have no direct experience of the events affecting them, learning about them only through the selective screen of centrally controlled media.

When that tiny segment of society whom it is fashionable to refer to as social scientists attempt to study the process of memory and forgetting, issues of power and self-determination are rarely (I am tempted to say never) at issue. As the editors of this fine book on collective remembering, David Middleton and Derek Edwards, point out in their informative introduction, memory is ordinarily considered the province of psychologists, and as 'everyone knows', psychology is the value- and power-free study of processes taking place inside the heads of individual human beings. For the past half-century, memory, the particular topic of this book, has been seen as either the accumulation of strength to habits resulting from reinforcement and frequency of occurrence, or as a system of storage and retrieval mechanisms operating in the manner of a digital computer. Working within a scientific division of labour that ceded to sociology and anthropology the explanation of behaviour of social collectivities, psychology could conceive of socio-cultural influences on memory in one of two ways. First, it could easily grant that the contents of memory are social in so far as they arise from social experience or are transmitted as lexical items in the course of communication. Secondly, it could accept that experience in different kinds of social environments may inculcate particular ways of remembering by influencing the particular social contexts that people inhabit. Thus, for example, children who have attended school may acquire special mnemonic techniques there.

A common persuasion uniting what might on other grounds be considered a quite heterogeneous collection of essays in this volume is the rejection of this view of human memory. Whether in an attempt to explain how Americans remember Abraham Lincoln or the British their Royal Family, the current authors both reject the interconnected set of dichotomies upon which the modern social sciences were founded and display a willingness to search for new paradigmatic frames for interpreting the phenomena of memory. Perhaps the most central belief that unites them is their rejection of the assumption that it is possible to maintain a strict separation between the individual and society, an assumption which can be traced back through Descartes to Plato. Once the mind and memory are seen as extending beyond the 'individual skin' to encompass both the cultural milieu and the 'body politic', other dichotomies fall too. The notions that psychological content can be strictly separated from process, or that science can be strictly separated from history by its reliance on the experimental method, come in for pointed, sceptical scrutiny.

What emerges from this examination of memory as a socio-culturally constituted process in which the individual and the social are united in cultural artefacts is both a challenge to the existing division of scientific labour and a roadmap to new forms of scientific practice. In these new practices, issues of power and the self-determination of people(s) will no longer be cut off from scientific inquiry into memory.

It should not go without note that, although the majority of the authors have obtained their degrees in psychology or sociology, only two are currently associated with departments bearing these disciplinary insignia. Instead, we see the emergence of new academic collectivities, all of a character that at present we label 'interdisciplinary'. It is out of such efforts that the new disciplines which await us in the twenty-first century will arise; and with them, hopefully, new and more powerful ways of conceiving of the phenomena of human remembering.

To return to the issue with which I began these remarks: this book has appeared at the present time and deserves the reader's full attention because of a world-wide rejection of the political and scientific common sense of the early twentieth century, and the concomitant search for a new paradigm for living.

List of Contributors

David Bakhurst Department of Communication, University of California, San Diego, USA

Michael Billig Department of Social Sciences, Loughborough University, UK

Katherine Brown Department of Sociology, University of Illinois, Urbana-Champaign, USA

Michael Cole Department of Communication and Laboratory of Comparative Human Cognition, University of California, San Diego, USA

Derek Edwards Department of Social Sciences, Loughborough University, UK

Ritva Engeström Department of Sociology, University of Helsinki, Finland

Yrjö Engeström Laboratory of Comparative Human Cognition, University of California, San Diego, USA

Kirsi Koistinen Department of Education, University of Helsinki, Finland

David Middleton Department of Human Sciences, Loughborough University, UK

Julian E. Orr System Sciences Laboratory, Xerox PARC, Palo Alto, California, USA

Carol A. Padden Department of Communication, University of California, San Diego, USA

Alan Radley Department of Social Sciences, Loughborough University, UK

Michael Schudson Department of Communication, University of California, San Diego, USA

Barry Schwartz Department of Sociology, University of Georgia, Athens, USA

John Shotter Faculty of Social Sciences, Rijksuniversiteit te Utrecht, Netherlands

1

Introduction

David Middleton and Derek Edwards

No one could claim that the study of human memory is a forgotten topic. Frances Yates, in her authoritative book *The Art of Memory* (1966) traces dispute on the topic back to the philosophical discussions of antiquity and in modern times memory is subject to a wide spectrum of scholarly and popular debate. The content of contemporary work also reflects a constantly changing emphasis on just what questions to ask, and how to conduct the enquiry. However, within that great variety of work, from psychoanalytic accounts of 'repression' to computer simulations of 'memory processes', the predominant focus of enquiry has been the study of memory as a property of individuals, or at the very best extending beyond individuals to include the *influence* of 'context' on what people remember. There exists a certain 'repression' for recognizing the social as a central topic of concern. When social 'factors' are considered, they are invariably treated as a social 'context' enriching the physical 'background' against which people exercise an individual 'capacity' to remember.

To treat the social as only situational to, or at best facilitative of, a person's memory is still to attempt what might be described as a 'single-minded' approach. The essays presented in this volume foregound a changing emphasis, or perhaps 'recollection' in approach – a shift from a predominant concern with individual memory, as process or content, to a direct consideration of remembering and forgetting as inherently social activities. Such an approach acknowledges the link between what people do as individuals and their socio-cultural heritage. These essays illustrate how to approach remembering and forgetting as activities that are studiable as part of the ordinary circumstances of daily life. Of particular interest is the way remembering and forgetting are integral with social practices that carry with them, in important ways, a culturally evolved legacy of conduct and invention, both material and social, central to the conduct of daily life.

Moves to consider the social aspect of remembering are not new. A heritage of late nineteenth-century and early twentieth-century

2 *Collective remembering*

European and American scholarship can be found across a wide range of disciplines. The French literature is particularly rich, including the sociological writings of Durkheim (1893/1984; 1895/1982), and especially those of his student Maurice Halbwachs (1925/52; 1951/80), and in addition the influential discussions of psychiatrist Pierre Janet (1928). While Durkheim's work has been taken up by European social psychologists, in the form of 'social-representation' theory (Moscovici, 1984), modern pyschological interest in the social basis of memory and remembering has a more direct source in the writings of the British psychologist Frederick Bartlett (1923; 1932). The anthropological discussions of Evans-Pritchard (1940) drew from both the French literature and Bartlett's early concerns with social institution and memory. There is the pathfinding psychological research of Vygotsky (1929) and his Soviet colleagues Alexander Luria (1968) and Alexander Leontiev (1981) within what is known as the 'socio-historical tradition' of psychological research (see for example Wertsch, 1987). In America the social behaviourism of George Herbert Mead (1934) and Grace de Laguna (1927) established a socially orientated research agenda on remembering.

Some Contemporary Background and Issues

This widespread literature, whilst certainly read and influential in its own right, never became established as representing 'mainstream' issues in the psychology of remembering and forgetting. Remembering and forgetting are widely recognized as socially significant issues. As Ulric Neisser observed recently, inverting an earlier admonition to psychologists on the dearth of socially relevant memory research, 'if X is an interesting or socially significant aspect of memory, some psychologist is probably trying to study it at this very moment' (Neisser and Winograd, 1988: 2). However, the study of human memory as a social process in its own right has still to receive the full attention of psychological research. Whether the work represented in this volume will contribute towards moving social issues more to the forefront of the psychological research agenda remains to be seen. However, there may be grounds for optimism because this volume does not stand as an isolated example of socially orientated approaches to the study of memory. Psychology, with its tradition of theory and method derived from the experimental study of individual memory, is no longer accorded a monopoly of interest in the topic. Beyond the boundaries of psychological discourse can be found a well established and burgeoning interest in the social nature of memory. These are to be found within the writings of oral history, folklore, museum studies, historical geography, communication studies, sociology and social theory. Oral historians come to the area through discussions of 'popular memory' (Johnson, McLennan, Schwarz and Sutton, 1982). The notion of 'popular memory' refers to commonly held representations to be found in the oral accounts people give of past events, traditions, customs and social practices. Discussions of popular memory immediately extend beyond a conceptualization of memories as the property of individuals. Two important issues within oral history are the reliability and verifiability of oral-witness testimony (for example, Davis, 1988). This concern for variability in oral accounts and testimony has an important bearing on a social perspective on remembering. David Thelen, in a detailed and informative introduction to a special issue of the *Journal of American History* on 'Memory and American History' (1989), makes the following point: 'In a study of memory the important question is not how accurately a recollection fitted some piece of a past reality, but why historical actors constructed their memories in a particular way at a particular time.' Variability does not have to be viewed as revealing mere methodological problems of how to establish the facticity of any person's account. It can become a resource for revealing the relationship between what people remember and the ideological dilemmas of their past and present socio-economic and political circumstances (Passerini, 1984/87; Schrager, 1983).[1] Thelen also reviews a number of ways in which the study of social history 'opens up promising fields in the study of memory' (1989: 1125). In particular, 'the struggle for possession and interpretation of memory is rooted among the conflict and interplay of social, political, and cultural interests and values in the present' (p. 1127). He observes also that the 'historian's narrative tradition' has 'deeply embedded' within it the recognition that the constructive nature of remembering 'is not made in isolation but in conversation with others that occur in the contexts of community, broader politics, and social dynamics' (p. 1119). Such discussion is part of a wider debate of the way history and memory bear an interdependent, yet contestive, relationship to one another (Davis and Starn, 1989).

Folklorists have an equivalent set of concerns with the social content and process of memory; but in addition 'variation through time and space is for folklorists a defining feature of their subject matter, oral or material. . . . Without significant differences around a core of similarity folklorists would not be able to detect the stamp of different tellers interacting with values and concerns held in common and made shareable through tradition' (Davis, 1988: 110).

Variability of re-presentation within particular genres, be they dance, song, theatre or story, carries with it a social memory marking continuities in the community of participation out of which any particular performance has developed. Unique features of individual performances become part of the tradition of presentation. Folklorists' explicit recognition of this collapses a distinction between the individual and the social aspects of memory. There is an interdependency between unique performances and tradition that cannot be inscribed as a property of an individual's memory, even though the performance they may witness and record is one rendered by an individual. It is in any case rendered for an audience, and is designed for that social purpose.

The significance of the constructed world of objects we possess and the environment in which we live, as collective memory, is also a topic of rekindled interest. The dilemmas of change and preservation of the urban and rural landscapes in which we live (Lowenthal and Binney, 1981), and the collections of artefacts that are intentionally brought together as celebration, commemoration and for archival purposes in public spaces, galleries, museums and libraries, are topics central to socially located studies of memory (Lumley, 1988; Radley, this volume). David Lowenthal's *The Past is a Foreign Country* is an authoritative treatment of a historical geography that sweeps away the arbitrary boundary between the individual and the social through a consideration of the linking of personal and communal memory. In his discussion of the artefactual legacy of history in building and landscape, he analyses how relics from the past 'remain essential bridges between then and now. They confirm or deny what we think of it, symbolize or memorialize communal links over time, and provide archeological metaphors that illumine the process of history and memory' (1985: xxiii). Lowenthal reveals the irony of a historical analysis in which versions of the past are variable, contested and subject to varieties of interpretation, as compared with a popular consensus that represents the past as a timeless mirror to be looked at for accurate reflections of historical events (Lowenthal, 1989).

A recent issue of *Communication* (1989) explores the topic of 'Social Memory' from a communicative perspective. Contributors to that volume discuss the implications of that notion for understanding communicative practices in the reconstruction and creation of shared memories. The editors note similar themes to the ones reported here. Common or social memories are variable, and that variability puts contest at the centre of any communicative practices that instantiate commonly held views of the past (Nerone and Wartella, 1989). Additionally they note the importance of considering the impact of the 'media as sites of the creation of social memory and as a body of available materials' for its study. Media, and their concomitant modes of presentation and discourse, constrain or shape what can and cannot be thought, said, written and remembered. The privileging effect of varieties of communicational means has important implications for what has been referred to in the sociological and philosophical discussions of social theory as 'communities of memory' (Bellah, Madsen, Sullivan, Swidler and Tipton, 1985; see also MacIntyre, 1981 for a related discussion of tradition). In their influential book, *Habits of the Heart*, Robert Bellah and his colleagues (1985: 152–5) examine how contemporary Americans talk and think about individualism and commitment. They identify two 'languages' of moral discourse. One is concerned with the language of the 'self-reliant individual', while the other articulates aspects of tradition and commitment in everyday life that are transcendent of an ahistorical individualism. That 'second language', as they call it, of moral discourse is rooted in communities that are 'in an important sense constituted by their past' (p. 153). They argue that it is possible to speak of a 'real community as a "community of memory," one that does not forget its past. In order not to forget its past, a community is involved in retelling its story, its constitutive narrative' (p. 153). Such 'communities of memory' are no mere celebration of the past. The argument is that 'they carry a context of meaning' that 'turns us toward the future'. This is contrasted with inhabiting the language of the 'self-reliant individual' which creates the grounds for a form of social amnesia concerning the nature of community.

The social institution of forgetting or structurally instigated amnesia has been taken up in Mary Douglas's recent work on *How Institutions Think* (1986). Working from the discussions of Evans-Pritchard (1940), who 'took systematic forgetting to be an integral part of the organization of a pastoral people in Sudan', and the work of Robert Merton (1965), who considered 'systematic forgetting to be an intergral part of the organization of science' and its institutions, she elaborates how institutional life has 'distinctive effects on remembering'. Intriguingly she uses as a case-study the work of Bartlett, a psychologist who placed great emphasis in his early work on remembering as a social process. Douglas argues that Bartlett's psychological career 'is a self referencing instance of the claim that psychologists are institutionally incapable of remembering that humans are social beings. As soon as they know it, they [psychologists] forget it' (1986: 81). Bartlett is portrayed as falling prey to the institutional constraints of a discipline that would legitimate the individual as its prime analytical concern. The legitimating priority of individual issues over social ones inexorably biased Bartlett's work away from his initial research agenda rooted in social anthropology with social issues as central.

A number of the chapters in this volume demonstrate the interest of psychologists in the socially orientated research agenda on remembering and forgetting (Billig; Middleton and Edwards; Radley; and Shotter). Whether these will be consigned to a form of 'socially constructed oblivion' (Douglas, 1980, after Michel Foucault) will presumably depend, if her argument is correct, on some form of institutional transformation within the discipline of psychology. It would have to be a transformation that affords some form of recognition that issues that are currently approached as the property of individual cognition require relocation within a broader epistemological framework. Psychologists have developed a sophisticated vocabulary and cadre of concepts acknowledging that memory of individuals does not just act as a passive 'storehouse' of past experience, but changes what is remembered in ways that enhance and transform it according to present circumstances. However, peeping over the boundary fences of psychology's backyard are any number of neighbouring and cognate disciplines who would 'want to show that one might handle *memory*, . . . in terms of the socially organized character of recollection and forgetting' (Coulter, 1979: 59). The studies in this book are certainly not the norm within psychology, despite continued efforts within the discipline to broaden the research agenda on memory (Scribner and Cole, 1981; Neisser, 1982; Neisser and Winograd, 1988; Norman, 1988). It is still not the norm to come by examples of studies that approach 'cognitive processes' as systemically organized within institutional practices of the sort described by anthropologists such as Suchman in her book *Plans and Situated Actions* (1987), or as Lave puts it, ' "cognition" observed in everyday practice that is distributed – stretched over, not divided among mind, body, activity and culturally organized settings' (1988: 1). Part of the purpose of this volume is to provide such examples.

There is a ferment of activity in this area that raises the expectation, and hope, that the priority of study will no longer be limited to memory as located in the processes and contents of individual minds, independent of social, historical and cultural circumstances.

Common Themes

Within this diversity of approach and interest in the social nature of remembering can be found a number of recurring themes which are also taken up in the chapters of this book. We can pose them as a series of questions, such as: Is it just that the contents of memory may be social, that we remember social occasions and events, while the processes of memory (its organization, how we do it) are essentially psychological and individual? Or does the social nature of memory extend deeper, into the very processes of remembering? Can studies of the social and the individual bases of remembering proceed independently of each other, or are they too intimately entwined for that? Is it that our capacity to remember develops in, and through, the joint action of remembering together? Or are even stronger claims being made about the social nature of memories as symbolically significant, communicable, conventionalizable, variable, manipulable and contestable features of a culturally located existence? How do we include the fact that, in many acts of 'commemoration', there is no requirement that the participants have had direct or personal experience of the 'remembered' events? How do public, political and commercial institutions in their archive and audit authenticate and legitimate what should or should not be remembered and forgotten? Is a claim being made that our individual consciousness is constituted by, and constructed within, symbolic social practices and the symbolic significance of a material world?

Remembering Together
It is self-evident that people share memories of events and objects that are social in origin. There is nothing particularly remarkable in such a claim. Of itself it merely highlights that people live in, and deal with, a world that extends beyond themselves. However, a discussion of the social and relational dynamic of *remembering together* reflects a concern to examine how people collectively constitute and 'function as integrated memory systems' (Wertsch, 1987). Such a view implies that more than mere pooling of experience and 'memories' is at issue. For example, when people reminisce about family photographs, or recount shared experiences of times of happiness and trauma at weddings and funerals, what is recalled and commemorated extends beyond the sum of the participants' individual perspectives: it becomes the basis of future reminiscence. In the contest between varying accounts of shared experiences, people reinterpret and discover features of the past that become the context and content for what they will jointly recall and commemorate on future occasions. Such distributed cognitive activity can also be observed where groups, in both work and leisure activity, work together to reconstruct and rediscover how to achieve some end which no one of them actually had the knowledge to

achieve independently (Hutchins, 1988; Middleton, 1987). They collectively reconstruct what the culture already 'knows' as part of its socio-historical evolution – what is potentially recoverable within the affordances of cultural artefacts and custom.

Social Practice of Commemoration

One aspect of joint recall that has attracted special attention is the *social practice of commemoration*, where the past, a person or event becomes the object of intentional commemoration and is ascribed some historical significance (Schwartz, 1986; Schwartz, Zerubavel and Barnett, 1982). In this way people recall and celebrate events and persons that are part of their jointly acknowledged generational and cultural identity and common understanding. In the gunfighters of the Western, in the statues of eminent citizens and places named after the famous, people 'in society' with each other evaluate their culture by establishing what is notable or notorious. However, acts of commemoration embody a continuing tension between immutable aspects of the past conserved in the present, in contrast with the past as transformable and manipulable – today's champions as tomorrow's villains, yesterday's radicalism as tomorrow's orthodoxy, set against past heroes or events as neither 'wearied nor condemned' by the passage of time. Commemoration silences the contrary interpretations of the past. The silent remembrance of those who died in battle also silences outrage at the courses of action entailing such loss.

Social Foundation and Context of Individual Memory

Both the joint reconstruction of the past (remembering things together) and the general process of commemoration can be taken as providing frameworks within which children, and indeed adults, actually learn what to remember and what it is to remember as part of a social enterprise. While conversational remembering is open ended, providing for lots of on-the-spot revisions, reconstructions, selections of what is remembered, public commemorations generally have a more fixed, ritualized and catechismic quality, to be repeated time after time. The morning recitation of the Pledge of Allegiance in American schools exemplifies both the joint and commemorative nature of the *social foundation and context of individual memory*. The unison of voices provides an environment of collectively realized performance within which the novice can bridge any gaps of individual incompetence. At the same time each re-performance consolidates the authority of this commemorative practice, and the authority of those who obligate the children's performance.

However, even the catechisms and ceremonies of ritual commemoration are the product of conversation and argument, as people have discussed how an event might best be commemorated, what precisely should be said and done and how it might be realized on each occasion. Billig (1987) makes the same point about the rhetorical basis for the formal rules of games such as cricket.

Rhetorical Organization of Remembering and Forgetting

Telling the *right* kind of story, at the right time, to the right person, about what went on, or did not go on, is what children, as 'unpractised' cultural participants, find difficult to do. The *rhetorical organization of remembering and forgetting* is also an emergent theme in the chapters of this book. Primarily it can be seen in argument about contested pasts and plausible accounts of who is to blame, or to be excused, acknowledged, praised, honoured, thanked, trusted and so on, that occur as part of the pragmatics of everyday communication. Such rhetorical skills can also be seen as being organized in relation to broader ideological considerations that place people in a contradictory relationship with what they would report or mark of the past in the present (Billig, Condor, Edwards, Gane, Middleton and Radley, 1988). For example, the tension between continuity and revision of the past manifests itself in a government's authority either to open archives to public scrutiny, or to limit, or only sanction 'sanitized' versions of the past. It is the dilemma that Orwell's 'Big Brother' sought to eliminate in the control of the future through the control of official records of events. Such dilemmas are voiced in any rhetoric of justification, or account, that is mounted in defence and legitimation of what should or should not be remembered or 'forgotten' of the past in the circumstances of today. The 'truth' of the past is always, at least potentially, at issue. It is not to be found unambiguously deposited in some objective social record or archive, nor yet as infinitely malleable in the service of the present. It obtains neither as 'fact' nor 'invention', but as an epistemological enterprise, created in dialectic and argument between those contrary positions.

Social Institutional Remembering and Forgetting

The rhetorical organization of remembering and forgetting also provides clues to the social institutional context within which the orthodoxy of the past is challenged so as to change the future. In the social organization of forgetting we have the basis of reconstructing anew what it was that was challenged and contested. The banning gives clues about the content and context of what it was that was banned. Milan Kundera's *Book of Laughter and Forgetting* illus-

trates this point. The very systematicity in repression of Czechoslo-
vakian culture after the Prague Spring of 1968 becomes a resource
for Kundera's reconstruction of the political and cultural events of
that period. The notion of *institutional remembering and forgetting*
is not simply a reference to the fact that social organizations create
records in the form of minutes, archives and financial audits, but
also refers to the large-scale manipulation of what should or could
be remembered – socially organized remembering and forgetting. It
relates to Robert Bellah's and his colleagues' discussion of
'communities of memory'. The significance of the notion of
institutional forgetting and remembering is that it shows that
collective remembering is essential to the identity and integrity of a
community. It is not just that 'he who controls the past controls the
future' but *he who controls the past controls who we are*.

The Forms of Social Practices in the Continuity of our Lives

From the perspective of the practices of institutional remembering
and forgetting it is possible to see how the continuity of social life, as
preserved in certain *forms of social practices*, and also who we are as
individuals, depends on the preservation of those practices. The
crucial notion in this recurring theme is the objectification of those
practices in the social environment, both material and communicative, such that the world we live in embodies in its very design a
relation to the past. The integrity of individual mental life is held in
place by participation in these practices. In its strongest form this
does not just refer to some form of coherence and sense of
continuity in our social lives but to the social constitution of
'individual' mind. The claim is that the very integrity of a person's
mentality depends upon participation in an environment which
owes its very shape to socio-cultural practices.

Such a view collapses problematic dualisms in the discussion of
remembering and forgetting as collective activities. From such a
perspective it makes no sense to talk in terms of what is an
individual as compared with what is social memory, what is past as
distinct from the present, what is specifically social and what
specifically physical, what part of memory is internal and what is
externally located. These are not separable categories but express
interdependent relationships which cannot be used reductively to
explain one in terms of the other. Remembering and forgetting are
to be taken as activities that are embodied and constituted within
the pragmatics of ordinary social and communicative practices, and
the symbolic significances of the natural and made world.

This set of themes characterizes the variety of claims being made when remembering and forgetting are identified as socially located and constituted activities. The essays presented here elaborate and exemplify these themes.

Central to our own contribution to this volume on conversational remembering (Chapter 2) is the theme of *remembering together* as an enterprise achieved in acts of communication. Our discussion invokes a reversal of the usual approach to the relationship between human consciousness and communication. We are not concerned with how conversational competence is represented cognitively, but with how cognition itself, and in particular remembering, is achieved and represented in people's talk with each other. Rather than wondering about how internal mental processes might represent past experience, we are interested in how people construct versions of events *and* their own mental process, within the practices of ordinary conversation. We illustrate our position with reference to a series of studies we have conducted, involving both children and adults, which examine the micro-processes of conversational remembering in relation to their broader societal and ideological location.

Our work also addresses the *social foundation and context of memory*. In so doing it re-positions three important issues that emerge as part of a research agenda on remembering collectively. First, *context* is treated not as mere background or social influence, but as the substance of collective memory itself, contestively established in talk. Secondly, *metacognition*, or talk about mental processes, is seen not as reflection upon internal mental processes, but as occurring in conversation in an occasioned manner, such that conceptions of mental processes are formulated, justified and socialized in the process of talking about them. Thirdly, we examine *inference and argument* in the construction of joint versions of events where remembering is the production of versions which are acceptable in so far as they succeed over other possible, foreseen or actual versions.

The overall aim of the discussion is to offer a perspective on remembering grounded in developments in the application of discourse analysis to issues in social and developmental psychology. This discourse-analytic approach orientates us to take people's accounts of the past as pragmatically variable versions that are constructed with regard to particular communicative circumstances. People's accounts of past events are treated not as a window on to the cognitive workings of memory, but as descriptions that vary according to whatever pragmatic and rhetorical work they are designed for, such that no single, decontextualized version can be taken as a reflection of the 'contents' of a person's 'memory'.

In Chapter 3, Alan Radley counsels against considering the social constitution of memory purely from the perspective of *remembering together* as realized through people's conversations with each other. He argues that if you want to set up a social-psychological theory of memory you must move 'away from the remembering subject to social practices in which people engage with the material world'. It is not just within the realm of communicative activity that a context for remembering is socially created.

In examining the role of artefacts in social life and their involvement in how people establish 'their individual and collective pasts', Radley demonstrates how 'the world of objects, as material culture' is constructive of *forms of social practices* that provide for *continuity in our lives*. The world of material artefacts embodies and organizes our relationship with the past in socially significant ways. The material world, as much as oral communication, provides a basis for a reading of the past in the present. It too provides for a rhetorically organized interpretation of collectively retrieved and reinstated ways of having done, and been, that are part of the *social foundation of individual memory*. Artefacts are rarely self-evident when displaced historically and as such provide for an 'argumentative' encounter with the past in the present.

The *rhetorical organization of collective remembering* is a theme continued in the contributions of Michael Billig (Chapter 4) and Barry Schwartz (Chapter 5). In addition their contributions also reflect a concern with the *social practice of commemoration*. Of particular interest is that although coming in from radically different topic areas, they converge on similar conclusions concerning the dilemmatic nature of collective memory as both marking continuity in the preservation of the past and altering the past in terms of the concerns of the present. Billig's focus is to explore ideology as a form of collective memory in the way the reproduction of power relations in society produces bias in what is commemorated or ignored of the past. He approaches this task through an illustrative analysis of the discourse of an ordinary family conversing about their views and recalling incidents in relation to an extraordinary family – the British Royal Family. Schwartz is concerned with the collective commemoration and transformation of Abraham Lincoln's political reputation at the turn of the century. His analysis is based on written texts. Both Billig's and Schwartz's analyses reveal equivalent contrary ideological themes crucial to the intentional commemoration of public figures – tensions between those figures as *ordinary versus extraordinary, equal versus privileged* and *traditional versus modern*.

The contradictory themes and arguments expressed in an ordinary family's conversations about an extraordinary family allow Billig to elaborate the notion of collective memory in two important ways. First, he demonstrates that an ordinary family's jointly produced and commemorated biography is expressed in ways that recapitulate their social position in British society in relation to a family that is accorded special status. As part of their discussions about the Royal Family, a family 'whose very extraordinariness is commonsensically assumed to guarantee its inherent memorability', aspects of the ordinary family's biography and mythology emerge. The content of this shared family narrative, symbolic of their own family unity across generations, reproducing family traditions and particular myths about tenuous contact with the Royal Family, is organized around the expression of contradictory themes according special privilege to a wealthy family in the context of a supposedly egalitarian and democratic society. Secondly, the idea of commemorating 'the past itself rather than the reconstruction of a past event' is an important point raised in Billig's discussion. This aspect of the family's discourse is also demonstrated to be organized around contradictory ideological issues concerning their positions on what status to accord the past, for example the loss of traditional values in the modernity of the present. The family, in their 'comemoration' argue both for 'the past against the present and the present against the past, just as they jointly possess discourses of equality and inequality'.

Schwartz approaches the *social practice of commemoration* through the collective commemoration of Lincoln's political reputation during a period of considerable social change in American society during the first twenty years of this century. The textual items he analyses reveal a major reworking of Lincoln's reputation during that period. Schwartz argues that the reworking of Lincoln's reputation is constituted in commemorative acts in relation to changing and contradictory ideological circumstances within American society at that time. The time he is concerned with has been dubbed the 'progressive era'. It saw expansion in the exploitation of natural reources and the transformation of America into a 'world power'. At the same time there was active concern to protect the rights of the common person in terms of equality of opportunity to share in that wealth and to engage in the democratic process without undermining the notion of 'free enterprise' as the means to achieve that economic opportunity.

His discussion is not a simple mapping between culture and the objects of collective memory. He adopts the economic rhetoric of the society he is analysing in construing 'memory-making' as 'an act of enterprise'. A person must be deemed commemorable by people who have an interest in marking and celebrating what they take to be the situated greatness in the actions of someone such as Abraham Lincoln. The quality of Lincoln's greatness is transformed from that of a simple and accessible figure to that of a remote and dignified personage while at the same time an essential continuity is maintained in the commemoration of the greatness of his reputation. Schwartz presents a view of commemoration as rhetorically organized in a way that both serves the function of marking continuity in *preserving* the past and also involves *altering* the past in terms of the concerns of the present.

Reputation as the focus of attention for discussions of the social basis of forgetting is taken up in Michael Schudson's contribution (Chapter 6). Schudson examines the 'misremembered' reputation of an American president. His contribution also shares with John Shotter's essay (Chapter 7) a concern to examine *social institutional forgetting and remembering*, and social memories as rhetorically organized in oral cultures. Schudson reveals the 'popularity' of Ronald Reagan as a socially constructed memory that defies the available poll data that such constructions of the presidency might ordinarily be thought to heed. He examines how Reagan's low ratings in the opinion polls in his first two years in office were virtually ignored in the public construction of Reagan's popularity. Schudson argues that the answer lies not in a distrust of polls but in the powerful face-to-face impression Reagan made with Washington élites, an impression political and media élites then projected on to the 'public' as a communicative resource in their work and political activities. In an age dominated and governed by the statistical and abstract, this case is taken to demonstrate the continuing salience in political life of personal, qualitative and anecdotal impression as a basis of judgement and presumed knowledge. The social memory of a political figure's reputation is seen to be constructed in the discursive practices of an oral and face-to-face political subculture. Within that collective construction of reputation, poll data are taken up or ignored, and are used as constructive of 'fact'. In Schudson's analysis, poll data are not seen a representing 'the truth of the matter' independently of the way they are deployed by those who earn their livings as members of any particular political discourse. Poll data are part of the oral culture. Schudson concludes that there is 'rhetorical structure to social institutions, a patterned way in which language comes to be used; once used, referred to; and when referred to remembered and drawn upon as part of what "everyone knows"'.

John Shotter's chapter continues the discussion of the social-institutional determinants of memory by examining the way in which the continuity of social life can be taken as being preserved in *forms of social practice*. His chapter outlines further examples of the sorts of criticism that can be brought to bear on many of the prevailing metaphors that underpin the psychological study of remembering and forgetting as being to do with the status of some 'individual' memory or process in the 'possession' of individual persons. He seeks to establish what he terms a 'non-cognitive' account of remembering and forgetting.[2] His main analytical focus is the early work of the British psychologist Frederick Bartlett (Bartlett, 1923; 1932).

Shotter highlights two important aspects of Bartlett's early work as corner-stones for the establishment of his non-cognitive agenda: 'the social and institutional determinants' of both remembering and forgetting; and Bartlett's discussion of what he termed 'conflicting tendencies' inherent in any social circumstances. It is through a re-examination of these two frequently 'forgotten' aspects of Bartlett's work that Shotter elaborates his 'non-cognitive' approach.

Shotter highlights the importance of 'accounting practices in human conduct' and the way in which ways of speaking serve to reproduce and maintain 'a certain established social order'. He also emphasizes the 'rhetorical nature of language'. This rhetorical perspective brings into question the idea that we possess language in a way independent of our communicative activities with others. Shotter argues that any claims we might make about the world, or our past, gain their authority by virtue of being 'adequate to an already intralinguistically constructed reality, rather than to the nature of an extralinguistic world'. The importance of this for the 'non-cognitive' agenda, and for remembering and forgetting as collective activities, is that no priority is being claimed for language over the nature of the world or of the nature of the world over language, 'but that one *must* assert both; for they owe their distinct existence to their *interdependency*'.

Institutional remembering and forgetting are further examined in the essay by Yrjö Engeström, Katherine Brown, Ritva Engeström and Kirsi Koistinen (Chapter 8) and in Julian Orr's contribution (Chapter 9). Both these contributions also share a common concern to ground their conceptual discussions in detailed analysis based on observations in the concrete circumstances of work within institutional settings.

Engeström and his associates examine the way *forgetting* impacts on the working practices of medical organizations. They seek to develop a conceptual framework for analysing organizational memory. To do this they draw upon the Soviet socio-historical tradition of psychological theorizing, a tradition frequently referred to as 'Activity Theory', in the European context (Leontiev, 1978; 1981), and one that has increasingly gained the attention of psychologists outside the Soviet Union (Wertsch, 1981). A guiding principle of such an approach is that human conduct cannot be understood through any simple form of reductive explanation, where the social is reduced to the individual, the individual to the biological or vice versa. The chapter offers a conceptualization of organizational forgetting based on what they term institutionalized 'silence' and 'solitude'. This 'silence' or 'solitude' is seen as having important implications for work contexts. If important details about particular cases, or innovative ways of overcoming the demands of everyday practice, fail to become part of the common knowledge of the medical team, be it in hospitals or in general practice, then the quality of service for any particular patient suffers; the patient's particular problems are 'forgotten' in that what the doctor deemed to be the salient features of the case are not recorded in ways that make them retrievable for others who might have to deal with the same patient. In addition, the team practice fails to build upon its members' innovative improvisations in their daily practice; the service remains disconnected and trapped in modes of practice that are solitary in nature. Such institutionalized 'silence' is not seen to be the product of any 'individual memory loss' or 'social amnesia'. It is conceptualized as a property of the forms of institutionalized social practice that have evolved as part of the history of the work settings where doctors practise their medicine.

The particular contexts discussed in this chapter are a Urology Clinic in a large American teaching hospital and a Finnish Health Centre where general practitioners work in teams. The overall aim of this work is to provide a conceptual framework that would allow participants, in the medical settings studied, to discover, in their existing practice, the basis for developing new ways of organizing and co-ordinating their work, thus avoiding the institutional forgetfulness endemic in 'silent', 'solitary' and 'disconnected' practice. Its practical goal is to encourage forms of team practice that sustain a collectively held understanding and remembrance of past case and precedence as a resource for the practice of today and tomorrow.

In Chapter 9, Julian Orr takes up the theme of how knowledge is shared and used as a form of collective memory in work settings. Rather than examining the structural properties of work practices and how they impact on the flexible maintenance of socially shared memories, he examines the role of orally related stories in and about work. The focus of his discussion is the working culture of photocopier service techicians.

Detailed fieldnotes and transcriptions of conversatons between technicians engaged in service tasks, and in subsequent discussions during periods of relaxation, provide the basis of analysing the construction of what Orr terms a 'community memory'. Orr argues that the most significant feature of this working talk is its narrative structure. Indeed, he claims that the very process of diagnosing technical faults has a narrative structure to it. The technicians face the problem of creating meaning and coherence out of a variety of disparate 'facts' that present themselves in relation to any malfunctioning machine. The weaving together of a coherent 'story' accounting for contradictory evidence as to the nature of a malfunction is a fundamental resource in the production of an accurate diagnosis of the problem and its resolution.

In elaborating his notion of 'community memory', Orr demonstrates how the socially situated actions of repair and maintenance entail more than the mere fixing of machines but are part of the active construction and 'repair' of a community of use. He illustrates how common knowledge concerning particular problems is established and maintained within oral re-narrations of past problems, and how these situated stories of past successes and failures allow for the handling of idiosyncratic and unpredicted failures and breakdowns that fall beyond the remit of current documentation in repair manuals.

The narrative structure of diagnosis, and any subsequent recounting of heroic struggles with intractable machines and faults, reveal two major themes of technical practice: 'the fragility of understanding and the fragility of control' of the technical objects, the machines, that are the subject of a technician's working life. Orr points out that service work is embodied in a relationship between technician, customer and machines. However, a person's identity as a technician stands or falls by virtue of their skill at actually fixing any faulty machine. So, although telling stories preserves potentially arcane and idiosyncratic pieces of information as part of the community of practice, a 'community memory', it also serves to establish a continued identity of the teller as a competent practitioner, as a 'member of the community, contributing to the community memory' of service practice.

The role of narrative is also examined in Carol Padden's essay (Chapter 10). She discusses folk explanations and narrative myths in deaf culture both as a *form of social practice* embodying a relation to the past and as a *practice of commemoration* in the social constitution of memories that maintain important elements of the culture. Her focus is to explicate how languages survive in adverse circumstances. Her particular concern is with the conditions under which American Sign Language (ASL) survives as a viable communicative medium in deaf culture. Deafness presents unique developmental problems for children with respect to their access to culturally generated solutions to the difficulties of their daily existence. Given that only 10 percent of deaf children are born to deaf parents who have direct experience of deafness as a condition of daily life, avenues for the intergenerational transmission of knowledge concerning the utility and functional significance of sign language are severely dislocated in deaf culture.

Language learning as a child-centred activity requires certain forms of input from the linguistic culture into which children are born. In particular, stable forms of social practices appear to make a fundamental contribution to the development of children within hearing culture. Because the majority of deaf children are not born into families where ASL is the first, or indeed a known, language, there exists an intergenerational dislocation of the social practices necessary for sign-language learning. There are strong arguments that language learning and language creation are cross-generational, and that a child requires exposure to varieties of discursive contexts in order to become a native speaker. For the deaf child to learn sign language as a *first language* there needs to be a form of social resource that bridges the lack of linguistic cultural continuity. The question is, what social resources are potentially available to bridge that cultural dislocation? Folk explanations and myths about sign language are identified as a social resource for achieving continuity. Such folk explanations and narrative myths about the origins and achievements of native signers are argued to be instrumental in marshalling social resources for the survival and maintenance of ASL under the normal conditions in which it is learned. They are seen as privileging patterns of social organization in the everyday life of the deaf child that afford possible contexts for the learning of ASL. Myth and folk explanation are therefore a form of collective memory bridging breaks in the intergenerational pattern of deafness. They maintain knowledge of the significance of signing, and the forms of social resource, that make its learning possible. In that way the 'folklore' of ASL contributes to the organization of social resources for maintaining its survival in the face of pressures from the outside.

Finally, in Chapter 11, David Bakhurst examines the issues of collective remembering from the perspective of the writings of Soviet psychologists and philosophers who have worked within what has come to be called the 'socio-historical tradition'. This tradition initially developed during the post-revolutionary period in the Soviet Union as a critical response to the dualisms of approach inherent in 'western' discussions of 'mind versus body'; 'individual versus social'; 'biological versus environmental'; 'social versus material'. The tradition's concern to establish a 'unit of analysis' that eliminates such conceptual dualisms in the study of psychology has subsequently received increasing international attention through the translation of the works of three influential Soviet scholars; Vygotsky, Luria and Leontiev.

Bakhurst mounts an argument from within the perspective of the socio-historical tradition for studying remembering as a collective or socially constituted activity. He does this through a review of three key issues frequently discussed within that tradition: the social origins of remembering as a 'higher mental function'; the social constitution of memories for individuals and for groups; and the conception of 'culture' as an embodiment of 'social memory'. In addition he argues that if that 'tradition' offers the basis for a strong claim about the social constitution of remembering, then (as Billig's and Schwartz's contributions would imply) the ideological circumstances of the persons who were committed to preserving it should also be considered. The suppression of Vygotsky's writings in the 1930s and the subsequent recollection of his ideas within what was essentially an oral 'tradition' within Soviet psychology from 1936 to 1956 represent an object lesson in collective remembering. Bakhurst shows that the very content of what was remembered and celebrated as the tradition's achievements demonstrates the *rhetorical organization of remembering and forgetting* as a collective activity. Again, the rhetorical organization of forgetting offers clues to the nature of what was repressed.

All these essays argue, in their respective ways, for the value of studying remembering and forgetting as kinds of social action, rather than as properties of individual mentality. It is not that there is no coherence to the notion of individual memory – of course there is. Rather, it is that the very heart of the topic, the sheer meaningfulness of memories, their content and organization (their personal and social significance), their contexts and occasionings in the flow of ordinary experience, cannot be accounted for by reference to mental processes alone. Those contents, processes and experiences are sensible only in the context of ideology and social action, collectivity and culture, and the everyday pragmatics of communication.

Notes

Many thanks to David Bakhurst for his written comments and discussion, and to Carol Padden for her discussion, in the preparation of this introduction.

1. This relationship is graphically illustrated in Luisa Passerini's study, *Facism in Popular Memory*. She gives the following example of the significant relationship between the memory of an Italian woman worker for the clothes she wore to work, and the ideological situation of that apparently mundane aspect of daily life. Passerini describes the 'multiplicity of meanings that a red outfit (clothes) could assume in the daily struggle and balance of forces in the factory' where the women worked in the years following the defeat of the Fascist regime. The factory at which she worked had refused to provide overalls and she had worn a red pair of her own. She recounted how

> they had called me into the office, they asked me why I was dressed in red. In fact I'd always gone into the office in my red overalls and they didn't like it. So that time in the studio they asked me 'And is it because you like red or is it because you are a Communist?' I replied: 'Because I like red, because I'm a Communist, because I wear what colour I like, and because G. doesn't give me overalls and I don't want to spend money on his account. Why haven't I the right to wear what colour I like? (quoted by Passerini, 1984/87: from Bosio, 1961)

2. This term is not to be confused with its common usage in moral philosophy where it is used to refer to a line of argument that claims the impossibility of determining ethics and values on the basis of rational or 'cognitively' determined considerations (see, for example, Blackburn, 1984; Mackie, 1977). There are of course certain parallels in the way Shotter is seeking to deploy the term in this context. His chapter is also an argument for taking into account the 'non-systematic' and 'conflicting process' in outlining a 'social-constructionist' approach to forgetting and remembering.

References

Bartlett, F.C. (1923) *Psychology and Primitive Culture*. Cambridge: Cambridge University Press.
Bartlett, F.C. (1932) *Remembering: a Study in Experimental Social Psychology*. Cambridge: Cambridge University Press.
Blackburn, S. (1984) *Spreading the Word*. Oxford: Oxford University Press.
Bellah, R.N., Madsen, R., Sullivan, W.M., Swidler, A. and Tipton S.M. (1985) *Habits of the Heart: Individualism and Commitment in American Life*. Berkeley: University of California Press.
Billig, M. (1987) *Arguing and Thinking: a Rhetorical Approach to Social Psychology*. Cambridge: Cambridge University Press.
Billig, M., Condor, S., Edwards, E., Gane, M., Middleton, D. and Radley, A. (1988) *Ideological Dilemmas: a Social Psychology of Everyday Thinking*. London: Sage.
Bosio, G. (1961) Preface to L. Musini, *Da Garibaldi al socialismo: Memorie e cronache per gli anni dal 1858 al 1890*. Milan.
Coulter, J. (1979) *The Social Construction of Mind*. London: Macmillan.
Davis, S.G. (1988) 'Review essay: storytelling rights', *Oral History Review*, 16(2) (Fall): 109–15.
Davis, N.Z. and Starn, R. (1989) 'Memory and Counter-Memory', special issue of *Representations*, 26 (Spring).
de Laguna, G.A. (1927) *Speech: its Function and Development*. Yale: Yale University Press.

Douglas, M. (1980) *Evans-Pritchard*. London: Fontana.

Douglas, M. (1986) *How Institutions Think*. London: Routledge & Kegan Paul.

Durkheim, E. (1893/1984) *The Division of Labour in Society*, tr. by W.D. Halls. London: Macmillan Press.

Durkheim, E. (1895/1982). *The Rules of Sociological Method*, tr. by W.D. Halls. London: Macmillan Press.

Evans-Pritchard, E. (1940) *The Nuer: a Description of the Modes of Livelihood and Political Institutions of the Nilotic People*. Oxford: Clarendon Press.

Halbwachs, M. (1925/52) *Les cadres sociaux de la mémoire*. Paris: Presses Universitaires de France.

Halbwachs, M. (1951/80) *The Collective Memory*. New York: Harper & Row.

Hutchins, E. (1988) 'The technology of team navigation', in J. Galegher, R. Kraut and C. Egido (eds), *Intellectual Teamwork: Social and Technical Bases of Collaborative Work*. Hillsdale, NJ: Lawrence Erlbaum.

Janet, P. (1928) *L'Évolution de la mémoire et de la notion du temps*. Paris: A. Chahine.

Johnson, R., McLennan, G., Schwarz, B. and Sutton, D. (1982) *Making Histories: Studies in History-writing and Politics*. London: Hutchinson in association with the Centre for Contemporary Cultural Studies, University of Birmingham.

Kundera, M. (1983) *The Book of Laughter and Forgetting*, tr. by Michael Henry Heim. Harmondsworth: Penguin.

Lave, J. (1988) *Cognition in Practice*. Cambridge: Cambridge University Press.

Leontiev, A.N. (1978) *Activity, Consciousness, and Personality*. Englewood Cliffs, NJ: Prentice-Hall.

Leontiev, A.N. (1981) *Problems of Development of the Mind*. Moscow: Progress House.

Lowenthal, D. (1985) *The Past is a Foreign Country*. Cambridge: Cambridge University Press.

Lowenthal, D. (1989) 'The timeless past: some Anglo-American historical preconceptions', *Journal of American History*, 75: 1263–80.

Lowenthal, D. and Binney, M. (eds) (1981) *Our Past before Us: Why Do We Save It?* London: Temple.

Lumley, R. (ed.) (1988) *The Museum Time-Machine: Putting Cultures on Display*. London: Routledge/Comedia.

Luria, A. (1968) *The Mind of a Mnemonist*. New York: Basic Books.

MacIntyre, A. (1981) *After Virtue*. London: Duckworths.

Mackie, J. (1977) *Ethics: Inventing Right and Wrong*. Harmondsworth: Penguin.

Mead, G.H. (1934) *Mind, Self and Society from the Standpoint of a Social Behaviourist*. Chicago: University of Chicago Press.

Merton, R. (1965) *On the Shoulders of Giants: a Shandian Postscript*. New York: Harcourt Brace.

Middleton, D. (1987) 'Dance to the music: conversational remembering and joint activity in learning an English Morris dance', *Quarterly Newsletter of the Laboratory of Comparative Human Cognition*, 9 (1): 23–38.

Moscovici, S. (1984) 'The phenomenon of social representations', in R. Farr and S. Moscovici (eds), *Social Representations*. Cambridge: Cambridge University Press.

Neisser, U. (1982) *Memory Observed*. Oxford: W.H. Freeman.

Neisser, U. and Winograd, E. (1988) *Remembering Reconsidered: Ecological and Traditional Approaches to the Study of Memory*. Cambridge: Cambridge University Press.

Nerone, J. and Wartella, E. (1989) 'Introduction', Special Issue on 'Social Memory', *Communication*, 11 (2): 85–88.

Norman, D. (1988) *The Psychology of Everyday Things*. New York: Basic Books.

Passerini, L. (1984/87) *Fascism in Popular Memory: the Cultural Experience of the Turin Working Class*, tr. by Robert Lumley and Jude Bloomfield. Cambridge: Cambridge University Press.

Schrager, S. (1983) 'What is social in oral history?', *International Journal of Oral History*, 4 (June): 76–98.

Schwartz, B. (1986) 'The recovery of Masada: a study in collective memory', *Sociological Quarterly*, 27 (2): 147–64.

Schwartz, B., Zerubavel, Y. and Barnett, B.N. (1982) 'The social context of commemoration: a study in collective memory', *Social Forces*, 61: 374–402.

Scribner, S. and Cole, M. (1981) *The Psychology of Consequences of Literacy*. Cambridge, Mass.: Harvard University Press.

Suchman, L.A. (1987) *Plans and Situated Actions: the Problem of Human–Machine Communication*. Cambridge: Cambridge University Press.

Thelen, D. (1989) 'Memory and American history', *Journal of American History*, 75: 1117–29.

Vygotsky, L.S. (1929) 'The problem of the cultural development of the child', *Journal of Genetic Psychology*, 36: 415–34.

Wertsch, J.V. (ed.) (1981) *The Concept of Activity in Soviet Psychology*. Armonk, NY: M.E. Sharpe.

Wertsch, J.V. (1987) 'Collective memory: issues from a socio-historical perspective', *Quarterly Newsletter of the Laboratory of Comparative Human Cognition*, 9 (1): 19–22.

Yates, F. (1966) *The Art of Memory*. London: Routledge & Kegan Paul.

2

Conversational Remembering: a Social Psychological Approach

David Middleton and Derek Edwards

Relations between Discourse and Memory

In cognitive psychology, the relationship between discourse and memory is generally seen as an issue of knowledge representation. The aim is to specify what we know about the world, which includes both how to hold a conversation, and also a mental representation of the world that conversations might be 'about'. This latter component would have to include both the general principles by which the world works, and also some sort of memory for particular events, an updatable record that can be drawn upon in talk and comprehension. In our work on conversational remembering, we have been concerned with similar sorts of issues, of how understandings are expressed in talk, but approached in a quite different manner. Rather than looking at how conversational competence is represented cognitively, we are interested in how cognition is represented in ordinary conversations. As far as memory is concerned, the aim is not to specify how putative mental models might represent knowledge and experience, but rather with how people represent their past, how they construct versions of events when talking about them.

This change of perspective has the effect of changing our theoretical concerns. We become sensitive to the pragmatics of communication, to the communicative uses to which people put their representations of experience. People present accounts of past events for all sorts of reasons, amongst which, as Bartlett noted, a concern for accurate and dispassionate accuracy is rather rare. Indeed, from the perspective of communicative pragmatics, dispassionately accurate reporting is merely one of a variety of actions to which talk might be orientated, or even, one of a variety of contentious claims, or positions, which a speaker might adopt with regard to an account. Once we are removed from the confines of some very special and formalized social occasions, such as courtroom testimony and experimental studies of memory, we find that many of the well known psychological distortions of recall, the importation of inferences, schema effects and so on (Bartlett, 1932; Bransford and McCarrell, 1974) come into their own as functional and contextually sensible aspects of ordinary conversation.

It is not only that conversation affords examination of the micro-processes of collective remembering, as these unfold with talk. Larger, societal themes are also available for examination, including historical, ideological and political ones (Billig et al., 1988; Billig, this volume), educational curricula and modes of thought (Edwards and Mercer, 1987), 'authenticity' in folk traditions and dilemmas of the work-place (Middleton, 1987; 1988). It is a feature of conversation that these themes are not merely available in the discourse for the analyst to discover, available like pebbles on a beach, to be picked up and examined, but rather, are worked on by the participants themselves. In doing education, or reconstructing a Morris dance, or remembering with one's children how they behaved on holiday, or jointly remembering the details of a problematic case as a member of a multi-professional team in the British National Health Service, cultural and ideological themes (even though they may not be named as such) are worked up, illustrated, used and commemorated by participants as part of the pragmatics of speaking.

We began our empirical study of conversational remembering in the time-honoured tradition of psychological research, with a group of undergraduates. We had been conducting a series of practical classes with them, which included Bartlett's serial-reproduction studies (Bartlett, 1932). We had been thinking for some time about the neglected social-cultural dimension of Bartlett's work as represented in his discussions of 'conventionalization' (Crook and Middleton, 1989; Edwards and Middleton, 1987), while also developing an interest in conversation and the analysis of discourse. It seemed to us that the method of serial reproduction was not really social *enough*. In Bartlett's studies, the output from each participant is passed on as the input to the next person in line. This has the methodological advantage of enabling the analyst to study the relationship between input and output, to note the discrepancies and to use these discrepancies as the basis for inferring things about the mental processes or representations that must have intervened – in other words, about the workings of memory.

This methodological advantage is, however, bought at a price. The direction of social influence is all one way, cut and dried, non-interactive. There are no conversations: the 'subjects' have no opportunity to engage with each other communicatively. It occurred to us that, however messy the data might get, there might be an advantage in allowing participants to talk to each other, and to create together, a joint version of remembered events. This might get us closer to the social creation of memory, which Bartlett himself sought. And in any case, unlike Bartlett, we had at our disposal tape-recorders, transcription units and a background of theoretical developments in the analysis of real conversations that the invention of tape-recorders has made possible (linguistic pragmatics, discourse analysis, conversation analysis: for succinct accounts of such developments, see Atkinson and Heritage, 1984; Brown and Yule, 1983; Heritage, 1984; Levinson, 1983; Potter and Wetherell, 1987).

Our procedure was to ask a section of the class to recall together something that they had recently witnessed, and that we would be able, if necessary, to examine independently. They recalled together, in recorded conversation, the feature film *E.T.* Extract 1 is a brief sample of the 35-minute conversation that followed. (Simultaneous speech is bracketed where it begins. & indicates speaker continues speaking. The full account is in Edwards and Middleton, 1986a.)

EXTRACT 1: *Joint Recall*

Karen: well he goes to the fridge to get something to eat first doesn't he with the dog following him
Diane: yeh that's it
Karen: mm
Diane: and he finds him feeding the dog
John: and then and then he finds the beer
Diane: and then he finds the beer and what is it there's a link between [Elliott and E.T. &
Karen: [Elliott's at school
John: [telepathic link
Diane: & that whatever happens to E.T. Elliott feels the same effects and E.T. got paralytic [*laughs*] and so E.T. is sort of going
Lesley: all a bit drunk
Tina: that's right I remember
Karen: Elliott is sitting at his school desk and they are doing experiments with frogs are they
Diane: and he lets all the frogs out
[*General hubbub of agreement*]
Tina: sets all the frogs out yeh
Lesley: and what's that little girl that he fancies
John: it's when he's watching E.T.'s watching television and John Wayne kisses the heroine in the film
Diane: oh so Elliott kisses [her
John: [and then Elliott kisses the little girl

The immediate impression is of a well practised activity which the participants could perform with ease and spontaneity. It was obvious that we were tapping into a familiar discursive practice, in which remembering is done jointly. The participants were skilled at pooling their accounts, dealing with issues of intersubjectivity, with the extent to which versions were jointly held, or disputed, or could be made joint through persuasion and agreement. Specific linguistic devices were identifiable, such as *tags* that signal or invite ratification (doesn't he); *overt agreements* (yeh that's it; that's right I remember); the operation of a *default continuity*, such that each successive contribution was taken to build upon the last as part of the construction of a sequential narrative; the *ratification* through repetition of previous speakers' contributions (and then he finds the beer; sets all the frogs out); *overt requests* for assistance in the joint task (and what's that little girl that he fancies); as well as *metacognitive formulations* of the process of remembering itself (that's right I remember). We shall begin by taking up three of the themes from Extract 1 for further analysis: the nature of context considered as collective memory and understanding; metacognitive formulations (talk about mental processes); and the use of inference and argument in the construction of joint versions of events.

Context as Shared Understanding

As any conversation proceeds, it does so on the basis of a continuously updated but contentious understanding of what has been said so far, what is understood, what is yet to be resolved. We have argued (Edwards and Mercer, 1987) that this 'context' has to be seen as intersubjective for the participants, rather than existing for the analyst in an objective record, such as in the back pages of a transcript, or in the surrounding circumstances of the speech event, Speakers can only act upon what they understand and remember, and it is a concern to which they address themselves, just what that 'context' at any time should be. Part of this shared context for speaking is a continuously reworked collective memory. In Extract 1, therefore, the joint account proceeds from event to event, each successively marked out and encapsulated in words, each added to the last by a default continuity such that order of mention corresponds to order of event, and each taken by default as jointly held, until some disagreement forces a reformulation, a relocation and a restart (see Edwards and Middleton, 1986a).

In Extract 2 (from Edwards and Mercer, 1989), we have a more institutionalized version of the process, in which a teacher is establishing with her pupils a shared representation of what they have done, and what they will therefore do next. She had earlier got them to suggest some hypotheses about which washing powders might work best, and they were about to put these notions to an empirical test. The teacher's privileged position as arbiter of a legitimate collective account contrasts with the student peer group recalling *E.T.* (Slashes denote pauses; bracketed dots denote undeciphered or omitted talk.)

EXTRACT 2: *Context and Collectivity in School*

> *T*: now the other day we were talking about which washing powder was going to wash best and when we began talking about it you gave me some positive firm answers / [*To Tom*] what made you say what you did say?
>
> *Tom*: well// we used a popular television things
>
> *T*: yes erm// well you were thinking about the ones that were advertised on television/ yes/ what did you say first of all? which washing powder did you think was going to wash best?
>
> *Tom*: Persil
>
> *T:* [*To Ellie*] what did you think?
>
> *Ellie*: Persil
>
> *T*: Persil somebody said Daz/ who was that? [. . .] and you were thinking *then* about what your mothers said.
>
> *Pupils*: yeh
>
> *T*: and what your mothers used
>
> *Pupils*: yeh
>
> *T*: weren't you? [. . .] then we went on and we looked at what the manufacturers said on the packets about their products and you then thought that which washing powder was going to wash ⌈best?
>
> *Mary*: ⌊Ariel
>
> *T*: Ariel and what made ⌈you say that Ariel
>
> *Mary*: [*interrupting*] ⌊it digests dirt and stains [. . .]
>
> *T*: yes it digests dirt and stains [. . .] [*Turning towards the washing equipment that is laid out on a table*] now when you're staining your fabrics you've got your stains out here// how much stain are you going to use?
>
> *Ellie*: two blobs// two blobs of five on the cloth.
>
> *T*: you're going to make two separate areas of five drops not squirts and then [. . .]

The teacher's method is one of elicitation. She builds up a shared account of what everyone has agreed to do, organizing the pupils' turns at speaking, so that each child's turn was accorded its position and significance in a teacher-generated list of items. What the pupils omit, she provides, or prompts them to provide. Pupils' contributions are further reworked in the teacher's responses, such that the various washing powders were ones advertised on television, and that the plan was to make 'two separate areas of five drops not squirts'. Each of these reformulations was pedagogically significant. The hypotheses to be tested were derived not merely from the appearance of the products on television, but from advertisers' claims that theirs was best. The point about five separate blobs related to the experimental necessity for controlling for amounts of powder used, so that any observed differences might be attributable to the substances themselves. Clearly, the collective account was driven not only by the teacher's privileged social position, her control of turns at talk, but also from her privileged position in relation to the knowledge at issue. The creation of a collective account served as a medium for the pedagogic socialization of scientific thought and practice. Similarly, in other lessons we observed and video-recorded (Edwards and Mercer, 1987; 1989), teachers routinely made use of lesson summaries to reconstruct what had supposedly happened previously. Through these 'reconstructive recaps', messy findings became neat and orderly, the significance of classroom events became routinely formalized in memorable phrases, errors of scientific method were tidied up and teacher and pupils would collude in the elicited creation of a joint version of what had been discovered, and what it all meant.

Discursive Metacognition

We discovered in the *E.T.* study, as elsewhere (Edwards and Goodwin, 1985; Edwards and Mercer, 1987; Edwards and Middleton, 1988; Middleton, 1987; 1988), how metacognitive formulations, rather than occurring merely as reflective understandings or observations that people are able to make about the nature of their mental processes (Flavell and Wellman, 1977), arose in an occasioned manner in particular sorts of discursive contexts. They generally occurred at points where the activity of remembering ran into trouble or difficulty, and especially, at moments when one person's account provoked sudden recognition, or disputation, from another person. There seemed in these data to be evidence of a social-discursive basis for metacognition itself, of the sort hypothesized by various theorists (Mead, 1934; Piaget, 1928), such that the very notion of mind, of mental life, of memory and experience as objects of reflective awareness, is given shape and occasion by discursive practices in which versions are being compared, conjoined and disputed. Indeed, it is possible to suggest a developmental process on the basis of this pattern. The awareness of having and using a 'memory', and the awareness of its properties, may well arise as a matter of difficulty – as a matter of *not* being able to remember something, of being suddenly reminded, of having something on the tip of your tongue, of trying to remember and of trying to square an offered version of events with what another speaker says.

In conversational remembering, therefore, the talk is revealed as more than just a window upon mental processes and metacognitive conceptions. Conversations emerge as a significant *environment* in which such thoughts are formulated, justified and socialized according to how other speakers talk about mental processes. In this sense, we should write not of metacognitive 'awareness', as if it were merely a matter of becoming conscious of the real nature of pre-existing mental processes, but rather, of metacognitive construction – acquiring a conventional vocabulary and discourse for mental life, which is designed to serve the social pragmatics of conversation. Metacognition can be analysed as the development of a culturally shared discourse for making claims about mental processes (cf. anthropological and social constructionist studies, such as Gergen, 1985; Harré, 1983; Heelas and Lock, 1981), for arguing, justifying, accounting to other people for what we claim to know. We shall consider some recorded conversations with children in a later section.

Inference and Argument in Collective Remembering

In experimental studies of memory, much of the interesting stuff of cognition is not visible in the data, but has to be theorized to make sense of the observed discrepancies between input and output. The existence and operation of mental 'schemata', 'scripts', 'models', 'scenarios', 'story grammars' and the related processes of plausible inference through which what people recall is not the same as what they experienced; all have to be inferred by the analyst on the basis of such discrepancies. One of the appealing features of studying conversational remembering is that we often find these processes of sense-making expressed overtly in the talk. When people remember things together, seeking to compare and contrast different accounts, to construct and defend plausible versions or to criticize or doubt their accuracy, they articulate the grounds and criteria for what is remembered. Inferential links are made overtly; plausibility is directly invoked. Furthermore, the articulation of these things occurs in a context that lends them additional significance – the context of communicative pragmatics. That is to say, the criteria for remembering are seen to be contingent upon the action to which the talk is orientated; they are occasioned by the developing context and purposes of conversation. This can be seen clearly in Extract 3 (from Edwards and Middleton, 1986a).

EXTRACT 3: *Inference and Argument*

  Diane: it's very confusing 'cause there's not really a basic story it's all

```
          just the fact ⌈ that
Lesley:                 ⌊ little things that
          ⌈ happen
Diane:    ⌊ yeh little things that happen that don't really make that much
          like er they met he met the other children
```
[. . .]
John: he's trying to explain first of all where he is from do you
         remember
Diane: yeh he's
Karen: that's after he has met all the ⌈ children because &
John: ⌊ 'cause he says Ell-i-ott like this
Karen: & all the children were there
[. . .]
Diane: so he meets the older boy um because doesn't he bring him in
         and says you know what I told you because before he'd been telling
```
         everybody that ⌈ he'd &
John:                    | that's right
Paul:                    ⌊ yeh
```
Diane: & got some sort of monster or whatever
[. . .]
Diane: she dressed him up
Karen: that's right
Diane: 'cause he looks so funny

At the start of Extract 3, the participants were experiencing some
difficulty in establishing the precise order of events. Diane and
Lesley duly switch to metacognitive mode, and agree that the
difficulty resides in the input, the film itself – it lacked something
that would normally make sequential remembering easier – 'a basic
story'. In the other parts of the extract, the point to note is the
speakers' use of the logical operators *so*, and *because ('cause)*. For
instance, Karen points out that the incident in question has to be
placed after E.T.'s meeting with the other children, because all the
children were now present. This is a recognizable connecting
inference, of the sort that psychologists are accustomed to through
the work of Bartlett (1932), Bransford (1979) and others. However,
this and the other uses of *because*, John's and Diane's, do not
merely link events together. In fact, John's and Diane's uses signal
no logical connection at all. They appear to be addressed to the
developing consensus itself – meaning, not 'this happened because
that happened', but 'this version should be accepted by everybody
because . . .'. They are used to introduce reminders, particularly
memorable images, that can serve as familiar benchmarks for the
placing of the more disputable items. John's '(be)cause' follows his
'do you remember' – it argues for why everyone should accept his
version of events – a communicative-pragmatic argument, rather
than that some events must logically have followed others.

Thus, we find in these data not only inferences that link events to those already established, but also a rhetorical, argumentative basis for the process. Inferences are sensitive to social considerations, framed so as to dispute or forestall alternative accounts, in favour of the one that is being offered. Remembering events is the production of versions of events, which are acceptable in so far as they succeed over other possible, foreseen or actual versions. Again, it is a temptation too strong for us to resist, to ponder the cognitive and developmental implications of this. It again suggests the plausibility of a dialogical basis for human thought (cf. Vygotsky, 1978; 1987; Wertsch, 1985), and specifically, for an origin of self-conscious, metacognitive, and rationalized remembering, from within communicative pragmatics – from within children's conversations and arguments.

Discursive Frames

There was, in fact, a rather gross communicative-pragmatic effect at work in these data, but nevertheless, one that is consistently ignored in psychological studies of remembering – namely, the effect of our experimental instructions, or the communicative context generally, in promoting a specific sort of remembering – a particular communicative frame within which everything would be recalled. The participants in our study took it as their task that they should proceed to reconstruct, point by point, in proper sequence, the narrative order of events. Many of the key characteristics of what they recalled, in which order and by which principles of organization, were dictated by this narrative frame. But there were signs of another, alternative frame at work, especially at the end of the session, when, having reached the end of the narrative and of the task proper, the subjects spontaneously carried on reminiscing about what had obviously been a pleasant and interesting experience. We left the tape-recorder running. But now, instead of reconstructing the story in sequential order, they proceeded to dip into it at lots of different points, back and forth, recalling what were, for them, particularly poignant, or significant, 'bits'.

EXTRACT 4: *Selective Reminiscences: the Good Bits*

> *Diane*: it was so sad
> *Lesley*: that little boy was a very good actor
> *Diane*: he was brilliant he really was
> *Tina*: especially at the end when he [. . .]
> *Karen*: he was quivering ⌈ wasn't he
> *John*:   ⌊ how many didn't cry at it
> *Lesley*: [*emphatically*] I didn't and I'm ⌈ proud of it too
>   ⌊ [*General laughter*]

John: I cried
Karen: I cried most when ⌈the flower came blooming back into life
Steve: ⌊wipe my eyes/ [*sarcastically, amidst general laughter*] I wept tears
Diane: tell you what got me the bit when he didn't get on the space ship right at the beginning
[. . .] the actual story line was really boring
            ⌈wasn't it
Karen: │yeh
Lesley: ⌊yeh dead boring
Tina: it was the effects that did it
[. . .]
Paul: it had some incredible little funny bits in it when he got
            ⌈drunk and things like that
Lesley: ⌊yeh
Paul: & but apart from that
Karen: I thought the best bit was when they found him lying there
Diane: yeh [*laughs, followed by general assent and laughter*]
Karen: the most realistic bit was that bit in the middle
Diane: yeh
Karen: when he was lying there he really looked
            ⌈something that was dead
Diane: ⌊oh that's right
Lesley: because they'd had such a panic of looking for him before hadn't they
Diane: yeh and it looked so realistic

It was a little disconcerting for us to hear the opinon, agreed explicitly in Extract 4 by three participants without any demurring from the others, that it was precisely these 'incredible little funny bits' that were especially memorable, while the actual story line, which had been so carefully reconstructed for our benefit, was in itself 'boring'. Not only that, but within this new discursive frame, lots of graphic descriptive details were introduced that had earlier been omitted from the narrative. The participants, having satisfied what they assumed to be the formalities of the task, clearly preferred to exchange reminiscences of what was best, worst, funny or incredible – memories based upon personal reactions and evaluations. But again, the data are not reducible merely to the expression of a set of individual reactions. Each reaction and evaluation was offered for general approval or disputation, as a candidate for social comparison, either for general acceptance as shared and ratified, or for marking out the offerer as distinctive. The group members operated with the notion that emotional reactions and evaluations were subject to the same sorts of social processes as simple versions of events. Participants expressed disagreement, agreement, sarcasm and embarrassment at each other's reactions, while generally orientating themselves to the creation of a consensus of evaluation. Diane's final few turns are remarkable in this respect; she was already agreeing with Karen that 'the most realistic bit was that bit in the middle' before she had heard which 'bit' Karen was referring to.

Text and Talk

This point about the importance of the communicational setting, or discursive frame, for what is remembered is a general one that goes beyond the confines of the *E.T.* study. It pervades all kinds of communicative remembering, including many experimental designs for individual memory, in which we can take the subjects' performance as communicational – occasioned as a response to the experimenter's instructions. For example, it arose in another study we did with a class of students replicating Bartlett. Here, we were interested in the differences between oral and written communication. A great deal has been written by psychologists, anthropologists and historians about this difference, about the different formal and functional characteristics of speech and writing, and the profound effects upon human thought and intelligence of the invention of writing (for example, Goody, 1977; Havelock, 1976; Luria, 1976; Olson, 1980; Ong, 1971; Scribner and Cole, 1981). For written text, some theorists claim all sorts of wonderful and controversial cognitive effects, from the growth of scientific thought to the creation of logical reasoning. But one point that most writers agree about, is the importance of written text for having transformed how we store and use information – written records can be systematically kept, stored and consulted, doing away with the need always to rely upon verbatim recall. The relation to memory is intriguing. We have a picture in which written text lends itself to verbatim copying, storage and repeated consultation. And yet, when it comes to the experimental study of memory, subjects are invariably presented with small bits, or extracts of written materials, and asked to recall them. It was, in fact, partly the prospect of dealing with spoken language, rather than written text, that had encouraged us to look at conversational remembering. People generally have to rely upon memory for what was said, but can consult the originals for what is written.

We asked our experimental group to try remembering, conversationally, some stories that they had encountered in the practical class the week before (see Edwards and Middleton, 1986b). One member of the group had been absent that week, and was asked to act as a 'scribe', making a written record of the story that the rest of the group then proceeded to reconstruct, talking their way through it, as in the *E.T.* study. Extract 5 shows a brief sample of data from that study. On the left are sections of the recorded conversation, and on the right is what the scribe wrote.

EXTRACT 5: *Text and Talk*

Talk	Text
1 'beautiful woman': 'messenger': 'serving wench': 'buxom wench': 'Chinese buxom wench': 'she had big tits'	Serving maid . . .
2 '. . . he meets the mistress who was the most beautiful intelligent . . .': 'what's happened to the purple wine . . . oh sorry purple wine and fornication . . . and he goes inside and they lie down on the couch well eventually chatting her up first they lie down on the couch and drink purple wine and fornicate'	. . . meets mistress. Beautiful and intelligent. Falls instantly in love. Goes in and they lie on couch, they drink purple wine and fornicate
3 'he goes back to the old nobleman's house'	Goes on to nobleman's house.
4 'he decides he quite likes the idea of purple wine and fornication'	Decides he wishes he was back with the woman.
5 '. . . so he keeps on organizing, he keeps on talking about visiting his parents when he is going to the house in the forest'	Says he's going home but really goes back to woman in cottage.
6 '. . . in town shopping', 'in the market-place'	. . . in the market.

What interested us were the qualitative differences between the conversation and its written record. The written version was considerably shorter, but was also qualitatively different, tidied up, serialized into a single coherent narrative and contained several interesting transformations and additions to what was said, such as those listed in Extract 5. The rather bawdy conversation was even bowdlerized in the written version, with most of the overt sexual references omitted or rendered euphemistically. Some things are treated as easier to say than to write, and some things are considered more appropriate to written text than to speech. Text is generally 'for the record', more formal, more condensed. Obviously what interested us was that going from speech to writing, we found many of the same phenomena that Bartlett had attributed to the workings of memory – condensations, additions, transformations, the imposition of coherence and so on. But the scribe did not have to rely upon memory. She wrote as the others spoke, and got them to pause, slow down, repeat things and occasionally questioned the accuracy of what she was writing. It was Bartlett without remembering. The effects seemed to be at least partly due to the different communicative conventions of talk and text.

In fact, there is evidence of similar, text-convention effects at work in Bartlett's own data. Extract 6 is from his classic 'War of the Ghosts' study (Bartlett, 1932: 65, 121).

EXTRACT 6: *The War of the Ghosts*

The original
One of the young men said: 'I have no arrows,' 'Arrows are in the canoe,' they said. 'I will not go along. I might be killed. My relatives do not know where I have gone. But you,' he said, turning to the other, 'may go with them.' So one of the young men went, but the other returned home.

Reproduction 2
'No,' they replied, 'we cannot fight, for we have no arrows.' 'There are arrows in the canoe, so come and tarry not.' 'Nay,' replied one of the Indians, 'I shall not come, for if I am killed, my people, who have need of me, will be sore grieved.' Then, turning to his companion, he went on: 'You go. You have no friends, and if aught befall you will not be missed.' 'Aye, go I will,' answered his friend, and bidding him adieu, he joined the men in the canoe; and the other went back home.

The second, reproduced version has clearly acquired embellishments of the sort that Bartlett himself, and subsequent cognitive psychology, has discovered: inferential links that fill in the gaps of narrative coherence, such as the notion that the Indian who 'went' was his companion's 'friend', and actually got into the canoe, and said goodbye to his companion, and the implication is also spelled out explicitly, that the possession of arrows bears upon whether the two men should go and fight. But in addition to these inferential links, other aspects of the transformation are essentially *literary*. It is imbued with the stylistic conventions of English and Scottish folksongs and tales (bidding adieu, tarrying not, being sore grieved, saying 'aye' and 'nay', and so on). Bartlett's subject was obviously not merely remembering the story. He was *rewriting* it, such that the nature of the remembering was significantly a function of the style of the discourse which constituted it.

Discourse Analysis and Versions of Events

Wertsch (1987) points out that conventional differences in versions of remembered events extend not only to speech and writing, but also to different sorts of written texts, such as police records versus newspaper reports. Indeed, this is a general point that any pragmatic approach to the construction of versions has to recognize; accounts are always designed to accomplish particular pragmatic actions, and will vary accordingly. This means that versions of events cannot be taken merely as windows upon individuals' mental representations, but have to be studied in their social, conversational context. Wertsch's perspective derives from the socio-historical tradition of Soviet development psychology, which originated with Vygotsky (LCHC, 1983; Vygotsky, 1987; Wertsch, 1985). The emphasis is upon the socio-historical construction of mind, a process in which cultural signs (including language) function as mediators of human social activity, and are the major origin of intelligent thought. Language is instrumental; signs are 'mental tools' that work, that mediate understanding of the past in action in the present (cf. Middleton, 1987).

It is not a far cry from this notion of the representational instrumentality of language to seeing versions of events as pragmatically variable accomplishments. Recent sociological and social-psychological developments in discourse analysis (Gilbert and Mulkay, 1984; Potter and Wetherell, 1987) offer an approach to text and conversation in which versions (of events, of persons, of scientific discoveries or whatever) are shown to be not only pragmatically occasioned, but also intrinsically structured and organized to accomplish particular sorts of pragmatic actions. We can illustrate this approach to the investigation of remembering with some recent work by Edwards and Potter (1989).

This study begins with a detailed examination of Ulric Neisser's (1981) classic paper on John Dean's testimony to the Senate Watergate committee. Through a close comparison of Dean's testimony with Nixon's subsequently published 'presidential transcripts' of tape-recorded conversations in the Oval Office, Neisser had been impressed by the extent to which Dean failed to remember all sort of details, and even important elements of the gist of things, while nevertheless managing to convey an accurate impression of Nixon's involvement, at least in the 'cover-up'. In seeking to clarify what Dean actually remembered, Neisser proposes a threefold set of types of accuracy of recall. These are: (a) verbatim recall, (b) gist and (c) repisodic memory. Verbatim recall is word-for-word accuracy; gist is getting the essential features correct despite detailed omissions and errors; repisodic memory is at a still more general level, and consists in doing what Dean did, recalling the overall nature and implications of a repeated series of events, despite lots of gross errors of recall: 'there is usually a deeper level at which he is right. He gave an accurate portrayal of the real situation, of the actual characters and commitments of the people he knew, and of the events that lay behind the conversations he was trying to remember' (Neisser, 1981: 4).

In adopting a discourse-analytical approach (cf. Potter and Wetherell, 1987), Edwards and Potter (1989) argue that people's accounts of past events, before they can be taken as data on the cognitive workings of memory, need to be examined as contextualized and variable productions that do pragmatic and rhetorical work, such that no one version can be taken as a person's real memory. Indeed, what is offered and taken to be an adequate summary, the 'gist' of things, is itself studiable as a participant's accomplishment, a matter for disputation or agreement. Similarly, as we noted earlier, Edwards and Mercer (1987; 1989) have analysed the way that summaries of classroom lessons are used by teachers to reformulate messy and problematical events according to their originally planned outcomes – in effect, articulating classroom events in terms of what 'ought' to have happened. Dean's rememberings can be examined, therefore, in their conversational context, as versions that are designed for the context in which they occur, as warrants under cross-examination for Dean's own essential truthfulness, for his lack of involvement and personal responsibility in the criminal events at issue. Thus, it is part of Dean's account that he was blessed with a particularly good memory for detailed conversation. This was warranted in various ways, including both direct claims, and also the offering of graphic descriptions of place and circumstances:

> . . . anyone who recalls my student years knew that I was very fast at recalling information . . . (quoted in Neisser, 1981: 5)
>
> . . . you know the way there are two chairs at the side of the President's desk . . . on the left-hand chair Mr. Haldeman was sitting . . . (p. 11)
>
> I can vividly recall that the way he sort of rolled his chair back from his desk and leaned over to Mr. Haldeman and said, 'A million dollars is no problem.' (p. 18)

These sorts of accounts served to bolster Dean's claim to an almost verbatim memory of conversations in the Oval Office.

Edwards and Potter (1989) proceed to analyse a series of newspaper accounts of a controversial press briefing given by the British Chancellor of the Exchequer, Nigel Lawson. Amongst the various devices and variances analysed is the sort of empiricist warranting (cf. Gilbert and Mulkay, 1984) of factuality of which Dean made use. Lawson had declared the initially published press accounts of the briefing to be 'a farrago of invention', 'inaccurate, half-baked' accounts which 'bear no relation whatever to what I said' (*Times, Guardian*, Tuesday 8 November 1988). The journalists concerned subsequently produced detailed narratives of the events, enriched with the sort of descriptive detail that made John Dean's rememberings so convincing:

> At one point I heard a click, and assumed the tape had run out. It was directly in front of me. When I looked to check, the spools were still spinning. The clicking I heard turned out to be Don Macintyre of the Sunday Telegraph, seated to my right, chewing a pen top. (*Sunday Mirror*, 13 November 1988)

It was noticeable that these sorts of descriptions occurred only after the issue of accuracy and fallibility of accounts had been raised, and indeed, as with Dean, after the competence and truthfulness of the rememberers had been called into question. Versions of events were constructed rhetorically, as parts of arguments (cf. Billig, 1987).

Conversations with Children

We have been speculating about developmental implications – about how children might come to use metacognitive formulations of the workings of memory, how they are inculcated into educated discursive practices and understandings (cf. Walkerdine, 1988), and how they may be socialized in family conversations into ways of representing the past – how to talk about it, what sorts of things are memorable and why. In a further study (Edwards and Middleton, 1988), we collected a set of tape-recordings of family conversations, in which mothers, and sometimes fathers, recorded themselves with their young children – usually pairs of siblings aged between four and six – talking through their collections of family photographs.

EXTRACT 7: *Learning Remembering*

> *Mother*: oh look/ there's when we went to the riding stables wasn't it?
> *Paul*: yeh/ er er
> *Mother*: you were trying to reach up and stroke that horse
> *Paul*: where? [*laughs*]
> *Mother*: would you like to do that again?
> *Paul*: yeh
> *Mother*: you don't look very happy though
> *Paul*: because I thought I was going to fall off
> *Mother*: you thought you was going to fall off did you?/ right misery/ daddy was holding on to you so that you didn't// did it FEEL very bumpy?
> *Paul*: yeh
> *Mother*: did it make your legs ache? [*Paul laughs*] Rebecca enjoyed it

Paul: yeh
Mother: she's a bit older wasn't she?/ you were a little boy there

Extract 7 (unpublished elsewhere) is a sample from one of these conversations. It contains many of the features that we have found interesting. Most of the work is being done by Paul's mother – she sets the scene, locating the picture in the context of the past events in which it was taken, a visit to the riding stables. She provides for Paul a description of what he is depicted as doing, and prompts him for an affective evaluation of the past that includes its relevance to the present and the future – 'would you like to do that again?' Paul's apparent unhappiness in the next picture is noted, and he is asked for, and provides an explanation ('I thought I was going to fall off'). Past events and emotional states are treated as essentially rational – they require explanations, motivational accounts for why they occur. Paul's mother recalls that he had been a 'right misery', enquires further about his feelings and reactions and points out that, in contrast, his elder sister had enjoyed herself. This in turn provides an occasion for some developmental comparisons – Rebecca was older, Paul was only a 'little boy' – the implication being that he can expect to react more favourably, like his sister, to future opportunities to go horse riding.

These conversations were used by parents as opportunities for marking past events as significant, recalling children's reactions and relationships, cuing the children to remember them, providing descriptions in terms of which those rememberings could be couched and providing all sorts of *contextual* reminiscences, prompted by the pictures, but of things and events not included within them. Children's identity and relationships change through time, and it is an important part of the developmental process that children come to see themselves as growing and changing, in specified, value-laden ways, within a culturally normative, moral world. This involves making sense of the past, of what one has been, and of the future, what one may become. Family photographs are a powerful mediator of such perspectives, especially when they are taken up in conversation with parents and siblings, and become the basis of comparisons and reactions shared between the people concerned. The children took an especially keen interest in seeing what they and their family looked like in other contexts (such as on the beach, undressed, with mummy bathing topless and daddy with hairy legs), and in recalling what they themselves looked like at an earlier age, reacting mainly with amusement, and making evaluations of the changes, comparing each other and sometimes mocking each other's earlier immaturity. The pictures and the conversational rememberings provided for a kind of family forum in which personal identities, social relationships and the milestones of developmental change could be marked out and interpreted, becoming the basis of an articulated family history.

If remembering is an occasioned activity, done for pragmatic purposes, and sensitive to its social and conversational context, then there is a sense also in which the children are being taught how to remember.

EXTRACT 8: *Inference and Argument Revisited*

1 With Helen (2 yrs 3 mths) and Sandra (4 yrs 11 mths)
Mother: . . . who's that?
Helen: I don't know
Mother: do you know where you were there?
Helen: [. . .]
Mother: whose house were you at there?/ do you recognize . . .
Sandra: . . . look there's Mummy on a boat/ I didn't go on boat [. . .]
  'cause look there's ⌈ [. . .]
Mother: ⌊ oh yes I bet that was in Liverpool when we went
  on the ferry/ ferry boat
2 With Paul (4 yrs 3 mths) and Rebecca (5 yrs 10 mths)
Mother: do you remember being on this beach?
Paul: yuk// no
Mother: don't you/ when we went to Jersey/ on the aeroplane//do you
  not remember that?
Paul: is that Jersey?
*Mother:*mm/ look Rebecca's wearing a hat that says Jersey on it
Paul: look/ what is that?
Mother: [. . .] probably a book we were going to go on that/ boat/ or a
  trip down the river/ and we took one or two books to keep you two
  occupied

The examples in Extract 8 (from two different families) are typical of many other such exchanges, in which the children could not recall something, and the mother then proceeded to invoke contextual reminders as an aid to recall. The mothers expressed directly the inferential, reconstructive basis of the process – 'I bet that was in Liverpool', 'probably a book . . .'. And Paul's mother offers him the evidence provided by the picture for concluding that they were on holiday in Jersey – the name of the place was written on his sister's hat. Paul's mother overtly demonstrates how recall (versions of the past) can be justified on the basis of inference and argument.

It is not possible to state definitively from these brief extracts what the children were actually learning; but it seems obvious that these kinds of family conversations are a rich learning environment, in which children's efforts at remembering are taken up by parents in conversation that centres on elaborations and explanations of things, resolving disputes between people, invoking context and using inference to work out and justify particular versions of events. It is an interactive environment, in which the parent takes pains to elicit perceptions, memories and judgements from the children, to examine and elaborate upon them, to contextualize and assign significance to them, in terms of a shared past in which personal identity, family relationships and the landmarks of development can be reconstructed. It is a process that can be well described by Vygotsky's concept of the 'zone of proximal development' (see Bakhurst, this volume), in which the development of mental processes proceeds within just such a social apprenticeship. The focus of our continuing analysis is upon the developmental implications of the rhetorical organization of family conversations.

Part of what the children are presumably acquiring is discourse itself – a shared way of talking about things, shared reference, shared evaluations, or criteria for evaluation, ways of describing and narrating, the selection of criteria, the offering of more or less interesting or convincing versions. Part of that process is defining what words to name things by. This is, of course, an aspect of most pedagogic transactions, whether children are at home acquiring language and everyday culture, or at school, doing classroom lessons. But it also occurs in adult conversation, as an intrinsic part of putting together common versions of things, where some manner of joint problem solving is involved. This is demonstrated in the difficulties a group of English Morris dancers had in reconstructing a dance which they wished to add to their performance repertoire (Middleton, 1987). Their problem was to re-create an 'authentic' version danced in time to the musical accompaniment. Among the resources they used to achieve this were a cryptic text of dance notation, a vocabulary of terms describing the dance moves and the beat of the dance tune. The reconstruction mainly centred upon the redefinition of the terms they used to describe and announce the moves in the dance. Through argument they improvised the redefinition of the dance terminology and how to fit the problematic moves to the music. The repair and development of the dance and the redefinition of the vocabulary were interdependent in achieving a commonly agreed version, a shared understanding of the dance's movements that would extend beyond any particular performance.

Discourse and Cognition

In offering a discourse-analytical approach to remembering, we are not proposing a simple reductionism. The phenomena studied in conversational remembering are not reducible to an account framed in terms of cognitive-neural processes, and neither would such an account be reducible to a description of social-discursive ones. But it is likely that the study of the everyday social-discursive basis of remembering will reveal some ways in which the exclusively individual-cognitive approach to memory can start to seem arbitrary. One of the most obvious benefits is a kind of ecological validity (cf. Neisser, 1982), the study of remembering as people actually do it, addressing the concerns and difficulties of everyday life, including both the ordinary and the extraordinary, rather than when posed in the psychological laboratory with materials and instructions that offer little resemblance to the situations in which remembering is ordinarily done. Indeed, it may be that the amount of control possible in experimental studies is made available only by altering the phenomenon to something which is unrecognizable to everyday practice.

For example, psychological experiments have arbitrarily reified particular aspects of everyday remembering: such as defining memory per se, in terms of a restricted sort of everyday setting in which remembering might be done – the specific communicative context of dispassionate, accurate reporting, usually dealing with materials which have very little personal significance for the rememberer. The experimental approach lends itself most readily to a conception of remembering as involving discrete factors which have separable causal influences upon discrete mental faculties. It is the legacy of Ebbinghaus's (1885) first studies of his own recall of lists of 'nonsense syllables' in preference for materials that might be contaminated by having some ready-made meaning or relevance to the rememberer. As Bartlett (1932) demonstrated, and much of cognitive psychology has done since, those elements of meaning and significance have to be replaced in order for remembering to work in anything like its normal manner. In experimental designs, meaning and context are defined as variables, factors whose effects on the accuracy of recall are manipulable. In the study of discursive remembering, significance and context are intrinsic to the activity, constitutive of it and constituted by it, rather than causally influential upon some other thing called 'memory'.

The individual-cognitive approach conflates method with theory, again producing an arbitrarily limited account of memory. The input–output discrepancy method encourages the notion of memory as being all about the cognitive processes that intervene between input and output – that take place in the time between, and in the space between the ears. Theoretically, this becomes the study of information processing – the method becomes the theory, as input is traced through stages of processing towards ouput. It is noticeable

how the problematical nature of perception is carefully circum-
vented in memory studies by its incorporation into methodology.
The 'original experience' become non-psychological, in that it is
identified as the 'materials' themselves, the stimulus materials,
objectively available for the psychologist and the reader to see. In
contrast, the study of discursive remembering deals with output
alone. Thus, in the study of teachers' recaps of what has been done
in classroom lessons (Edwards and Mercer, 1989), what we have is
two discourses at different points in time, each doing constructive
work on what everyone is doing, seeing and thinking. The later
'recaps' are reformulations in situated discourse of earlier situated
discourse, which is studiable in just the same way. There is no
neutral 'input'. As with our study of Dean and Lawson (Edwards
and Potter, 1989), the nature of the true original event is precisely
the point at issue for the participants, and is studiable as such
through their discourse. What we have for comparison is not input
and output, but two outputs at different times, serving different
communicative purposes, and requiring the same sort of analysis. In
our initial investigation of recall of the film *E.T.*, that topic was
chosen because we imagined it would be useful, if not necessary, to
have recourse to the original experience. In fact, no such recourse
was taken, nor felt necessary (indeed, one of us did not see the film
until some four years later). Of course, had such recourse been
taken, it is not obvious how it would have avoided constructive
work on the part of the investigators that would be, from however
advantaged a position, of an essentially similar sort to that of the
rememberers. With discourse analysis, we do not have to say
anything about what has happened in the space or time between –
we merely have to deal with a socially occasioned variability from
one time to another. The methodological advantage is considerable
– like the behaviourists, our analysis remains at all times close to the
observable, recorded conversational record. But unlike the behaviourists, we are not shackled with the severe limitations of stimulus–
response psychology.

The study of remembering in conversation affords unique
opportunities for understanding remembering as organized social
action. Reports of past events are studiable as pragmatically
occasioned versions whose variability is due not only to the nature
and vicissitudes of individual cognition, but to the conversational
work that those versions accomplish. Collective versions of past
events are available as grounds for justifying current and future
action; and because they are so 'useful' it is quite ordinary to find
them being reconstructed and contested.

44 *Collective remembering*

References

Atkinson, J.M. and Heritage, J. (eds) (1984) *Structures of Social Action: Studies in Conversation Analysis*. Cambridge: Cambridge University Press.

Bartlett, F.C. (1932) *Remembering: a Study in Experimental and Social Psychology*. Cambridge: Cambridge University Press.

Billig, M. (1987) *Arguing and Thinking*. Cambridge: Cambridge University Press.

Billig, M., Condor, S., Edwards, D., Gane, M., Middleton, D.J. and Radley, A.R. (1988) *Ideological Dilemmas: a Social Psychology of Everyday Thinking*. London: Sage.

Bransford, J.D. (1979) *Human Cognition: Learning, Understanding and Remembering*. Belmont, CA: Wadsworth.

Bransford, J.D. and McCarrell, N.S. (1974) 'A sketch of a cognitive approach to comprehension', in W. Weimer and D.S. Palermo (eds), *Cognition and the Symbolic Processes*. Hillsdale, NJ: Lawrence Erlbaum.

Brown, G. and Yule, G. (1983) *Discourse Analysis*. Cambridge: Cambridge University Press.

Crook, C. and Middleton, D. (1989) 'Bartlett's significance for a cultural psychology of cognition', paper presented at the Annual Conference of the British Psychological Society, St. Andrew's, Scotland, April.

Ebbinghaus, H. (1885) *Über das Gedächtnis: Untersuchungen zur experimentellen Psychologie*. Leipzig: Duncker & Humboldt.

Edwards, D. and Goodwin, R.Q. (1985) 'The language of shared attention and visual experience: a functional study of early nomination', *Journal of Pragmatics*, 9 (4): 475–93.

Edwards, D. and Mercer, N.M. (1987) *Common Knowledge: the Development of Understanding in the Classroom*. London: Methuen.

Edwards, D. and Mercer, N.M. (1989) 'Reconstructing context: the conventionalization of classroom knowledge', *Discourse Processes*, 12: 91–104.

Edwards, D. and Middleton, D. (1986a) 'Joint remembering: constructing an account of shared experience through conversational discourse', *Discourse Processes*, 9 (4): 423–59.

Edwards, D. and Middleton, D. (1986b) 'Text for memory: joint recall with a scribe', *Human Learning*, 5 (3): 125–38.

Edwards, D. and Middleton, D. (1987) 'Conversation and remembering: Bartlett revisited', *Applied Cognitive Psychology*, 1: 77–92.

Edwards, D. and Middleton, D. (1988) 'Conversational remembering and family relationships: how children learn to remember', *Journal of Social and Personal Relationships*, 5: 3–25.

Edwards, D. and Potter, J. (1989) 'The chancellor's memory: rhetoric and truth in discursive remembering', unpublished mimeo, Loughborough University.

Flavell, J.H. and Wellman, H.M. (1977) 'Metamemory', in R. Kail and J. Hagen (eds), *Perspectives on the Development of Memory and Cognition*. Hillsdale, NJ: Lawrence Erlbaum.

Gergen, K.J. (1985) 'The social constructionist movement in modern psychology', *American Psychologist*, 40: 266–75.

Gilbert, G.N. and Mulkay, M. (1984) *Opening Pandora's Box: a Sociological Analysis of Scientists' Discourse*. Cambridge: Cambridge University Press.

Goody, J. (1977) *The Domestication of the Savage Mind*. Cambridge: Cambridge University Press.

Harré, R. (1983) *Personal Being: a Theory for Individual Psychology*. Oxford: Blackwell.

Havelock, E. (1976) *Origins of Western Literacy*. Toronto: Ontario Institute for Studies in Education Press.

Heelas, P. and Lock, A. (eds) (1981) *Indigenous Psychologies*. London: Academic Press.

Heritage, J. (1984) *Garfinkel and Ethnomethodology*. Cambridge: Polity Press.

LCHC (Laboratory of Comparative Human Cognition) (1983) 'Culture and cognitive development', in W. Kessen (ed.), *Carmichael's Manual of Child Psychology: History, Theories and Methods*. New York: Wiley.

Levinson, S.C. (1983) *Pragmatics*. Cambridge: Cambridge University Press.

Luria, A.R. (1976) *Cognitive Development: its Cultural and Social Foundations*. Cambridge, MA: Harvard University Press.

Mead, G.H. (1934) *Mind, Self and Society*. Chicago: University of Chicago Press.

Middleton, D. (1987) 'Dance to the music: conversational remembering and joint activity in learning an English Morris dance', *Quarterly Newsletter of the Laboratory of Comparative Human Cognition*, 9 (1): 23–38.

Middleton, D. (1988) 'Talking work: argument in co-ordination, commemoration and improvization in team work', paper presented at University of California San Diego Conference on Work and Communication. 11–15 July.

Neisser, U. (1981) 'John Dean's memory: a case study', *Cognition*, 9: 1–22.

Neisser, U. (1982) *Memory Observed: Remembering in Natural Contexts*. Oxford: W.H. Freeman.

Olson, D.R. (1980) 'Some social aspects of meaning in oral and written language', in D.R. Olson (ed.), *Social Foundations of Language and Thought: Essays in Honor of J.S. Bruner*. New York: Norton.

Ong, W.J. (1971) *Rhetoric, Romance and Technology: Studies in the Interaction of Expression and Culture*. Ithaca, NY: Cornell University Press.

Piaget, J. (1928) *Judgement and Reasoning in the Child*. London: Routledge & Kegan Paul.

Potter, J. and Wetherell, M. (1987) *Discourse and Social Psychology*. London: Sage.

Scribner, S. and Cole, M. (1981) *The Psychology of Literacy*. Cambridge, MA: Harvard University Press.

Vygotsky, L.S. (1978) *Mind in Society*, ed. by Michael Cole, Vera John-Steiner, Sylvia Scribner and Glen Souberman. Cambridge, MA: Harvard University Press.

Vygotsky, L.S. (1987) *Thought and Language*, ed. by A. Kozulin. Cambridge, MA: MIT Press.

Walkerdine, V. (1988) *The Mastery of Reason: Cognitive Development and the Production of Rationality*. London: Routledge.

Wertsch, J.V. (1985) *Vygotsky and the Social Formation of Mind*. Cambridge, MA: Harvard University Press.

Wertsch, J.V. (1987) 'Collective Memory: Issues from a Sociohistorical Perspective', *Quarterly Newsletter of the Laboratory of Comparative Human Cognition*, 9 (1): 19–22.

3

Artefacts, Memory and a Sense of the Past

Alan Radley

Although psychologists acknowledge the personal significance of particular objects, the place of the material world in the study of memory has, as in other areas of the discipline, been of marginal interest (see, however, Wertsch, 1985). The history of the study of memory is a tale of the search for a faculty, a quest for the way in which the mind-brain codes, stores and retrieves information. Only with the recent interest in language and in cultural aspects of thinking has there emerged the wider view of remembering as something that people do together, reminding themselves of and co-memorating experiences which they have jointly undertaken (Edwards and Middleton, 1986; 1987; Shotter and Gauld, 1981). This line of inquiry draws upon the work of Bartlett (1932) in his study of remembering as a form of constructive activity, emphasizing that memory is not the retrieval of stored information, but the putting together of a claim about past states of affairs by means of a framework of shared cultural understanding. Where Bartlett had described memory as a constructive act 'inside the head' of the social individual, this modern perspective locates memory within the discourse of people talking together about the past. Memory, as a problem for study, is liberated from the constraints of faculty psychology to become the subject of social psychological research.

This movement, however, still falls short of addressing questions relating to remembering in a world of things – both natural, and products of cultural endeavour – where it concentrates upon memory as a product of discourse. The emphasis upon language tends to hide interesting questions which arise once we acknowledge that the sphere of material objects is ordered in ways upon which we rely for a sense of continuity and as markers of temporal change. As an example of continuity, we remember the layout of our homes without needing to speak of it or to recollect where everything is. Indeed, we rely upon this ordering of the house and its contents in order to achieve other aims; climbing stairs, reaching for a light-switch or the coffee-pot are successful because the objects in question remain stable in relation to each other. The way in which these material forms embody categorization processes should not, however, be dismissed as idiosyncrasies or made secondary to 'habit'. Cultural considerations enable us to recognize that this reliance on an ordered material world extends to other people's houses and to other social environments which are specially designed to facilitate not only what should be remembered (for example, in a supermarket, a church) but how this remembering should be conducted.

In this chapter I shall take up the question of what might be learned from redirecting our view away from the remembering subject to social practices in which people engage with the material world. The discussion is guided by the argument that signification within memory is inadequately understood by reference only to a cognitive ordering of neutral or passive objects: how and what we remember is also objectified in material forms which are sometimes (but not always) arranged to embody categories and thereby mark out the objects' significance. To pursue this argument will necessitate examining the role of artefacts in social life as well as indicating how, specifically, they are implicated in how people go about establishing their individual and collective pasts.

At a mundane level, many objects in the everyday world are inextricably tied up with memory. A study of people's personal possessions shows, as would be expected, that objects are used to establish a link with the past which helps to sustain identity, and that this increases as individuals become older (Csikszentmihalyi and Rochberg-Halton, 1981). When put aside or gathered into collections, everyday objects can be used, either informally as memorabilia or formally in museums, to evoke a sense of their time and place. It is often the ordinariness of such objects, sometimes coupled with the circumstances of their acquisition, that enables the owner to indulge in particularly pleasurable forms of remembering (Taylor, 1981). Museums, as with other edifices in the community (cathedrals, town halls, castles) are repositories of objects which exist as special artefacts, by reference to which past epochs may be read and understood. In these cases, people do not remember a series of personal events which touched their own lives but enjoy 'a sense of the past' through the understanding of a history which other people appear to have created. These points give the impression that artefacts serve each and every one of us in the same way. This, however, is not the case and it will be one of the purposes of this essay to show why our different reactions to and sensibilities of objects are important for an understanding of remembering.

One of the hallmarks of individual psychology is its disregard of social differences, of the fact that people are constituted differently in their sense of what is memorable or is worthy of collection and recollection. A social-psychological theory of memory cannot start from this position, nor should it remain with the notion that remembering, if not a purely mental phenomenon, is limited to being a verbal one. People do not only remember about things – how they looked or what happened to them – but they also remember what to do with them, how to engage with objects so that such and such an event might occur. Remembering is a broader phenomenon than is signified by either of the terms recall or reminiscence.

There are objects which are made specially in order that they might help us to remember. They do this by their form and location as well as by the text which they often bear. Some of them are relatively permanent features of the environment, such as a tombstone or a plaque unveiled by a local dignitary. Others are transitory markers of an event to be recorded (a flag planted on a mountain top) or of an action which is yet to be undertaken (a knotted handkerchief) (Harris, 1984). In both cases – transitory and permanent – people are fashioning objects or installing artefacts in order that something be remembered, or even commemorated in the future. The world of objects, as material culture, is therefore the tangible record of human endeavour, both social and individual. As part of that endeavour certain objects are marked out intentionally as things which will help their makers – or those who come after them – to remember an event, activity or principle. Other artefacts are not so intentionally created, but only later come to be marked in a way which designates them as special possessions, as part of the cultural heritage or of one's memorabilia.

With the focus in psychology upon remembering as an 'internal event', it is perhaps not surprising that most attention should have been paid to the role of objects as triggers for the recall of certain events or experiences. Ever since Proust wrote of the effect of the *madeleine* upon poor Mr Swann (was ever a tea-time so encumbered with unwanted memories?), the place of objects as constitutive of affect-laden images has been part of treatises on everyday remembering (Bartlett, 1932). This by itself, however, does far less than justice to the ways in which people are not only re-minded by objects in their environment (cf. Lynch's (1960) landscape as a vast mnemonic), but, through being variously engaged in the fabrication of material culture, constitute the opportunities and directions for the appreciation of what has gone before, can be re-assessed or re-enacted once again.

Memory in Time and Place

Outside of the psychological laboratory and the examination room, the world of everyday memories embraces not only personal experiences but social ones as well. In the neighbourhood, in the home or in the work-place people remember things that they or others have done, things that have happened to them and changes which have taken place. The character of these long-term memories is biographical, stressing the shared background within which those concerned can appreciate their common past. As such, these memories are part of culture and depend, in various ways, upon the physical setting for how people remember the course of events leading up to the present. It is not just that individuals remember specific things, or are reminded of the past by particular objects figured against the background of a shared discussion of the past. Artefacts and the fabricated environment are also there as a tangible expression of the basis from which one remembers, the material aspect of the setting which justifies the memories so constructed. What this means for a social psychology of remembering is that one must look beyond the idea of a single cognitive faculty which people have in common to the proposition that their ways of remembering may be different depending upon their relationship to their community, including the world of objects it produces and preserves.

This can be illustrated by reference to a study of the socio-cultural identities of different sections of an ageing Swiss population (Lalive d'Épinay, 1986). Working-class respondents (as designated in the study) lived in a neighbourhood which they had adapted to their personal use. However, in spite of frequenting it they were subject to it being changed by planners and other authorities in ways which they had learned to 'put up with'. Their relationship to their physical environment – 'making little journeys . . . gazing at the pageant of life and history' – makes the form of their memories understandable. These are concrete, stoical and without nostalgia: 'We were very poor at the time. My father died when I was 2½. I had a brother of 3½ and another of 18 months. My father met his death in the mountains. It wasn't easy at the time, there wasn't any insurance' (Lalive d'Épinay, 1986).

These memories are contrasted, in their form, to those of the middle-class property-owners, for whom the sense of their history is marked by their ability to steer their own lives, and to negotiate their way through the constraints of the economic and physical environment. As Lalive d'Épinay remarks, these respondents explicitly avoided the concrete details of their lives: 'Well, I don't think we'll go into lots of details which are quite unimportant'. For these people, what was remembered were personal achievements and important transition points in their lives. The sense of the past, expressed by members of the two communities, was different in form because they had lived through different cultural contexts. It is not just that one group mentioned physical objects more than the other but that the form of their recollections was different. This is not to say that, given a specific task of recall to carry out, they might not have performed in a similar way. However, the point is that the usual bracketing procedure which psychologists often carry out when studying memory has the effect of obscuring the distinction which Lalive d'Épinay's study brings into focus. (Differences between social classes have also been noted following people being forced to relocate their homes, particularly in that special form of remembering which we call grieving (Fried, 1963).) When one speaks of class differences here, one must assume that shorthand reference is being made to a multiplicity of related distinctions. A world of manual labour in a neighbourhood of which the people own relatively little is contrasted with a life of professional activity undertaken in a sphere of owner-occupation. The different relationships of people to the material world through both their work and their consumption of goods indicate a distinction in how they premise their remembering upon 'the world' in which each has lived.

Remembering, then, is an activity intimately bound up with a sense of the past. It is not a mental exercise which takes place in segmented presents, but describes an activity characteristic of the establishment of biographical identities, by groups as well as by individuals. It is not at all surprising, therefore, that we find remembering to take up much time among the ageing in society, among those who feel that most of their lives (or the significant parts of it) have already been lived. (The implication that reminiscing is limited to the aged is not intended.) Among the elderly, possessions are marked by their mnemonic quality, as a gateway to recapturing experiences and the satisfaction of relationships with loved ones who are now either dead or at some distance. With increasing age, and with increasing marginalization, the elderly cling to the few cherished possessions which they own. Sherman and Newman (1977–78) examined the meaning of personal possessions in a group of elderly people in a nursing home. They found that these objects were, indeed, concrete instances of past events, the meaning of which was sustained in the retelling:

> a gold cross – It was a gift from my son when he was a youngster. He had a paper route and worked and saved very hard to get it for me.

> pictures (photos) – They mean I was a woman. I had children and built my life around them. Happy memories.

In this case the significance of the artefacts, now removed from the temporal and spatial context for which they were obtained, is made through their being the object of discourse. Not only the artefact but the person as subject has been displaced, so that the use of the possession as a vehicle for such remembering is part of a narrative whose purpose may be to repair a biographical disruption which the individual concerned has suffered. In these examples the place of objects in remembering is not only part of getting older (an ageing body) but of the elderly being removed from the centre of the socio-economic stage of their culture. This 'sense of the past' is revealed through efforts to evoke either a sense of continuity with, or a discrete break from, what has gone before.

The different ways in which people furnish rooms – some choosing antiques or displaying heirlooms, while others buy modern artefacts – is evidence of a difference in the maintenance of a particular conception of 'the Past' and the effort to be given over to remembering (Pratt, 1981). Stylistic differences need not be reduced to matters of self-expression, but can be considered as material codifications of continuing social orders, some of which deliberately evoke a sense of continuity, deliberately invite remembering, and in so doing create a temporal perspective which claims for the group who own these artefacts its entitlement to a superior moral status (Douglas and Isherwood, 1979). It is in this context that we have to see the histories of the Victorian chaise longue, the brass telescope or the Regency chair as facets of remembering which are also marks of social distinction for those who can afford them and who are concerned to display them.

The Past Collected Together

We are used to the idea that objects serve as reminders or as a focus for recalling time spent with others or in particular places. However, from what has been said already in this essay, it can be argued that this is a very partial view of the role of artefacts in people's remembering. Objects do seemingly present themselves unexpectedly to 'evoke memories', but they are also very much part of the material world ordered to sustain certain myths and ideologies, both about people as individuals and about particular cultures.

At the level of the individual, we are used to the idea of personal possessions being kept as mementos of times which we wish to remember. The assembly of such items is likely to be more haphazard than planned; a silver cigarette lighter from one's smoking days, a cribbage board from the times when the family came round to play cards. Tossed into drawers or boxes and left for some years, these objects eventually become interesting because they are displaced from their time, from the context shared with other items, and from social practices as part of which they were perhaps merely functional. This is the fate of a small proportion of artefacts which belong to each epoch, surviving through hazard into a period when their displacement is perceived as significant, and in being then deliberately set aside, become marked out as indices of the past, as objects to 'remember by'.

Assembled together by interested individuals, this is one way in which many museums have put together collections over the years. Therefore, the question of what or how objects evoke memories cannot be separated from the issue of the ways they have been displaced over time, and the forms of order to which they have been subject in marking them out as significant. What people remember when they see a gas-mask owned by a member of their family during the Second World War, or what they remember about English history when they view the block and executioner's axe at the Tower of London, are products of particular myths and ideologies in which these objects are significant images. That these kinds of objects play a powerful role in shaping and maintaining people's memories of their collective past – as far as the USA is concerned – has been demonstrated vividly by Hawes (1986) who asked people to produce narrative accounts of selected objects in a folk museum. He found that, on being shown objects such as a candlestick, cooking pot and axe grouped together, his subjects, without exception, produced accounts of the pioneer myth of the nuclear family's role in building colonial America. Hawes argues that these material aspects of myths play a central role in maintaining a particular ideology of American history, part of this being the relation of the present to the past. That is to say, certain artefacts are significant in re-invoking cultural beliefs and feelings, the directions of which imbue these objects with a definite political character. For example, the stories of the 'Wild West' are embodied in the trappings of the cowboy and the indian, and are re-enacted through the adoption of items of clothing and the use of appropriate weapons. Not only are the original objects collected together in museums, but they are replicated in modern theme-parks devoted to entertaining people by encouraging them to re-engage in activities embodied in the objects' ritual uses.

The argument is made that social remembering – the collective recounting of a shared past and the commemoration of events which may be prior to each individual's own experience, is not only sustained by the world of objects and artefacts, but is, in part, shaped through the ways in which the world of things is ordered (Kavanagh, 1989). The displacement of objects from one context to another is not always haphazard, but is often deliberate. What has been called a process of 'singularization' of objects (Kopytoff, 1986) is linked to power relations in society as to who may determine what is to be removed from the sphere of exchange (of wear and decay) and declared significant (and permanent). To take one example from the realm of museology, it has been argued that with the establishment of the Republic of France came the redistribution of objects which had been the property of the king and his followers; these were placed in a museum open to the gaze of the people (Hooper-Greenhill, 1989). The selection, arrangement and labelling of these objects served to commemorate and to justify the revolution. They became the material aspect of a narrative which reconstructed the past of the French people in a particular way.

It is not claimed that every individual's memories are determined by the ordering of objects by sections of society – these inevitably will be coloured by the idiosyncrasies of each encounter. What, instead, is being argued is that no account of social remembering can ignore that everyday life involves the fabrication of the past through a construction of the material world, either in its transformation or in its re-ordering.

To take a further example, this time from the world of art, Berger (1972) has argued that the work of oil paintings commissioned by the wealthy was to create, through the assembly of pictured objects, a celebration of their social position which would be sustained through being viewed by others over the years. (He gives the example of Gainsborough's picture 'Mr and Mrs Andrews', showing a wealthy couple painted against the background of the very substantial estate which they owned and over which they enjoyed power and, through this, privilege in society.) What we, as spectators, then remember is a function of these material forms which, paradoxically, are obscured by the new symbolisms of the art expert. This therefore leads to an important point having considerable implications for cultural memory; that the displacements of objects from one context to another over time (such as the removal of a religious painting from a church to an art gallery) allows certain features of the object to remain significant while making us forget (if we ever clearly knew) by what transformations the artefact achieved its present importance. By comparison with students of material culture, psychologists studying memory through a serial remembering study (Bartlett, 1932) are privileged to see the processes of transformation taking place under their eyes. However, in the compression of events, and from the researcher's position of temporal authority, the psychologist creates an ahistoric time in comparison with changes in the material world. The form and the duration of transformations in the ordering of artefacts – their historical progression and decay – suggest possibilities for the study of a cultural sense of the past which go beyond inquiries into the memories of recent collective experience.

The Making of Memories

In the previous section I focused upon the way in which social, or rather cultural, remembering is sustained by the re-ordering of objects in terms of chosen enduring qualities. Indeed, it is the enduring nature of objects that allows them to proceed, often relatively unchanged, through the various periods of people's lives so that they can 're-invoke' the contexts of which they were once a part. From what has been said already, it is clear that the use of objects for remembering is both intended and has unintended features. I have tried to show that the intended aspects need to be sought in social relationships and group differences. They are also reflected, however, at the level of individual actions when people seek to use objects to shape how others will remember them in years to come. This is particularly appropriate at the time when someone has either just died, or is about to die. In the former case, it is a matter for the relatives of the deceased person to decide how the person's possessions should be treated. The death of a person is a displacement of a special kind, through which the ownership of an entire estate is subject to cultural rules (and laws) about its transition. At an informal level, within the family, the possessions of the deceased person can be held, as it were, in suspension – untouched – making them sacred in their being marked as being beyond disposal or exchange. Unruh (1983) has described these and other ways in which people's possessions are employed to establish memories of what they were like before they died, which are chosen as special in order to be identified with the individual concerned.

Equally intriguing, from the perspective of the making of memories, is the way in which people who are either approaching death, or are of an age where they feel it not to be too distant, use material objects to create in their survivors the kind of memory of themselves which they desire. This can be done through passing on treasured possessions known to be of significance by the recipient. It is something 'owned and used' by that person, showing the marks of their personal attention. Its special quality arises not only from the fact that it was theirs, but that it was chosen, by the owner, for the recipient. Unruh (1983) notes, however, that it is rare for the new owner to feel the same way (that is, to remember) about the object as did its original owner. As an alternative strategy, the elderly or dying might arrange to buy special gifts for their dependents, relatives or friends, as a way of establishing through the nature of the gift, as well as the giving, a special context which will mark out the object – that is, make it memorable in a particular way – while it is in that person's possession. At the level of individuals, too, memory is fabricated by people for people, through either the shaping or exchange of objects. There can be no guarantee, of course, that the recipients of such gifts will always, if ever, remember the donor in quite the way that it was hoped or intended. There is always this 'mix' of intentional and fortuitous circumstances surrounding memory involving things. This is a significant matter, and one to which I will turn attention in the concluding section. At this point I want to illustrate this peculiar relationship between the intended and the unintended aspects of things in memory by making recourse to a well-known narrative. In Antoine de Saint-Exupéry's story of *The Little Prince* he recounts the meeting between the prince and the fox (a true psychologist among subjects):

> My life is very monotonous [said the fox] . . . I hunt chickens; men hunt me. All the chickens are just alike, and all men just alike. And, in consequence, I am a little bored. But if you tame me, it will be as if the sun came to shine on my life. I shall know the sound of a step that will be different from all the others . . . And then look: you see the grain-fields down yonder? I do not eat bread. Wheat is of no use to me. The wheat fields have nothing to say to me. And that is sad. But you have hair that is the colour of gold. Think how wonderful that will be when you have tamed me! The grain, which is also golden, will bring me back the thought of you. And I shall love to listen to the wind in the wheat . . . (1974: 66–7)

This little passage is interesting in this context because it directs our attention to the way in which intended actions, which might or might not centre upon objects, are caught up with features of the material world in ways that make them significant. Classically, psychological treatments of these phenomena refer the problem inside the heads of the participants, accounting for what happens in terms of sensory or conceptual connections. What is there, as object to be seen or thought about, is quite fortuitous; 'it just happened to be there and then'. Everything that has gone before in this essay suggests that this is a mistaken idea. The world of objects is ordered – is a plane in which culture can be read – so that the 'interests' and 'organised settings' which Bartlett (1932) saw as determining features of remembering can be explicated in their technical, artistic or functional forms. We are indeed 'reminded' by objects, but we are also 'mindful' of them in lives constrained by ownership and by patterns of exchange.

For Bartlett, it was through the function of images that things appeared to play their part in remembering. Images – as mental constructs – serve to pick out significant features of experience through the affective colouring of a number of interrelated interests. These interests, as mentioned already, are not haphazard but are constituted within the culture of social groupings who adopt or fashion objects to serve as condensed symbols. These artefacts are the material aspects of the relationships in which people act together, the object of the 'attitude' engendered by their interests and ideals. (I am deliberately staying with the terms which Bartlett used when discussing his theory because I wish to open his thesis to a wider consideration of the place of objects in memory.)

If we consider remembering as a constructive act, the justification of an attitude towards 'the massed effects of a series of past reactions' (1932: 208), then one function of artefacts – as material images – is the 'bringing into relation' of attitudes and interests which constrain and lead the memories of people concerned. From this position – that of an observer concerned primarily with sensing the world – the appearance of objects is haphazard, they 'pass before the eyes'. From all that has been said in this essay so far, this does an injustice to the fact that the material world is ordered, is constraining, is formative of our subjectivity through bringing us into definite relationships. The status of objects as things for remembering is a matter of social definition, framing some artefacts (through displacement) as mementos, some as of historic interest and others so that they remain merely functional. This marking of objects as being worthy of attention for remembering – that is, as serving the 'image function' which Bartlett described – can be illustrated by the discovery of an old heirloom in the attic which is brought into the living room, or of the selection of clockwork toys for display in a museum. There is here a definite invitation to attend to these objects in a special way, to *allow* the interests and attitudes which they evoke to be revived through the elaboration of meanings made possible by talking with others about them (Edwards and Middleton, 1986). This re-framing of objects is not, however, only a mental activity; it is brought about by a re-ordering or transposition of the artefacts themselves or of their context. Museums do not exist in the minds of individual rememberers.

Before returning to the discussion of objects in the social world it is necessary to pursue, briefly, the experience of remembering which this re-framing makes possible: for it brings into focus the difference between objects as functional parts of the world and as special items by which to remember. In its functional form an object – say a screwdriver – is used unreflectingly to carry out a range of tasks. It may undergo a series of happenings – become lost, get found, be borrowed and returned. Its very ordinariness is evoked by these examples of variability in its use and fate; its status is a means for achieving other things in the world. Only later, in being redesignated an object from the past, does it serve the material aspect of the image function which Bartlett described. This redesignation may be unintended (for example, discovering a pen which has lain unseen for years in a drawer) or else it may be invited by another person, or even demanded by its inclusion in a museum display or a history lesson. These material displacements, either by accident or design, then produce the object as a 'memento', a 'historic artefact' *with* which to define the world of which it was a part rather than (as before) *through* which to achieve ends within a particular time and space.

This brief excursion into the phenomenology of remembering with things is necessary to show that the forms of arrangement of the material world – an aspect of social action and ideology – are not distant from, or contextual beyond, the pale of remembering as either a communicated or solitary happening. The apprehension of artefacts as things 'fit for remembering by' or else as mundane objects is a matter both of mental 'attitude' (in Bartlett's sense) and of social relationships as produced through the ordering, fabrication and ownership of the objects concerned. This extends beyond the realm of personal memories to the past which a culture or society refers to as its history or inheritance. The designation of buildings or other edifices as worthy of preservation or as of special historic interest not only alters their status as 'things' (by removing their mundane function), but produces (constructs) a Past of which they are held to be a part and to which people then owe (or disavow) a certain allegiance (Shanks and Tilley, 1987). About such matters there is often fierce disagreement and debate, which shows that restricting the role of objects in memory to the evocation of images is a shortcoming which derives from thinking of memory only as the reflections of the solitary individual.

Concluding Remarks

This essay has argued that remembering is something which occurs in a world of things, as well as words, and that artefacts play a central role in the memories of cultures and individuals. What makes memory a social affair is not just that people remember together, or that memories are discussions about what has happened in the past. These, it is acknowledged, are key aspects of the way that remembering happens: they are not, in themselves, constitutive of the wider field in which memory takes place, is encouraged or is hindered by people concerned. Because the material world endures, because it can outlive its makers, it can serve as a monument to their efforts and ideals; and yet for that same reason, artefacts survive in ways unintended by makers and owners to become evidence on which other interpretations of the past can be reconstructed. This property of things – shared to some degree with written texts – has given some artefacts a special place as symbols of the past. Cultures differ as to the degree to which artefacts are used in this way, and in modern societies, with their inequalities in ownership and control of consumption, classes and groups differ in their relationship to things as potentials for remembering past times. Implicit in this argument is the idea that objects may be transformed in their function, both at a personal and at a cultural level. Yesterday's functional artefact can become tomorrow's memento or museum piece, although today its displacement may remove it to a limbo where it has outlived its usefulness though not yet been rediscovered or been marked as of special interest. This idea of a gradual, and perhaps meandering transition contrasts with the notion of a complete re-ordering of artefacts, such as the previously mentioned display of objects which followed the French Revolution. Together, these descriptions point to the fact that objects are employed deliberately and are met, as it were, accidentally. The latter circumstance is made possible by the fact that artefacts are functional, concrete and apparently trivial. These three features have been used to account for the way in which objects, though considered as unworthy of direct contemplation, are eminently suitable to be used to frame social relationships (Miller, 1985). In the very variability of objects, in the ordinariness of their consumption and in the sensory richness of relationships people enjoy through them, they are fitted to be later re-framed as material images for reflection and recall. It is for this reason that Miller (1985: 204) concludes that, in relation to abstractions of thought and language, 'the actual ability of such [material] forms to affect all these areas is therefore at present underestimated'.

References

Bartlett, F.C. (1932) *Remembering: a Study in Experimental and Social Psychology.* Cambridge: Cambridge University Press.

Berger, J. (1972) *Ways of Seeing.* London: BBC/Penguin Books.

Csikszentmihalyi, M. and Rochberg-Halton, E. (1981) *The Meaning of Things: Domestic Symbols and the Self.* Cambridge: Cambridge University Press.

de Saint-Exupéry, A. (1974) *The Little Prince.* London: Pan Books.

Douglas, M. and Isherwood, B. (1979) *The World of Goods: Towards an Anthropology of Consumption.* London: Allen Lane.

Edwards, D. and Middleton, D. (1986) 'Joint remembering: constructing an account of shared experience through conversational discourse', *Discourse Processes*, 9: 423–59.

Edwards, D. and Middleton, D. (1987) 'Conversation and remembering: Bartlett revisited', *Applied Cognitive Psychology*, 1: 77–92.

Fried, M. (1963) 'Grieving for a lost home', in L.J. Duhl (ed.), *The Urban Condition*. New York: Basic Books. pp. 151–71.

Harris, J.E. (1984) 'Remembering to do things: a forgotten topic', in J.E. Harris and P.E. Morris (eds), *Everyday Memory Actions and Absent Mindedness*. London: Academic Press.

Hawes, E.L. (1986) 'Artifacts, myths and identity in American history museums', in V. Sofka (ed.), *Museology and Identity*. ICOFOM Study Series, 10. pp. 135–9.

Hooper-Greenhill, E. (1989) 'The museum in the disciplinary society', in S. Pearce (ed.), *Museum Studies in Material Culture*. Leicester: Leicester University Press.

Kavanagh, G. (1989) 'Objects as evidence, or not?', in S. Pearce (ed.), *Museum Studies in Material Culture*. Leicester: Leicester University Press.

Kopytoff, I. (1986) 'The cultural biography of things: commoditization as process', in A. Appadurai (ed.), *The Social Life of Things: Commodities in Cultural Perspective*. Cambridge: Cambridge University Press. pp. 64–91.

Lalive d'Épinay, C. (1986) 'Time, space and socio-cultural identity: the ethos of the proletariat, small owners and peasantry in an aged population', *International Social Services Journal*, 107: 89–104.

Lynch, K. (1960) *The Image of the City*. Cambridge, MA: MIT Press.

Miller, D. (1985) *Artefacts as Categories: A Study of Ceramic Variability in Central India*. Cambridge: Cambridge University Press.

Pratt, G. (1981) 'The house as an expression of social worlds', in J.S. Duncan (ed.), *Housing and Identity*. London: Croom Helm. pp. 135–80.

Shanks, M. and Tilley, C. (1987) *Social Theory and Archaeology*. Cambridge: Polity Press.

Sherman, E. and Newman, E.S. (1977–78) 'The meaning of cherished personal possessions for the elderly', *Journal of Aging and Human Development*, 8: 181–92.

Shotter, J. and Gauld, A. (1981) 'Memory as a social institution', paper presented at Cognitive Psychology Section of The British Psychological Society conference, Plymouth.

Taylor, L. (1981) 'Collections of memories', *Architectural Digest*, 38, 36–42.

Unruh, D.R. (1983) 'Death and personal history: strategies of identity preservation', *Social Problems*, 30: 340–51.

Wertsch, J.V. (1985) *Vygotsky and the Social Formation of Mind*. Cambridge, MA: Harvard University Press.

4

Collective Memory, Ideology and the British Royal Family

Michael Billig

The concept of collective memory is a potentially important one for the study of ideology. A number of general points can be made about the potential connections between collective memory and ideology. If, as Maurice Halbwachs (1951/80) suggested, memory is collectively determined, then it is also ideologically determined, for the collective processes which enable memorization to occur will themselves be part of wider ideological patterns. That being so, investigators should seek to locate the ways in which ideological forces affect, and indeed constitute, the psychological processes of memory. However, the relations between ideology and memory will not be causally one way, with preformed ideology impinging upon individual psychology. Ideology itself will be a form of social memory, in as much as it constitutes what collectively is remembered and also what is forgotten or what aspects of society's history continue to be commemorated and what are relegated to the unread archives. In this way, memory will be both a part of ideology, as well as being a process by which ideology, and thereby the power relations of society, are reproduced.

These points will nevertheless remain somewhat vague so long as the concepts of ideology and collective memory are used without specification. As has often been remarked, the concept of ideology is one of the most notoriously slippery and contested in the social sciences, with different schools of thought using the concept in very different ways (for discussions of the history of the concept, see, for instance, Billig, 1982; Larrain, 1979; 1983; McLellan, 1986). The notion of collective memory may not have been as widely used by analysts as that of ideology, yet it too lacks clear definition. As first formulated by Halbwachs, the concept covers a range of related phenomena, relating to the situations in which memory occurs, the process by which it occurs and the contents of what is remembered. These will need careful differentiation as investigators seek to uncover the ways that memory is both collectively, or ideologically, realized and constituted.

Therefore, a few preliminary remarks can be made about the present use of both concepts. Ideology refers to the patterns of beliefs and practices in society, which ensure the reproduction of power relations (Thompson, 1986). In contrast to many conceptions of ideology, the present approach does not treat ideology as a sort of giant, internally consistent schema, which rigidly determines and distorts the thoughts of those who live under its influence. Billig et al. (1988) stress the dilemmatic aspects of ideology, claiming that what ideology presents as commonsensical will contain contrary themes. If there were not such contrary themes in common sense, then the ideological subject would be nothing more than an 'ideological dupe' who reacts to situations in a pre-programmed and unthinking way. Instead, the ideological subject is a rhetorical subject: that is, people use ideology to think and argue about the social world, and, of course, ideology in turn determines the nature of such arguments and the rhetorical forms which they take (Billig, 1988a; 1988b; in press).

This position suggests that ideologically constituted rhetorical elements will be involved in the processes of collective memorization. However, this too is overly simple, at least so long as collective memory is treated as an undifferentiated concept. In particular, the present investigation will seek to illustrate some rhetorical features in three different aspects of collective memory. In order to examine these different aspects it is necessary to distinguish between memory as a process and memory as an object of thinking.

Memory as a process but not object of thought   When an element of common sense is used in discourse it must be recalled, or to use an archaic term, it must be 'memorated'. If one uses a proverb, it is being memorated rather than invented, and re-created rather than created. Using the terminology of ancient rhetoric, one might say that the use of common-sense discourse frequently involves little *inventio*, but much reproduction of *loci communes*, or commonly shared and commonly used themes (Billig, 1987; Perelman and Olbrechts-Tyteca, 1971). This is memory as a psychological process but not as an object of thinking, and, as will be seen, this sort of memoration can be jointly achieved in discourse. However, speakers using common-sense discourse may not recognize what they are doing as memorizing, if the topic of the discourse is not the past. As Halbwachs has written of everyday opinions, 'we are unaware that we are but an echo' (1980: 45). A similar point is made by Moscovici (1983), in discussing the way in which shared social beliefs, or 'social representations' shape thinking: 'Social and intellectual activity is, after all, a rehearsal or recital, yet most social psychologists treat it as if it were amnesic' (Moscovici, 1983: 10).

More generally, Moscovici writes that 'memory prevails over deduction, the past over the present' (p. 24: see Billig, in press; Jaspars and Fraser, 1983; see also McKinlay and Potter, 1987; Potter and Litton, 1985, for criticisms of social-representation theory). Thus, on the level of psychological processes, the past may prevail over the present, but this need not be reflected in the content of the discourse, or in the phenomenological experience of the speaker, who is unaware that anything is being echoed.

Memory as a process by which past events are reconstructed   This is the sort of memoration process examined by Edwards and Middleton (1986, 1988), who have shown how the processes of memory can be socially accomplished through conversation. Past events are jointly reconstructed through discourse and typically the discussants, or some of them, will be presumed to have participated in those past events. In this way, the discourse takes the past as its topic, and memory is both the process and object of thought. One might say that past events are jointly memorated or commemorated. Edwards and Middleton (1988), for example, demonstrated how families collectively remembered past events by talking about photographs (see also Beloff, 1986 and Musello, 1979). This sort of process can occur on a collective level much larger than a face-to-face collective such as a family. National groups can create their own history by jointly recalling, or commemorating, a reconstructed past (Hobsbawm, 1983; Schwartz et al., 1986). In these cases, there will not be the assumption that the speakers themselves directly participated in the past events, although there might be an identification with long dead participants, as 'we' the members of the nation recall what 'we', or 'our forefathers', did in distant former times. In this sense, a national celebration recalling a past event, such as the storming of the Bastille, or the declaration of National Independence, commemorates past events, just as the family, gathered around the snapshot album, commemorates the holidays of former years. In both cases the reconstruction involves the use of common-sense themes or shared ideology, so that the commemoration of the past is accomplished as an object of thought by the process of memoration.

Commemoration of the past itself rather than reconstruction of a past event   It is possible for a collectivity to have as its object of commemoration the past itself rather than a specific past event. What is recalled is not an event, whether genuinely historical or mythical, but the feeling that the collectivity possesses a history. In a broad way, this involves the collective sharing of a philosophy of history or sense of the past, and as such its content is more general than the memoration of specific event. This sort of memoration may be collectively achieved, but its focus may not be upon a specific past event.

It is the present intention to look at these different aspects of collective memory in relation to a corpus of ideologically significant discourse – namely, the discourse of an ordinary family talking about the extraordinary family which sits upon the throne of Britain.

Ideology and the British Monarchy

It is easy to think of the British monarchy as a topic which is essentially trivial and undeserving of scholarly attention. Such a thought will come easily to any serious student of world affairs who, when watching televised news in Britain, is forced to see pictures of royalty meeting civic dignitaries, sightseeing in foreign countries or just sitting upon horses. Even self-consciously serious newspapers contain enough of such items to irritate academic readers with a different set of priorities about what should constitute world news. The British Royal Family may not possess overt political power, and the lives of its members may not be filled with heroic deeds or great personal achievements. Yet this in itself is sufficient to make the topic worthy of study. The news items about the Royal Family essentially report trivial incidents, but the triviality of such items serves to underline the seriousness of the basic issue: why in an ostensibly democratic society should there be such deep interest in the country's richest family, whose very position symbolizes undemocratic privilege and inequality?

Attitude researchers have tended to ignore the study of public views on the monarchy possibly because they have traditionally sought to discover attitudinal differences between individuals or between the beliefs of demographic groups. The studies that have been conducted reveal very little demographic difference, at least by contrast to the general consensual support for the notion of monarchy (Blumler et al., 1971; Rose and Kavanagh, 1976; Young, 1984). Certainly Republicanism is not an issue in contemporary British politics, and the overwhelming majority of survey respondents reveal an unwillingness to imagine Britain without its monarchy (Harris, 1966; Ziegler, 1977). Perhaps it is for this reason that the British monarchy has not excited much interest amongst academic researchers of attitudes. However, those interested in studying ideology might well pay particular attention to those matters which do not appear to excite divisions of public opinion.

General uniformity, as indicated by opinion polls, might be held to indicate a topic of particular ideological interest. Thus, the ideological discourse used about monarchy may be based upon broadly accepted commonsensical notions.

Over a century ago, the political commentator Walter Bagehot wrote that having a family on the throne was 'an interesting idea', for it 'brings down the pride of sovereignty to the level of petty life' (1867/1965: 85). Even Bagehot would not have predicted the extent to which the interesting idea has attracted mass interest. Practically every television news broadcast and every issue of the popular newspapers in Britain today has its royal item (Nairn, 1988). The theoretical importance of this interest does not merely lie in its extent. The interest itself can be considered qualitatively, as well as quantitatively, ideological. Bagehot advocated the notion of an interesting family on the throne as a way of ensuring that the ill-educated masses did not turn to revolutionary discontent. An interest in, and reverence for, the 'dignified' aspects of the state would distract attention from the 'efficient' parts, in which real power was exercised. It is not difficult to recaste this notion in a Durkheimian way, in order to view royalty as the sacred symbol, which provides unity to the community. One of the few academic studies of British royalty adopts such a perspective. Shils and Young (1953), concentrating upon the Coronation of 1953, saw that event as producing a great national communion, in which sacral values were celebrated in a mood of quasi-mystical union. It was as if the modern mass public was stepping back from its own age into a distant past to partake of an ancient collective conscience (for alternative views of the Coronation, see Cannadine, 1983; Chaney, 1983). However, this Durkheimian notion hardly explains the contrary themes in the representation of monarchy. Reverential presentations of formal ceremonies exist alongside the continual search for scandal and intimate detail. Durkheimian theory does little to explain the desire to know whose beds the sacral symbols are sharing. Sensing a scandal, involving the father of the wife of the Queen's second son, the most popular newspaper in Britain filled its front page with the headline: 'Fergie Dad Vice Girl: Blonde Barbara was "favourite" ' (11 May, 1988). The headline, and the accompanying story and photograph of the scantily clad 'Blonde Barbara' hardly indicate reverence either to Durkheim's sacral values or to Bagehot's dignified aspects of the Constitution.

On the other hand, it is reasonable to suppose that in such stories there are ideological values. The fact of a wealthy man frequenting a brothel is not itself interesting. What gives the story its interest is, of course, the royal dimension. One way to investigate the ideological themes in this regal dimension would be to study the media representations of royalty, and some work has been done in this direction (Coward, 1983; Williamson, 1987; see also Billig, 1988a, c). The present approach, by contrast, is based upon an examination of the way that 'ordinary' people talk about the 'extraordinary' family upon the throne. The assumption will be made that ideological themes flow constantly through this 'ordinary' discourse. As people talk about royalty, they are talking, directly or indirectly, about the nature of society and family, privilege and equality, morality and duty, and so on. In particular, such discourse will contain themes about history and nationality, and about the conception of historical time, and in its use of common sense and by its content it will demonstrate the properties of collective memorization.

The Ordinary Family

The analysis is based upon a recorded interview from a wider project looking at the way that British families talk about the monarchy. The project has involved over forty recorded conversations with families. The present study is based upon an interview with a single family, comprising father, mother, teenage son and daughter. There was a younger son, who took no part in the proceedings. The interview, which lasted over an hour, was part of a series, in which families were asked in their own homes to talk about the Royal Family. The family was lower-middle class, living in the East Midlands. The interviewer provided prompts for discussion, and, as much as possible, attempted to set the conversation in motion, rather than direct it along predetermined paths.

One problem which faces discourse analysis is that of representativeness. A piece of recorded conversation may contain all manner of interesting aspects, but there is always the worry that the particular conversation may be unusual and the thoughts expressed may be peculiar to the participants rather than being widely shared views. Obviously if ideology and social representations are to be studied, the analyst hopes to study aspects of discourse which are widely shared, rather than being the peculiar property of the speakers in question. Fortunately, such problems are lessened with the topic of monarchy. Public-opinion surveys have revealed the broad consensual support of the British public for the monarchy, and this particular family could be placed within this consensus on any standard attitudinal questionnaire. All the members agreed with the idea of Britain having a monarchy. None, in fact, could imagine Britain without a Royal Family. The idea of a President seemed strange. In addition, the members seemed at pains to locate themselves within some assumed, rather than statistically defined, moral consensus, especially when it came to describing their own interest in the Royal Family. Uttering the sorts of disclaimers, which Hewitt and Stokes (1975) claim deflect criticism whilst establishing the desired identity of the speaker, all four family members were united in claiming that they did not have the sort of over-zealous interest, which leads either to scandal-mongering or to prying. They said that they liked to know what was going on regarding royalty, but, as they pointed out, they were not *too* interested. An implicit assumption of a moral consensus lay behind the father's insistence that he did not show unseemly interest: 'I don't like reading all the, err, scandal, for want of a better word.' They all agreed with the mother when she declared that 'I'm not interested in their private lives or anything'. According to the father, 'we watch the news, but if there's anything about them, you know scandalwise, I just turn it off, mindwise; it might still be on, 'cause you don't know what else is coming on the news.'

In such discourse, the family was using common-sense notions about the presumed consensus itself. They were talking about the proper amount of interest to be shown in the Royal Family, whose continued existence all sought. Moreover, they were expressing common-sense views about the 'normal', 'decent' behaviour of 'ordinary' men and women. Just as attitudinal survey researchers would have placed this family within the 90 or so per cent of the British population who support the monarchy, so this 'ordinary' family were at pains to stress their own ordinariness by locating themselves within the presumed moral consensus of the nation. And in this way they were using, and laying claim to, the ideological values of the community.

Joint Argumentation

The notion of a moral consensus does not mean that discourse, which locates itself within that consensus, is composed of nothing but statements to which all speakers harmoniously assent. Rather than consensus suppressing argumentation, it permits discussion and disagreement. The issue of royalty can be used to illustrate the point. There might be consensus that there should be a family on the throne. This would not then be a topic for argument. In fact, the family in question had little to say on the issue, for none of its members was prepared to take the republican stance. However, an agreement that there should be a family on the throne is not sufficient to make that family an interesting idea. If the family is to be interesting, then people can wonder how it should disport itself, and, indeed, how they should disport themselves in relation to this extraordinarily situated family group. The very anomalies of the Royal Family make it interesting. It embodies hereditary privilege in a democratic age; its members possess no special talents which have qualified them by meritocratic competition for the position which they occupy; above all, in terms of personalities and personal qualities, it is an ordinary family in an extraordinary location. And all this gives ample scope for the consensus to provide material for thought and argumentation.

Thus, one should not expect the discourse about monarchy to be entirely composed of harmonious themes, but it could include commonly shared, but contrary, themes. The discourse of the mother and father provides an illustration of the consensual nature of contrary themes. The father, a special policeman, expressed his love of the pageantry of royalty and its traditions. The mother was keen that members of the Royal Family should behave with appropriate morality. They both would be likely to tick the items on a questionnaire scale of conventional moral belief. And yet, despite obvious agreement and shared conventionality, their discourse at times showed an argumentative structure. The interviewer (I) had asked whether the existence of royalty heightens the differences between the very rich and the very poor:

F: We should all be on the same level
I: Do you think that having a Royal Family makes that worse, you can't attain that with such conspicuous wealth?
F: Well sometimes with this pomp and ceremony, there's a lot of waste, but having said that I suppose really the waste is paying other people, keeping other people in work anyway. Well you know, all this and the garlands and what have you, paper flags, for want of a better thing could be better spent perhaps. But having said that, people have got to make them, so it's giving people work in that respect, so it's a vicious circle anyway
M: You'll never get everybody on the same level, well moneywise

The extract begins with a statement from the father of the sort of populist principle, which he recognizes to be in conflict with the idea of monarchy: if we should all be on the same level, then monarchy cannot be on the 'pedestal', to which his wife referred several times in the course of the interview. The father then goes on to criticize the expense of the sort of pageantry which he finds attractive. Criticism, however, is followed by justification: jobs are created by the demand for garlands and paper flags. But then criticism reappears, and the father seems to recognize that this dialectic between criticism and justification could be infinite: 'it's a vicious circle anyway.' The mother then adds what appears to be a statement of unequal reality to criticize the opening populist statement of egalitarian principle: it's impossible to get everyone on the same level. But she adds a coda, which seems to open the way for further argumentation, rather than close the issue with the discourse of conservative practice triumphing over egalitarian hope: 'well moneywise'. Perhaps the wealth of the Royal Family is not to be criticized on the basis of some egalitarian principle, but the coda suggests that the principle is not being entirely discarded: there are other levels of existence, apart from the financial, which monarch and people might be expected to inhabit equally.

The point is that the argument is not one between a supporter of egalitarianism and a supporter of privilege. The discourses of egalitarianism and inequality are intermixed. Moreover, the argumentative structure is not confined to the argument between persons, but the structure is to be found within the discourse of the father. He himself offers reflexively criticisms and qualifications to his own statements. In fact, his discourse, with a mirror change of prepositions, could be recast as a discourse between two different people with two different attitudinal positions. He does not need his wife to point out that the manufacture of paper flags creates jobs and therefore is in the interests of ordinary, non-royal flag-makers. His own phraseology recognizes that his statements can be countered by further statements: 'Having said that', he says, now putting the qualification, or other side. But it is he himself who has just said the 'that' and is now uttering the argumentatively critical 'this'.

Another example occurred when the discussion moved to the topic of the younger members of the Royal Family and their behaviour on a popular television programme. The mother was concerned that royalty was coming down off its pedestal: 'I think they're coming down off the pedestal and that's not really a good thing.' The father, in common with the children, disagreed:

> F: Mind you I think it was good it shows to the public that they are human the same as us, whereas if they're up there you can't touch them
>
> M: But then you see when they get down to our level, get down to the same/
>
> F: You might undermine them then or undermine the authority/
>
> M: Saying things that we do and everything (F: Yeah) and then you stop admiring them and then the next generation admires them even less and so on

At first sight this seems like a straightforward disagreement. The mother, not wanting royalty to be brought down to the same level as everyone else, objects to their being seen as ordinary human beings on the television. It is destroying the mystique of monarchy, she is arguing. Her argument is based, not so much on an expression of identification, but upon a lay psychological theory of identification. She is not sayng that she looks up to the Royal Family: in fact, she is criticizing members of the family for unsatisfactorily unroyal behaviour. Instead, she is saying that admiration depends upon the objects of admiration appearing exalted, otherwise examples will neither be set nor followed. The spatial metaphor runs through this discourse: whether royalty should be above us, beyond the reach of the ordinary touch, or whether they should be brought downwards to the level of ordinariness, to be like 'us'. The father, continuing the egalitarian theme, sees it as desirable that royalty should move downwards, in order to be 'the same as us'. Yet it is the father who interrupts the mother to provide the justification for the pedestal position and criticizes his own populism. He mentions the undermining of authority before the mother, in so doing adding again the 'this', having uttered his own 'that'.

Jointly the mother and father are re-creating the positions for and against the topics of which they are talking. The point is not merely that they are using the contrary themes of an ideological common sense, but that the common sense is being jointly re-created in their discourse. This involves the discursive processes of memoration which do not have memory as the object of discourse. This re-creation does not involve the invention of new themes, nor in this case the addition of unique personal narratives. What are being reproduced are commonplace themes which, like the *loci communes* of ancient rhetoric, are common in two related senses: they are commonly, or socially, shared (the places of the community) and they are commonly cited in discourse on this topic (frequently visited places). As such, the resulting rhetorical *loci communes* are platitudes, or unremarkable scraps of common sense, and in this sense the re-creation of social representations relies on jointly produced memoration. The father has not worked out the economic implications of paper flag-making, but he is repeating the common sense of contemporary economics. In a third sense, the commonplaces are shared: it is the shared activity of discourse which is reproducing them.

The father would probably be unable to identify the source of his economic assumptions. In Halbwach's terms, he is unaware what he is echoing, and perhaps indeed that his discourse is in a real sense not merely *his*, but is an echo of other nameless discourses. He presents his discourse as common knowledge and, significantly, this common-sense economics seems to be accepted, or at least unchallenged, and is another theme to be taken into account. However, for it to be so presented, without *inventio*, it must be re-presented and, thereby, recalled from some sort of collectively maintained memory. And, indeed, the other participants in the discussion are on hand to add other factors that must be taken into account to qualify the 'this' with a countering 'that'. These are matters which the participants must remember to take into account if they are to discuss the issue.

One might say that the discourse of the mother and father is repeating the commonplace, ideological themes of monarchy: ordinariness and extraordinariness, privilege and equality are topics to be raised, if the matter is to be adequately discussed. The discourse has the feel of remembrance, as the participants remember the factors which must be taken into account. Having said one thing, then there is another which must be said. In an obvious sense the extracts quoted have an argumentative structure, as the hierarchical discourse of the mother seems to collide with the egalitarian themes of the father with each theme countering criticisms with justifications and vice versa. However, if mother and father, not to mention son and daughter, are combining to reproduce the themes which are commonly shared, then the structure of argumentation is not an argument between individuals. Rather the common sense of monarchical themes is itself argumentatively structured. The father shows this, and his own reflexive awareness of the situation, when he draws attention to the potentially endless (or viciously endless) circle of criticism and counter-criticism. Thus, the consensually agreed-upon themes, far from excluding argumentation, permit, even necessitate, argumentation. If this discourse could be said to be revealing the nature of the social representation of royalty, then the representation, as structured through discourse, is structured argumentatively. More generally, one might say that this sort of discourse re-creates, and thereby reveals, the argumentative structure of ideology itself.

Commemorating the Family's History

The link between commonsensical elements and memory is a general one, in that the link exists regardless of particular content. The topics of such commonsensical discourse are not memoration, although collectively memoration may enable their topics to be discursively realized. However, some social phenomena are consensually agreed to be memorable and lend themselves to conversations about memories. The monarchy is one such phenomenon. The records of the Mass Observation are based upon reports of overheard conversations and carefully kept diaries by informants, principally in the 1930s and 1940s. Ziegler, commenting on these records, states that 'again and again one finds that the most tenuous brush with royalty is lovingly recorded' (1977: 77). A conversation with the monarch, or a trip to Buckingham Palace to receive personally some sort of award, is not likely to be forgotten, but it will be described, discussed and probably photographed. It can be jointly recalled at a later time, as the family talks over past events, and such talk will not only literally co-memorate its past, but it will commemorate it. It will become a family story (Martin, Hagestad and Diedrick, 1988). In short, the event will take its proud place in the history of the family group, although never meriting even a footnote in the history of the nation.

The interviewed family reported two brushes with royalty, both of a most tenuous nature but both recalled after years. The mother reported that as a young child she had seen the Queen: 'I've only seen her once in my lifetime and that time I swore to me mother that she'd got a tiara on as she passed by on a train and she said, "you silly girl".' Not only has the event been remembered but it has been cast into a narrative. Moreover, it is not a narrative about the Royal Family but about the ordinary family, which is co-memorating the event: the Queen passes by briefly off-stage in this narrative, or, at least, we presume it was the Queen who passed by. What is recalled is the conversation about the Queen and what the mother said to her daughter. What the Queen actually looked like is not recalled, and, in fact, that is the whole point of the co-memorated episode. And many years later, this conversation between mother and daughter is still being re-created, when so many other conversations are lost beyond recall. This most tenuous of tenuous brushes continues to be preserved in the oral tradition of the family.

The same basic features appear in the second tenuous brush, which occurred once when the family had been walking by the seaside on holiday:

S: When they were at Margate, we went to see them there, the Queen Mum/
F: That's right
D: Oh, did we? Oh yes
S: Oh yeah, don't you remember when she says 'hello Ray' as she goes past
D: That's what he said

Again the event has been cast as a narrative, although without the clear structure of the mother's story about the Queen in the train. Part of the reasons for the lack of clarity is that the story is jointly recalled, rather than being singly narrated. At first the daughter does not remember the incident, but then she is prompted by the son. She then remembers the episode because it was the time when the father jokingly claimed that the Queen Mother greeted him with familiarity ('Hello Ray'). The joke has become a piece of family folklore, and the daughter feels the need to explain the family joke to the outsider, lest the interviewer miss the point by interpreting the event literally. Therefore, she says helpfully, 'that's what he said', with the 'he' being her father.

In both narrations the speaker(s) were participants in the events of which they are talking. The mother is recalling her own experiences, and the family participated in the holiday at Margate. They may be recalling events about royalty, yet the actual memory of royalty is unimportant. A claim of clear recall is not crucial for the successful reproduction of the story. In fact, the successful telling of both stories, whether individually or collectively re-counted, depends upon the absence of a claim of veridical recall of the past. It does not matter whether the Queen actually wore a tiara all those years ago: the mother's credentials for telling the story do not depend on such recall. The second story consciously records a detail which never took place. Thus, the stories do not function to summon up mental images, which eidetically repeat this non-occurring event. Instead, previous tellings of the history of this non-occurring event can be repeated. In both the train and the seaside stories, a well-told story is being repeated, and, if one teller seems to be omitting matters or faltering, another member can take up the family story which has now become history. In this way, perceptual memory has taken second place to a historical narrative. This occurs in a way that, on a mundane level, bears out Pierre Vidal-Naquet's more general point that 'between memory and history there can be tension, even opposition' (1987: 8).

There is a further point of similarity between both narratives, for both express contrary themes, although they have been cast as unified narratives, telling a coherent, or unified, story. Each story plays on the ambiguity of royalty being both ordinary and extraordinary. The Queen may be Queen, but she is also a railway passenger. The Queen Mother might be walking on the sea-front, but she is still regal, recognized by ordinary members of the public but unrecognizing them. The stories derive their humour by acknowledging the contrary themes, but telling of their past non-acknowledgement, in the one case by an innocent child and the other by a knowing, but playful, adult. The listeners know that the Queen would not be wearing her crown whilst sat on a train, nor would the Queen Mother say 'Hello Ray'; but they also know both that Queens do wear crowns and that they have their ordinary moments.

The stories, which can be jointly memorated, commemorate the family's own history, and the act of their being told reproduces the family traditions and helps to solidify the family itself. The telling of both stories expresses and symbolizes a unity within the family, especially an intergenerational unity. The mother is telling a story in front of her children about her experiences as a child. The Queen passes by off-stage, as it were, in a train, but the story derives its force from the fact of the continuity between both the ordinary and the off-stage, extraordinary family. The father, very much a believer in traditional values and good behaviour, is seen to act like a child in the presence of regal authority, at least on holiday, when not everything is for real. In the presence of his acknowledged social superior, he comes down to the level of the naughty child, and, significantly, his children tell his story for him in the interview.

Lévi-Strauss (1967) suggested that a culture's myths have the function of expressing contradictions, which have to be suppressed in normal discourse. The stories of the tenuous brush with royalty may constitute part of the family's own mythology, but the contrary themes of the narrative are not to be suppressed. The narrative mode of discourse might unify the contradictory themes, but when speakers switch to the argumentative mode, the contrary themes can tumble out to provide the overt content of discussion. Speakers quite openly discuss the ambiguity of the royal role, debating whether the Royal Family should be more or less ordinary in its behaviour; whether its members should metaphorically wear their crowns on trains or whether they should greet passers-by with jocular familiarity. In this sense, the contrary themes of common sense are not to be hidden, until they can be obliquely expressed in odd, historical myths which are neither real nor unreal. But it is the contrary themes which can provide the interesting family commemorations, as well as the interesting wider arguments.

In this way, the processes of co-memoration, or joint recall, can reproduce discursively the memorative content, although what is memorated may never have occurred. In fact, the possible non-occurrence makes it an interesting story to tell. The telling of the story helps to commemorate the immediate family, in which the joint memoration is occurring, and about whose members the story tells. It also serves to commemorate another family: that extraordinary family, whose very extraordinariness is commonsensically assumed to guarantee its inherent memorability. In this way a wider ideology about family and about social position is being reproduced as the family tells of its tenuous brushes with the most memorable family in the country.

National Commemoration and Ideology of History

One reason why royalty is conceived of as being intrinsically memorable is that it is part of the collective memory of the nation. Just as individuals might believe they own royalty – it is *their* Queen – so they own the history of their group – it is *their* history. Royalty represents the continuity of this history, as the present Queen stands at the end of a long line of kings and queens, whose lives and deaths have formed the narrative themes of the nation's history (Cannadine, 1983; Nairn, 1988). Thus a tenuous brush with royalty is also a tenuous brush with the living history of the collectivity. For royalty to be experienced in this way it is necessary for people to have a historical consciousness, which is more than a memory for historical events, but which is a consciousness, or ideology, of history itself. As such, history itself, rather than historical events, can become the object of co-memoration and commonsensical argument.

If there is such an ideology, it can be assumed that it will be expressed in ordinary discourse. As the family members talked about royalty and their own selves, they revealed not a single account of history but two contrary accounts. Again, the argumentative, or contrary, structures of common sense were re-created in two opposing social representations of history. There was history as a record of liberal progress, with modernity as the civilized and enlightened counterpart to the barbarity and unfairness of distant dark ages. Then there was history as recording a loss, with modern society as inauthentic and morally impoverished as compared to the moral stature of past times.

Such contrary themes occurred in the interview, and they provided the basis for argumentation. Again, however, the argument was not between defined attitudinal positions, but all could draw upon the consensually shared, but opposing, images. At different stages in the discussion the roles of traditionalist and modernist could be reversed. for all shared the beliefs. Such contrary themes were apparent in the interview. Like many British families, this family liked to visit the past on its holidays. Castles and the historic homes of the aristocracy were regularly toured. According to the father, 'Yeah we always visit the castles and local attractions and see, you know, it's all part of history.' All agreed with the daughter that it was fun to imagine oneself living in the old buildings. Significantly they did not imagine themselves stepping back in time, but they imagined themselves living there presently: they did not like to imagine life without the conveniences of modern life. The image of the past was that of barbarism: 'Dungeons and tortures' interjected the son as they talked about the life of olden days.

Hewison (1987) has argued that a nostalgic concern to preserve ancient heritage characterizes contemporary British public opinion (see also Urry, 1988). Feelings of nostalgia might be firmly rooted in modernity, but they also express a criticism of modern life. They constitute an argument, which is formulated by the present for the past against the present. Yet, of course, the present, which is phrasing the argument, also retains some criticisms of the past with which to defend itself. This internal argument between present and past time was expressed at one point in the interview:

> *F*: I think sometimes it would pay us to go back in time/
> *M*: The trouble is we probably wouldn't be in the castle, we'd be serfs
> *D*: Oh yes
> *F*: So we haven't got all the mod cons you see
> *M*: We wouldn't like it like that, see
> *F*: If we haven't got all the mod cons let us live like that, 'cause I think that's where I think we're losing out, or our kids are losing out
> *I*: What are you losing?
> *F*: Everything, anything they want, you've only got to press a button and it's there. Before, there was no television, no videos, no pop, you know everything was live, for want of a better word, live music as he keeps saying, playing it himself [*laughs*]

It is the father who is arguing for the past, not the mother, who on other occasions argues for a return to some of the traditional privileges of kingship. Now, she has taken up the case for modernity and its 'mod cons', possibly thinking of the modern machinery of domestic labour. Her history here is one of increasing equality, for she tells a populist story, in which serfs have won their rights from their traditional betters. In this account, she identifies with the history of the serfs: *we* would have been serfs, having worse lives, materially and socially, than we have at present. Her ideology of history here is an ideology of progress. It is a very different image from that which she expressed, when arguing against the present for a return to the privileges of the past. Speaking of royalty she commented: 'I like the idea in the old days when they could get away with anything actually.'

A similar ambivalence can be found in the discourse of the father. Having seemed to voice the progressive argument, when countering his wife's criticisms of equality, he now champions the past for its authenticity. Something has been lost in the present. He has difficulty in expressing what exactly. His own knowledge of history, despite all the visits to castles, is, as he recognized, very limited: 'I failed it at school, I wished I'd took it up at school but didn't, so I think I'm missing out on that.' His lack of historical knowledge becomes apparent, as he struggles to find something to say about Henry VIII and his wives, but forgets even that king's name. However, gaps in the historical memory about historical events do not mean that there can be no representation of history itself, as opposed to its specific content. However, the father lacks the words and the images to describe exactly what it is that the past possessed which modern life is lacking. He defends traditions, saying that 'we're getting rid of too many now, and it's, you know, forcing the country apart.' This seems to suggest that what has been lost is some sense of *gemeinschaft*. There seems to be a notion of a communal life, united by tradition and living out authentic experiences. The divisions between serfs and aristocrats seem to have little place in this image, which is of a united, not class-antagonistic, past. The father admits his inability to describe the life he wants to recapture, beyond describing it as the negation of the present. It is as if the present has swamped the collective memory, although in point of fact it is, as always, re-creating it. Reflexively, he comments upon his own discourse, and the choice of words he uses to describe the authenticity of the past: 'live music'. He knows that this is a phrase which, far from belonging to the past, is taken from the vocabulary of his son's generation and describes just the sort of modern entertainment he wishes to criticize. Yet the words, which might more suitably describe what is lost to the present themselves seem to have been lost.

Both images of the past, that of the barbarity and that of community, seem to be negations of the present, and the contradictory nature of these images of the past represents the mirror image of contradictions in the perception of the present. The image of barbarity is the negation of the material and political progress of the present, which enables the descendants of serfs to spend holidays wandering rightfully around the ancestral homes of the aristocracy. The image of past community is an image of present dislocation: if once people knew their place, and the appropriate codes of conduct associated with that place, then the corollary of this belief is that people no more possess any moral or social certainty. Royalty fits into this image of moral dislocation, not so much by offering the image of ideal morality and past standards, which the mother wants royalty to uphold, but as a topic for debate. When the family discussed the behaviour of young members of the Royal Family, the mother stood alone. Her children and her husband all approved of the informality shown by the young royals. The mother took a historical perspective, seeing present moments as part of a chain of events leading away from the mythic past, when codes were strictly clear. She suggested that informality threatened the very notion of royalty: 'I think, it'll get lax, more lax, more lax, until it's just nothing.' She expressed her fears for the future in terms of the past:

> If you look back to the time of Victoria, I mean, I mean, say for instance Charles and Di they kissed on the balcony, right, when they got married, that would never have been allowed in Victoria's time, would it? So, it's, again it's bringing them down a little bit. I mean to me it was all right, it didn't bother me, but the morals are going as, as, the time goes on and it's just reaching them as well.

Here again she has slipped back into the nostalgic recollection of the past. No longer is history the history of oppressed serfs, but the morally authentic past society is given a definite location in the nineteenth century. There is a sense that the present, ever moving forward into the future, is becoming further and further detached from this past: the unimaginable might have to be imagined, as royalty becomes nothing, or at least nothing extraordinary, in its descent into egalitarian ordinariness. Yet there is no sense that the past can be reproduced. She herself recognizes that she is part of the historical movement flowing away from the time of Victoria, when lax standards were not allowed. Her argument for traditional morality and past generations, voiced in front of her own children, has its internal ambiguities. The discourse of the present simultaneously champions and undermines the past. The mother uses the very language of present, whilst arguing for a greater degree of formality; she talks of 'Charles and Di', not even Charles and Diana, let alone His and Her Royal Highness. She criticizes their kissing in public, but then adds that it is 'all right by her': she personally does not disapprove. It is as if she is dissociating herself from her own views. Moreover, she conveys a sense of awareness that she is to be located in the present, as part of the historical movement away from that morally authentic past. She might argue with her own children as they move further towards the lax, informal future, but she with her 'Charles and Di' and with her condoning of the public informality has moved further than the woman who held her up to see the train pass by all those years ago. Perhaps she argued with her mother, just as her children might argue with her, and so, by championing the past, she continues a tradition of argumentation, which needs the past to be criticized for its continuation. She might be criticizing the present, but she possesses the wherewithal for 'taking the side of the other' (Billig, 1987; 1988b). Faced by a defence of the past, which frowns upon the descendants of serfs showing too much familiarity when discussing their social betters, she could switch sides: the virtues of informality and modernity could then be defended. In this way she, like the other members of the family, possesses the discursive repertoires to argue both for the past against the present and the present against the past, just as they jointly possess the discourses of equality and inequality. Because the contrary themes are simultaneously held, each individual's discourse will show variability, as the themes are produced on different occasions, or at different moments in the same conversation (on discursive variability, see Potter and Wetherell, 1987; Wetherell and Potter, 1988; Billig, 1989).

One might say that ideology, far from conditioning people not to think, provides the interesting and contrary topics for debate and argumentation (Billig et al., 1988). Yet if people think about one set of issues or dilemmas, then their attention is removed from other matters, and the effects of ideology might be gauged by what is *not* a matter for interesting discussion. In analysing ideological discourse, therefore, one should be aware of the gaps in discourse, or those possible topics of conversation which fail to be mentioned. The discussions of the family about history revealed a tension between images of the past and the present. Royalty is a link with a past or, by its informal displays of all-too-human emotion, an egalitarian improvement of the past. What this debate between past and present, or between contrary views of the relation between past and present, crowds out is any image of the future, which might be more than a pale continuation of the present. At worst the future is to be feared, for it will be a time when familiar objects, such as the Royal Family, will disappear. At best it is a continuation of the present.

The daughter expressed the latter theme. She said that it was 'nice' to look at the royal babies: 'It will be nice when they're older and you can think "well, I saw them, when they were babies and now look at them, they're so grown up"; I mean that is nice.' Here again, memory is a topic of discourse, but in this case the present, or at least the royal aspect, is being talked of as a possible memory for the future. In this instance, the young woman anticipates the future as little more than a collective memory of the present being forwardly projected in time. Moreover, it is a future for which she presently hopes. The fact that this hope incorporates a wish for the continued well-being of the richest family in the land is itself highly ideological. So too is the lack of space left for talk of a future which is qualitatively different from the present. It is in the silences of these discursive gaps, just as much as in the noise of the expressed words, that the continuing march of ideology can be heard.

Note

The project on the way that British families talk about the monarchy has been funded by the ESRC. I am grateful to Marie Kennedy for conducting the interviews.

References

Bagehot, W. (1867/1965) *The English Constitution*. London: Fontana.

Beloff, H. (1986) *Camera Culture*. Oxford: Blackwell.

Billig, M. (1982) *Ideology and Social Psychology*. Oxford: Blackwell.

Billig, M. (1987) *Arguing and Thinking: a Rhetorical Approach to Social Psychology*. Cambridge: Cambridge University Press.

Billig, M. (1988a) 'Rhetorical and historical aspects of attitudes: the case of the British monarchy', *Philosophical Psychology*, 1: 83–103.

Billig, M. (1988b) 'Social representation, anchoring and objectification: a rhetorical analysis', *Social Behaviour*, 3: 1–16.

Billig, M. (1988c) 'Common-places of the British Royal Family: a rhetorical analysis of plain and argumentative sense', *Text*, 8: 191–217.

Billig, M. (1989) 'The argumentative nature of holding strong views: a case study', *European Journal of Social Psychology*, 19: 203–222.

Billig, M. (in press) 'Studying the thinking society', in G. Breakwell and D. Canter (eds), *Empirical Approaches to Social Representations*. Oxford: Oxford University Press.

Billig, M., Condor, S., Edwards, D., Gane, M., Middleton, D. and Radley, A.R. (1988) *Ideological Dilemmas*. London: Sage.

Blumler, J.G., Brown, J.R., Ewbank, A.J. and Nossiter, T.J. (1971) 'Attitudes to the monarchy: their structure and development during a ceremonial occasion', *Political Studies*, 19: 149–71.

Cannadine, D. (1983) 'The context, performance and meaning of ritual: the British monarchy and the "invention of tradition"', in E. Hobsbawm and T. Ranger (eds), *The Invention of Tradition*. Cambridge: Cambridge University Press.

Chaney, D. (1983) 'A symbolic mirror of ourselves: civic ritual in mass society', *Media, Culture and Society*, 5: 119–35.

Coward, R. (1983) *Female Desire*. London: Paladin.

Edwards, D. and Middleton, D. (1986) 'Joint remembering: constructing an account of shared experience through conversational discourse', *Discourse Processes*, 9: 423–59.

Edwards, D. and Middleton, D. (1988) 'Conversational remembering and family relationships: how children learn to remember', *Journal of Social and Personal Relationships*, 5: 3–25.

Halbwachs, M. (1951/80) *The Collective Memory*. New York: Harper & Row.

Harris, L.M. (1966) *Long to Reign over Us?* London: William Kimber.

Hewison, R. (1987) *The Heritage Industry*. London: Methuen.

Hewitt, J.P. and Stokes, R. (1975) 'Disclaimers', *American Sociological Review*, 40: 1–11.

Hobsbawm, E. (1983) 'Introduction: inventing tradition', in E. Hobsbawm and T. Ranger. *The Invention of Tradition*. Cambridge: Cambridge University Press.

Jaspars, J.M.F. and Fraser, C. (1983) 'Attitudes and social representations', in R.M. Farr and S. Moscovici (eds), *Social Representations*. Paris: Presses Universitaires de France.

Larrain, J. (1979) *The Concept of Ideology*. London: Hutchinson.

Larrain, J. (1983) *Marxism and Ideology*. London: Macmillan.

Lévi-Strauss, C. (1967) 'The myth of "Asdiwal"', in *The Structural Study of Myth and Totemism*. ASA Monographs. London: ASA.

Martin, P., Hagestad, G.O. and Diedrick, P. (1988) 'Family stories: events (temporarily) remembered', *Journal of Marriage and the Family*, 50: 533–41.

McKinlay, A. and Potter, J. (1987) 'Social representations: a conceptual critique', *Journal for the Theory of Social Behaviour*, 17: 471–88.

McLellan, D. (1986) *Ideology*. Milton Keynes: Open University Press.

Moscovici, S. (1983) 'The phenomenon of social representations', in R. Farr and S. Moscovici (eds), *Social Representations*. Cambridge: Cambridge University Press.

Musello, C. (1979) 'Family photography', in J. Wagner (ed.), *Images of Information*. Beverly Hills, CA: Sage.

Nairn, T. (1988) *The Enchanted Glass: Britain and its Monarchy*. London: Radius.

Perelman, C. and Olbrechts-Tyteca, L. (1971) *The New Rhetoric*, Notre Dame, IN: University of Notre Dame.

Potter, J. and Litton, I. (1985) 'Some problems underlying the theory of social representations', *British Journal of Social Psychology*, 24: 81–90.

Potter, J. and Wetherell, M. (1987) *Discourse and Social Psychology*. London: Sage.

Rose, R. and Kavanagh, D. (1976) 'The monarchy in contemporary culture', *Comparative Politics*, 8: 548–76.

Schwartz, B., Zerubavel, Y. and Barnett, B.M. (1986) 'The recovery of Masada: a study in collective memory', *Sociological Quarterly*, 27: 147–64.

Shils, E. and Young, M. (1953) 'The meaning of the Coronation', *Sociological Review*, 1: 68–81.

Thompson, K. (1986) *Beliefs and Ideology*. Chichester: Ellis Horwood.

Urry, J. (1988) 'Cultural change and contemporary holiday making', *Theory, Culture and Society*, 5: 35–56.

Vidal-Naquet, P. (1987) *Les Assassins de la Mémoire*. Paris: La Découverte.

Wetherell, M. and Potter, J. (1988) 'Discourse analysis and the identification of interpretative repertoires', in C. Antaki (ed.), *Analysing Everyday Explanation*. London: Sage.

Williamson, J. (1987) *Consuming Passions*. London: Boyars.

Young, K. (1984) 'Political attitudes', in R. Jowell and C. Airey (eds), *British Social Attitudes: the 1984 Report*. Aldershot: Gower.

Ziegler, P. (1977) *Crown and People*. London: Collins.

5

The Reconstruction of Abraham Lincoln

Barry Schwartz

'Abe Lincoln the rail-splitter', 'the rude man from the prairie and the river bottoms', the 'people's President' – these conceptions reveal much of the essential content of Abraham Lincoln's present-day image. However, the people's belief in Lincoln's common touch, in his simplicity and other homely virtues, was never enough to make him into a true national idol. Indeed, the attribution of these common qualities to Lincoln after his death prevented his being universally perceived as such. Lincoln's name, declared Reverend George Briggs in his 1865 eulogy, 'is to be hailed, in the coming time . . . with a truer, deeper homage than it wins today (1865: 28).'[1]

To relate the ebb and flow of Lincoln's reputation to America's changing conditions, from his death in 1865 to the present, is beyond the scope of this essay. Events that occurred during a narrower time frame comprise its subject-matter. Lincoln became a national idol during a period that began with Theodore Roosevelt's presidency in 1901 and ended with Warren Harding's presidency in 1921. These were the years of the Progressive Movement. These were also the years that spanned the Spanish–American War and the First World War – a period in which America became a world power. The Lincoln that we know today is a product of this period. What the nineteenth-century Lincoln image looked like, how that image was reconstructed in the first two decades of the twentieth century and how that reconstruction was linked to the ideological and emotional issues of the time, is what this essay will attempt to show.

The purpose of the exercise is to deal not only with the collective memory of Lincoln but also with collective memory as a general category of knowledge. Two analytic approaches now inform our understanding of this matter. The first approach assumes that the past is a social construction shaped by the concerns of the present. Every conception of the past, declares George Herbert Mead, is construed 'from the standpoint of the new problem of today' (1929: 353; see also Mead, 1932; Maines, Sugrue and Katovich, 1983). For

Maurice Halbwachs, 'collective memory is essentially a reconstruction of the past [which] adapts the image of ancient facts to the
beliefs and spiritual needs of the present' (1941: 7). 'The prime
function of memory', David Lowenthal (1985: 210) concludes, 'is
not to preserve the past, but to adapt it so as to enrich and
manipulate the present.' Mead, Halbwachs and Lowenthal pursue
different research goals and proceed from different assumptions
about how present conditions affect perceptions of the past. The
thrust of their arguments, however, is the same. They present an
atemporal concept of collective memory, one that relates things
remembered in a given context to beliefs, interests, aspirations and
fears of the here and now.

Every society, however, displays, and perhaps even requires, a
minimal sense of continuity with the past, and its memories cannot
be serviceable to the present unless it secures this continuity. If
beliefs about the past failed to outlive changes in society, then
society's unity and continuity would diminish. Emile Durkheim was
among the first to develop this point systematically. Ties to the past,
in his view, are cultivated by means of periodic commemoration
rites. The function of these rites is not to transform the past by
bending it to the service of the present but to reproduce the past, to
make it live again as it once was. Thereby, society 'renews the
sentiment which it has of itself and its unity' (1912/1965: 415, 420).
Edward Shils's concept of tradition expresses this same idea. The
image of an epoch or a historical figure, he observes, is not
conceived and elaborated anew in each generation, but is rather
transmitted according to a 'guiding pattern' (1981: 31–2) that
endows different generations with a common heritage.

In the contrast between Mead, Halbwachs and Lowenthal on the
one side, and Durkheim and Shils on the other, inheres the broader
question of how the need for cultural continuity and cultural
revision reconcile themselves to one another and to society. Alfred
North Whitehead spoke to this question many years ago when he
noted that

> The art of free society consists in the maintenance of the symbolic code;
> and secondly in fearlessness of revision, to secure that the code serves
> those purposes which satisfy an enlightened reason. Those societies
> which cannot combine reverence to their symbols with freedom of
> revision must ultimately decay either from anarchy, or from the slow
> atrophy of a life stifled by useless shadows. (cited in Peterson, 1960:
> 332)

Society's memory of its great men is one part of this 'symbolic
code'. Emphasizing the revisions and discontinuities of collective
memory, men like Mead and Halbwachs make this code seem more

precarious than it actually is. By stressing the continuities of collective memory, however, men like Durkheim and Shils underestimate the extent to which the code is maintained by revisions that conform to society's immediate needs and inclinations. These contrasting theoretical approaches and their problems are resolved in many places and in the memory of many people, but nowhere more clearly and more dramatically than in America's memory of Abraham Lincoln.

I

Abraham Lincoln was shot on Good Friday, 14 April, 1865 and died the next day. The immediate reaction of every State government to his death was an official proclamation of grief and condolence, along with the appointment of a committee to decide on how the State should participate in the national mourning. Every city government, and most local business, professional, trade and ethnic organizations went through these same deliberations and planned similar kinds of ceremonies. Announcements and ceremonies, however, would not be enough. These dramatized the fact of Lincoln's death, but for that death to make sense it had to be interpreted. Was Lincoln really shot by an assassin? Was his murder related to the war that everyone thought was over? Is the government still intact? Will the war be resumed? Who is the new President, and what will he do? These were the kinds of questions that flew through the air on the day Lincoln died.

On the next day, Easter Sunday, the churches were filled to capacity long before the hour of service. 'There was great excitement' among the congregants, 'many being moved to tears', and if the typical Sunday sermon failed to interest the typical churchgoer, this day's sermon was 'listened to with profound attention' (*New York Times*, 17 April 1865, p. 8). The people had talked to one another about the murder the day before; now they would get an authoritative religious account of what had happened.

Crucial to the religious interpretation of Lincoln's death is the fact that he was not an overwhelmingly popular president. He had come close to losing his bid for re-election six months earlier and was opposed since then by a large percentage of the Northern population (Oates, 1977). His assassination, traumatic as it was, did not reverse these negative attitudes. He was an imperfect martyr. Most people felt sympathy for him, many liked him, some loved him, but few were certain that his assassin had caused the nation an irreparable loss. The clergymen, unawed by their subject, never hesitated to mention his flaws, and there was often a painful bite to their discussions. Lincoln's failings were defined not as peripheral imperfectons, but rather as the distinguishing feature of his presidency.

Apparent from the very beginning of the war, Lincoln's forgiveness and compassion were the objects of special criticism. The very traits that induced Lincoln to hear the petitions of the powerless and to pardon army deserters under death sentence also prevented him from dealing decisively with the nation's enemies. Indeed, the one theme that cuts through the most eulogies is that after the loss of so many Northern lives, Lincoln was too forgiving, too compassionate towards the Southern traitors, and that he had become the victim of his own leniency. If Lincoln was a Moses who brought his people within sight of the Promised Land, there had to be a Joshua to see the cause to its completion. The merciful Abraham Lincoln had to be removed and replaced by the stern Andrew Johnson. The term 'removed and replaced' is apt, for Lincoln's assassination was deemed an essential part of God's plan. People throughout the North were told, and believed, that God 'permitted' the murder because He needed a stronger man to effect the righteous punishment of the Confederacy.

Yet no one benefited more from God's design than Lincoln himself. If the people 'were not, indeed, always pleased with his deeds', the assassin's bullet, in Reverend Stone's words, made him 'safe from all possibilities of error, frailties, and failures' (Boardman, 1865: 5; Stone, 1865: 349). By dying as he did, Lincoln not only preserved his own reputation but also alerted the Union to the South's desperation and treachery. 'Who shall dare deny', asked Reverend Hepworth (1865: 120), 'that Lincoln dead may yet do more for America than Lincoln living'. This is a peculiar way to compliment a fallen leader: to claim that his place in the nation's posterity resides not so much in what he did to others, as in what others did to him.[2]

The Easter Sunday characterization of Lincoln was reiterated in a second wave of sermons, delivered on Wednesday, 19 April, the official day of mourning.[3] Wednesday the 19th was also the day Lincoln's remains were taken by train from Washington. His body was carried for two weeks and viewed by multitudes in the Northern cities before it was placed to rest in the Oak Ridge Cemetery in Springfield, Illinois. So massive and dramatic was this funeral procession that many people today believe that by 4 May 1865, the date of his entombment, Abraham Lincoln had become a god. Beyond that day, however, a different picture emerged. The more ambivalent part of the public attitude toward Lincoln may have been suppressed by the glare and emotion of his funeral procession, but it was not suppressed for long. On 1 June 1865, one month after Lincoln's emtombment, the nation observed a Day of Humiliation and Prayer, and on this day was delivered the third wave of Lincoln eulogies. The tone of these eulogies was no different from those delivered in mid-April: Lincoln remained the honest and well-meaning man of the people, but too tender, too merciful, for his own good.[4]

Six months later, in his Lincoln's Birthday address to a joint session of Congress, America's most influential historian, George Bancroft, gave an even more negative portrayal. He explained that the martyred President 'was led along by the greatness of [the people's] self-sacrificing example; and as a child, in a dark night, on a rugged way catches hold of the hand of its father for guidance and support, he clung fast to the hand of the people, and moved calmly through the gloom' (1866: 35). Bancroft's inversion of the conventional metaphor is striking. There is no trace of a political father here. Lincoln is the child; the people are the father on whom he depends for guidance. Bancroft also inverted Lincoln's reputation for sympathy and tenderness. Most Americans (along with their religious spokesmen) believed that Lincoln's soft heart often caused him to be slow on urgent matters. Bancroft, however, was less generous. The President's slowness, he revealed, was due to simple indecisiveness and 'not from humility or tenderness of feeling'. Indeed, Lincoln's sensibilities were not acute: 'he had no vividness of imagination to picture to his mind the horrors of the battlefield or the sufferings in hospitals . . .'[5]

Few of the Republicans in Congress, let alone the Democrats, found anything objectionable in Bancroft's unflattering address. In this reaction the congressmen reflected the most negative aspects of their constituents' attitude towards Lincoln. Democrats who opposed the war were glad to learn that they were not the only ones who believed Lincoln to be insensitive to its costs. Republicans who supported the war were reinforced in their belief that Lincoln lacked the will to pursue it vigorously. As to Lincoln's reliance on popular opinion, no group knew this better, or was more pleased to hear it criticized, than the abolitionist Republicans. While most Republicans shared Bancroft's view that Lincoln was a patriotic man, they also shared his opinion about Lincoln's modest historic role. And not only did Bancroft convince his own audience. As Richard Current (1983: 185) explains: 'Bancroft and his fellow Brahmins contributed to forming the popular image of Lincoln that was to prevail for many years. In this picture the wartime president had little to do, as an agent in his own right, with the events of the Civil War.' A truer appreciation, Current adds, lay in the distant future.

II

The most prominent feature of the reaction to President Lincoln's assassination was its symbolic complexity – specifically, the differences between what the people's representatives said about Lincoln in funeral sermons and public orations, how these same spokesmen related Lincoln to other national figures, particularly George Washington, and how people participated in ceremonies to honour his memory. That same man whose death had been attributed to his own failings was compared with the great Father of his Country and visited in death by the multitudes. As the remaining years of the nineteenth century unfolded, Lincoln's place in history became more secure. Commentaries and poems about him appeared frequently. Biographers worked extra hard to meet the public demand for greater and more detailed information about the martyr's life. Still, something was missing, something that made the difference between an intensely admired man and a great man, between a folk hero and an epic hero.

Among the characteristics missing from the Lincoln cult was universality. Lincoln's predecessor, Washington, died as 'the man who united all hearts', and communities in every part of a still localistic nation vied with one another to show him reverence. When civil war broke out 65 years after Washington's death, he was embraced by both sides as the personification of their cause: union in the North, liberty in the South. No such consensus graced the memory of Lincoln. The Southerners whom he defeated in war may have been saddened by his assassination, but they were not inclined to revere him. They were busy building a cult around one of their own leaders, Robert E. Lee. Puritanical people from New England, genteel people everywhere, often found the President's homely manners and emotional expressiveness unattractive. Others were repelled by Lincoln's policies. Many pro-Confederate ('Copperhead') and anti-war Democrats on the one side, and radical abolitionists and Republicans on the other, were glad to see him dead. Even among the black people, who as a group loved Lincoln intensely, there were prominent and influential exceptions (see, for example, Douglass, 1962).

Although not universally adored in the post-war decades, Lincoln was a greatly admired man. The post-war biographers and publicists did much to sustain this admiration, even though none of their hundreds of biographical accounts really captured the public imagination. Josiah Holland wrote the first popular Lincoln biography, but it never approached Parson Weems's (1800) life of Washington, which went through more than forty editions before

Weems died in 1825. Among the three most serious lives of Lincoln, two were scarcely read. William Herndon and Ward Lamon sincerely felt that the truest version of Lincoln's life would be the best tribute to him. It was a wonderful thing, they believed, for a man to be a national treasure and at the same time joke about Christianity, sell liquor, tell dirty jokes and make do without a handkerchief. The reading public, however, was not ready for this kind of biography, and when the publishers realized how offensive it was they stopped the presses and cancelled arrangements for subsequent volumes. John Hay and John Nicolay, both secretaries to President Lincoln, were less intimate in their revelations; however, the resulting biography confined itself almost exclusively to the public man – so much so that Lincoln often got lost in the very war he was fighting. (For details, see Fehrenbacher, 1987: 182–4; O'Neill, 1935: 119–39.)

Still, the writings about Lincoln accumulated, and if they failed to transform him into a national idol, they did keep him alive in the people's imagination and reflected the people's affection for him. Meanwhile, the other lineaments of his cult were developing. In both private and public places, portraits of Lincoln multiplied. Postage stamps bore his image. His countenance appeared in conspicious places throughout the United States Capitol Building. Counties, towns, streets and businesses were named for him. By the end of the century there was talk in many states of his birthday becoming an official holiday. On the other hand, Lincoln's was not the only claim on America's collective memory. The last quarter of the nineteenth century was filled with reminders of the Revolutionary era. From 1876 to 1889, and beyond, great centennial celebrations marked the nation's independence and its first government, and these enlarged George Washington's already paramount role in that nation's representation of itself, overshadowing Lincoln's and leaving him in second place.

III

In the early years of the twentieth century began the developments that made Lincoln the most cherished of national possessions, greater even than Washington. One aspect of Lincoln's growing reputation can be indexed by the relative frequency with which he was written about in the popular media. Citation counts from the *Reader's Guide to Periodical Literature* are by no means a precise measure of Washington's and Lincoln's standing over time, but they do reflect something of the changing demands of a general adult reading audience and the way these demands were met. As we trace the volume of articles from 1890 to 1904 (Table 5.1), we find a declining trend for both Washington and Lincoln, with about one Lincoln article published for every Washington article. In the next five-year interval, 1905–09, two Lincoln articles appeared for every Washington article. Thereafter, the ratio grew even more in Lincoln's favour.

Table 5.1   *Reader's Guide Entries on Abraham Lincoln and George Washington, 1890–1921*

Period[1]	Number of entries (mean per year)	
	Lincoln	Washington
1890–99	9.0	10.0
1900–04	7.6	7.2
1905–09	14.2	7.0
1910–14	14.0	5.4
1915–18	23.0	4.5
1919–21	20.7	6.3

[1] Unequal intervals follow the *Reader's Guide* method of accumulation.

The *Congressional Record* entries in Table 5.2 go back to 1875. Between then and 1890, as the table shows, there are 4.2 entries on Washington for every one on Lincoln, a ratio that reflects the centennial events associated with the nation's founding. From 1890 to 1905, the fluctuation in the number of entries follows the same pattern revealed by the *Reader's Guide* article counts: Washington and Lincoln are the subjects of almost the same number of entries. For the next 15 years, 1905–19, Lincoln surpasses Washington by a ratio of about 1.5 to 1.

Similarly, in the *New York Times* the number of articles about Washington far exceeds the number about Lincoln until the very turn of the century (reaching a peak in 1889, the year of Washington's Inauguration centennial). During the next five years, the volume drops sharply for both men, with Washington only slightly ahead of Lincoln. After 1905, the volume rises and the Lincoln coverage outpaces Washington's by a ratio of almost two to one.

An analysis of the February issues of the *New York Age*, a black newspaper, reveals the same trend. Prior to 1905, Table 5.2 shows, the *Age* contained few entries on either Washington or Lincoln. However, the Washington count remained negligible (except for the last years of the First World War), while the Lincoln count grew: 36 articles on Lincoln appeared between 1905 and 1909, followed by 54 and 73 articles during the next two five-year intervals.

Table 5.2 *Entries on Abraham Lincoln and George Washington:* Congressional Record, New York Times *and* New York Age

Period	Congressional Record		New York Times		New York Age[1]	
	Lincoln	Washington	Lincoln	Washington	Lincoln	Washington
1875–99	4	22	55	58		
1880–84	21	66	74	80		
1885–89	8	51	45	309	1	
1890–94	12	11	30	111	1	
1895–99	35	34	52	120		
1900–04	15	19	18	30		
1905–09	55	33	236	82	36	3
1910–14	76	46	125	81	54	5
1915–19	61	47	164	104	73	31

[1] February issues only.

Table 5.3 *Unveiling of outdoor statues in bronze of Abraham Lincoln 1865–1919*

Period	Number of Statues
1865–69	1
1870–79	5
1880–89	1
1890–99	3
1900–09	11
1910–19	21

Source: *Bulletin of the Lincoln National Life Foundation*, February, 1962

The enlivening of Lincoln's memory in the early 1900s is also manifested in the production of heroic-size, outdoor bronze statues. Table 5.3 shows that from Lincoln's death to the turn of the century, a period of 35 years, only 10 such Lincoln statues were unveiled – about one every 3½ years. In the first decade of the century, 1900–09, 11 statues appeared – about one a year. The second decade, 1910–19, witnessed the unveiling of 21 statues – about two a year. Scripture and icon thus display an identical pattern, and that is an abrupt growth of interest in Lincoln during the first twenty years of the twentieth century.

A year-by-year analysis of *The New York Times Index* reveals a definite turning-point in Lincoln's popularity. Between 1875 and 1907, a 33-year period, no trend in the production of *Times* articles on Lincoln is evident. A mean of 9 articles appeared annually during this period. In 1908, however, the number of articles rose to 36, a level higher than it had ever been before, then leaped to an extraordinary quantity, 163 articles, in 1909, before settling upon a new equilibrium. The number of articles varies substantially from one year to the next, but the average is three times as high after 1909 (29 articles annually), as before. Likewise, an average of 3.2 entries a year on Lincoln appeared in the *Congressional Record* between 1875 and 1908. In 1909, the number of entries rose to 41 and averaged 13.7 annually during the next ten years.

The number of *Times* and *Congressional Record* entries rose as high as they did in 1909 because that year was the one-hundredth anniversary of Lincoln's birth, because that anniversary was perceived by local officials everywhere as an opportunity to celebrate his life and achievements and because that celebration was one in which the people at large were eager to participate. Concentrated as they were in one year, and even more noticeably on one day of that year, the Lincoln centennial events made for a cogent instance of the truth in Emile Durkheim's (1912/1965: 474–5) theory of periodic assemblies. In order to retain in the collective memory some great person or event, Durkheim believed, society must set aside a time for people periodically to assemble and to contemplate in common the things they cherish and wish to preserve. The point of such an event is to mark off the day from others, and to bring people into the presence of one another. The resulting social mood is expansive, effervescent and facilitates communion with objects in society which transcend the private lives of its members and infuses them with collective purpose and meaning. Centennial anniversaries of events critical to the nation, like birthdays of national heroes, serve this end effectively.

The number and kind of Lincoln Centennial activities defy adequate description, but the range of these activities tells something of the function they performed. Centennial activities did more than Durkheim would have expected. They not only helped the people remember Lincoln but also enlarged Lincoln by encasing his memory in ritual and associating it with personal interests and national symbols. The most elaborate celebrations of this kind were found in America's cities. In Chicago, public meetings were held by almost every religious, ethnic, trade and neighbourhood organization. Throughout the city, tens of thousands of people watched massive and colourful parades. The city itself was 'fairly buried beneath flags' and its stores were full of Civil War relics, including portraits of Lincoln. In New York, the nation's largest city, the commemorative activities were attended by more than a million people. Participation was effusive everywhere in the North. In almost every classroom, from the biggest cities to the smallest towns, Abraham Lincoln's portrait appeared. Southern cities and Southern schools did not go so far, but they too conducted exercises, most for the very first time, to bring Lincoln to respected, if not honoured, memory.

In every city the nation's most eminent men took part in the leading ceremonies. William Jennings Bryan, the 'Great Commoner', spoke in Springfield, Illinois; Woodrow Wilson, in Chicago. At the Cooper Union Hall in New York, site of the Lincoln speech that 'won the East', Booker T. Washington appeared and made a speech of his own. The festivities in New Orleans were presided over by President-elect Howard Taft, while the President himself, Theodore Roosevelt, dedicated Lincoln's birthplace in Kentucky. In each case, Lincoln's greatness was magnified by the prestige of the man who honoured him. In each case, the integrative character of the observance was underscored by the simple fact that this man came from out-of-State. By this 'ritual exogamy' local solidarity was ignored, national solidarity reaffirmed.

These extraordinary centennial celebrations were attended by people who had already begun to change their perceptions of Lincoln. They had begun to regard him as not merely the most prominent of the last century's public men, but as the one man whose qualities transcended his age. This new perception of Lincoln's historical status finds expression not only in citation counts from popular periodicals but also through direct attestation. Thus, in March 1906 a commentator for the *Review of Reviews* observed that 'During each succeeding decade, since the tragic end of that remarkable life, the American people have through the perspective of time, found their appreciation of his great character and achievements constantly growing' (p. 294). Another commentator, in *The World's Work*, noted on the centennial of Lincoln's birth (February 1909, p. 11,186) that the man 'became larger and larger as we get further from his physical presence'. At the very same time, Lord James Bryce declared that 'it remained for later years for both Americans and Europeans to recognize Lincoln's greatness' (*Outlook*, 20 February 1909, p. 364). So evident was the growth of Abraham Lincoln's stature during the first decade of this century that one commentator deemed inappropriate any kind of finished memorial to him (*Review of Reviews*, September 1908, pp. 334–41). It would take something that could be enlarged as the years pass (like a memorial highway from Washington to Gettysburg) to do him justice. In 1913, four years after the centennial excitement had died down, a *Nation* (27 February, p. 196) contributor found that 'Lincoln's rank as an embodiment of popular ideals and as an object of national homage is today vastly higher than it was when a quarter-century, instead of a half-century, separated us from the time of his labors and his martyrdom.' As the twentieth-century's second decade progressed, the Lincoln image became even more appealing. In 1917, the United States entered the First World War and Abraham Lincoln became 'America's most quoted man' (*Literary Digest*, 6 January 1917, p. 18). At the end of the war he was more revered than he had ever been before. As one *New York Times* (15 August 1920, p. 2) editor put it, Lincoln has 'been revalued year by year, with the result of an ever mounting fame'. Contemplating the same epoch, an *Outlook* (29 September 1920, p. 186) contributor declared: 'At no time in a long period has more attention been given to the character, influence, and steadfast qualities of Abraham Lincoln than seems to have filled the minds of men, both here and abroad, during the last two or three years, especially since the armistice.'

In this series of observations, we have additional evidence of a rapidly growing reputation for Lincoln during the first two decades of the twentieth century. During each year there was someone to say that Lincoln had become more exalted than he was in previous years. Corresponding changes appeared in the relationship between Lincoln and the great standard: George Washington. On this matter, all commentators trod gingerly, not wanting to insult the memory of the Founding Father. Still, they got their message across. Readers of the February 1913 issue of *Nation*, for example, learned that 'while the birthday of Washington had been observed for more than a century, Lincoln's birthday has within the last two decades assumed something like a coordinate place in the national thought' (p. 196). However, the writer waxed bolder as he moved along: ' "We are doing just what Lincoln would do if he were living" has become a familiar catchword in these latter days. But nobody says "we're doing just what Washington would do" ' (p. 197). Another observer came to the same conclusion. 'No longer', he declared, 'is Washington first in the hearts of his countrymen. Lincoln [is] secure in that place'[6] (*Dial*, 9 August 1919, p. 93). That Lincoln was more secure in some hearts than in others is certain. He was more secure in the hearts of Northerners than Southerners, of black men than white men, of Midwesterners than Easterners. Among all categories of people and sections of the country, however, his reputation had grown, and by 1920 he had become the principal occupant of the American pantheon.

IV

Abraham Lincoln emerged as a national idol during a critical phase in America's historical development, the beginnings of which were apparent only in the last decade of the nineteenth century. In order to understand which of Lincoln's personal characteristics and achievements had the most significance for the twentieth-century American, and why the commemoration of these qualities became so persistent and widespread, the main aspects of this critical phase must be made known.

Prior to the 1890s, the voice that announced America's identity came from the past. America's cultural institutions saw their mission in both the preservation of the inspired design of the founding era and the realization of that design in institution building and individual moral development. As the twentieth century approached, however, the orientation changed from past to future, from preservation to growth. In Henry Steele Commager's words:

> The decade of the nineties is the watershed of American history. . . . On the one side lies an America predominantly agricultural; concerned with domestic problems; conforming, intellectually at least, to the political, economic, and moral principles inherited from the seventeenth and eighteenth centuries. . . . On the other side lies the modern America, predominantly urban and industrial; inextricably involved in a world economy and politics; troubled with the problems that had long been thought peculiar to the Old World; experiencing profound changes in population, social institutions, and technology; and trying to accommodate its traditions and habits of thought to conditions new and in part alien. (1950: 41)

Implied in Commager's statement are two lines along which early twentieth century American social development can be plotted: first, the expansion and use of national resources and power in global arenas, and secondly, a concern for the way these resources and this power were distributed internally. The Spanish–American War, more than any other single event, initiated the first line of development. Fought and won in about ten weeks, at low cost and few casualties, this 'splendid little war', as John Hay, former secretary to Lincoln, called it, yielded high returns in unity and self-conception. John Henry Barrows, President of Oberlin College, called the event of 1898 a 'miracle'. All previous conceptions of national pride, like the insular nationalism of the pre-Civil War years, must be repudiated. 'God has made us a world power' (Nagel, 1971: 258–9). And so, as America moved into the twentieth century the nationalistic uproar became shrill and strident.

The second aspect of America's turn-of-the-century development, concern for the internal distribution of resources and power, defined the programme of the Progressive Era. Against the problems of the industrial revolution – unregulated immigration and urban growth, massive slums, decline in moral values and, above all, a widening gap between rich and poor – the Progressives harnessed and exerted federal power. Anti-trust legislation, a pure food and drug law, child and sweatshop labour laws, federal workmen's compensation, the progressive income tax – these and other measures helped to transform the competitive jungle of the nineteenth century into the humane capitalist order of the twentieth. No less extensive in their social effect were the democratic political reforms, including the direct election of United States senators, the voter initiative, the referendum, women's suffrage, the Primary Election and Corrupt Practices Acts.

These reforms brought no social revolution. They were meant to protect, not undermine, free enterprise and property. Indeed, the gap between rich and poor was greater at the end of the reform era than at its beginning. Racial and ethnic animosities, too, became more, not less, pronounced. For contemporaries, however, the distinction of the Progressive Era was its climate of aspiration rather than its concrete economic and political achievements. This was very much an ideological era, an era that witnessed the arousal of a new political spirit, a revitalization of democracy, an unprecedented concern for the rights and well-being of common people. Progressivism, then, 'must be understood as a major episode in the history of American consciousness', a 'spiritual growth in the hearts of the American people . . . a moral movement in democracy' (Hofstadter 1963: 15, 36). Animated by 'civic alertness', 'revolutionary feeling' and a 'combative mood', the extraordinary texture of the Progressive Movement is perhaps best attested to by the phrase 'Return to normalcy', which was the slogan of those who wanted to see the Movement end. (See also Commager, 1950; Mann, 1962; Noble, 1970; Roosevelt, 1961; Wilson et al., 1979).

Begun in the early years of the twentieth century, these changes in American society set the stage for a reconstruction of the American past. It was in this context that the need for a new Lincoln revealed itself.

V

The traits most celebrated in great leaders reflect the main premises of their culture. To understand leaders as political symbols, then, we must be able to move from the categories in which they are thought about to the categories of political thinking in general. Thus, the main issues of the early 1900s – the exercise of expanding power beyond national borders and the redistribution of power within – placed limits on the kind of man that Americans could make of Lincoln. Great and powerful nations cannot be represented by common, weak men. Democratic nations cannot be represented by élitist, strong men. The Lincoln image was for these reasons pulled in two opposite directions: toward stateliness, authority and dignity on the one hand, and toward plainness, familiarity and homeliness on the other. These two sides of the twentieth-century Lincoln image reflect two fundamental strains of American political culture: the equalitarian strain, rooted in the Republican-antebellum Democratic tradition, and the hierarchical strain, rooted in the Federalist-antebellum Whig tradition (de Tocqueville, 1946; Ellis and Wildavsky, 1989; Howe, 1979; Meyers, 1960). Both themes, the equalitarian and the hierarchical, were personified by Lincoln from the very moment he died, but they have formed his image unevenly. The post-Civil War Lincoln was composed largely of equalitarian stuff. In the early, Progressive decades of the twentieth century, Lincoln's majesty was super-imposed upon his commonness and brought into balance with it.

The equalitarian dimension of the Lincoln image not only retained its salience in the twentieth century but was also promoted in new ways. Many of those people who moulded the new image were mature adolescents or young adults engaged in the Civil War effort when they had come to know Lincoln, or to converse with him, or to see him enacting his presidential duties. This contact induced in many a profound sense of attachment to him.[7] As the celebration of the 1909 Lincoln Centennial drew closer, more and more reminiscences by Lincoln's young contemporaries were published, and almost all writers told of the President's closeness and accessibility to common people like themselves. 'Recollections of Lincoln', 'An audience with Lincoln', 'Intimate personal recol-lections', 'Impressions of Lincoln', 'Lincoln as I knew him', 'A boy at Lincoln's feet' – these are the kinds of titles that filled popular magazines during the first decade of the twentieth century.

Article-writers articulated this equalitarian theme in many ways, the most common of which was the comparison between Abraham Lincoln and George Washington. The need for such comparison signalled the Americans' awareness that their country was under-going a significant cultural transition, and the content of the comparison embodied an interpretation of the transition itself. The flurry of 'Washington and Lincoln' articles that came out in the early twentieth century shows Lincoln's fame surpassing Washington's and thus reveals the growing nation's increasingly democratic con-ception of itself and a corresponding alienation from its early past. For the first time, post-revolutionary America took on the look of a foreign country. As Charles Beard, William Allen White and other 'Progressive historians' were revealing the anti-democratic inspira-tion of the Constitution's designers, popular writers were discover-ing the essential difference between America's old hero, George Washington, and its new hero, Abraham Lincoln. In this connection, Lyman Powell (*Review of Reviews*, 1901, p. 192) made use of a metaphor from nature. Washington and Lincoln, he said, are two trees, two giants of the American forest. Washington is the tree that draws the eye upward toward leafy crown and sky; the Lincoln tree draws the eye downward to massive roots and to the earth in which they are set. To this contrast between leafage and roots, high and low, sky and earth, corresponds another contrast – that of Old World and New. The leaves that crown the Washington tree reflect 'the autumnal tints of Europe' (p. 192), while the roots of the Lincoln tree go deep into the New World soil.[8]

The contrast is ironic. Washington was the real farmer; Lincoln, the townsman. Yet Lincoln became the man of the soil. The association meant only one thing: to be of the earth is to be of the people: 'Ay, Earth's he is; not hers alone/ Blood of our blood, bone of my bone,/ Love folded him to rest upon a people's breast' (*Atlantic*, February 1909, p. 278). The logic was extended to Lincoln's personal background and enlarged to incorporate other symbols. If to be of the earth is to be of the people, then to be of the people is to be of the West. Coming from 'the backyard of the nation', another observer (*Everybody's*, February 1910, p. 217) explained, the East could not see, let alone understand, Lincoln's greatness. With Lincoln's coming, however, that old civilization of 'prudish colonials' and 'icicled Puritanism' began its demise. The West rolled back the East. Lincoln became the embodiment of America itself as the log cabin in Hodgenville replaced Mount Vernon.

Celebration of Lincoln's commonness, so much a part of the nineteenth-century idea of the man, took on a new, almost militant meaning in the twentieth century. The primacy of soil to sky, New World to Old, West to East, were metaphors for the renewed dignity and power of the common people. Correspondingly, Lincoln's growing prestige, its articulation in terms of symbols of commonness and simplicity, was a restatement of democracy's rediscovery, a way of bringing it down out of its abstractness, making it known to the people in a concrete and dramatic way. Many Centennial speeches and commentaries on Lincoln made explicit reference to this point. When Theodore Roosevelt laid the corner-stone for the Lincoln shrine in Hodgenville, Kentucky, he remarked on the 'social and industrial problems of the day' and how Lincoln's own 'reform' would apply to them. Many other spokesmen worked away at this theme. Lincoln would oppose child labour and the exploitation of adult labour. He would recognize that 'socialism is the new slavery', but would say the same about 'corporations that break the laws with insolence and impunity'. Lincoln was a natural 'labour leader' who recognized not only the legitimacy of property but also the essential rights of the working man. He was a supporter of universal suffrage: 'I go for all sharing the privilege of government . . . by no means excluding women', quoted suffragette billboards bearing his picture, as well as the February issues of the *Woman's Journal*. The Lincoln image insinuated itself into many other political discussions. An *Arena* (July 1909: 480) commentator defined the centennial of Lincoln's birth as a major event, giving 'a new inspiration and hope to thousands who were all but despairing of the success of popular rule. . . . It has flooded the imagination of the rising generation with the light of democracy, so hated and feared by the reactionary interests of privileged wealth'. In the centennial edition of the *Chicago Tribune*, the editorial explained that 'demand for popular-ization of the senate, for the democratization of party organization . . ., for the initiative and referendum, and even the recall' have all converged into a 'tide of democracy'. And 'in this ripe hour the American people turn to their noblest memory. . . . For Lincoln's life and Lincoln's character illustrate more perfectly than that of any other of America's great men the essential rightness and prac-ticability [of these political reforms]' (*Atlanta Constitution*, 13 February 1909, p. 2; *Outlook*, 27 February 1909; *Chicago Tribune*, 19 February 1909, p. 1; 13 February 1909, p. 2, 4; 7 February 1909, p. 4).

It was precisely with Lincoln's life and Lincoln's character that the vast majority of Centennial and later writings concerned themselves, for in the end it was not as important to know what particular contemporary measures Lincoln would have supported or opposed as to know what traits of character were revealed in that support and that opposition. Hence the inexhaustible reminiscences of Lincoln's authentic simplicity and unpretentiousness, his merciful attitude towards condemned soldiers, his accessiblity and respon-siveness to people without influence and power, his profound sympathy for the casualties of war and their families. Saturating the February issues of popular magazines and the Lincoln's Birthday edition of local newspapers, these reminiscences depict the blurring of hierarchical distinction; they depict the common person in interaction and close moral affinity with the state. Lincoln's character and life on the one hand, and twentieth-century political and economic reforms on the other, were thus seen to be infused by the same egalitarian principle, such that the invocation of one invariably brought to mind the other. In Lincoln the people found the most compelling emblem of the Progressive Era's democratic aspirations.

VI

To depict Lincoln as the common man, the man who represents the masses but never leaves them, is to depict a kind of folk hero. Folk heroes symbolize their societies' most general tendencies. They are embodiments of *la vie légère*[9] – the most mundane, least consequential aspects of life. In the talk, actions and troubles of these heroes the people readily see themselves. As embodiments of the common life, folk heroes are imitable as well as touchable. They are also 'touching' in that they evoke sentiments which become central to their own public identities. Thus, Lincoln's signature emotions – his brightness and humour, his dark foreboding and overwhelming grief – distinguished him from other public men and brought him closer to the people.

Epic heroes, on the other hand, remind the people of their ideals rather than their actual conduct and feelings. They point to the concerns of *la vie sérieuse*. The extraordinary talents and virtues of epic heroes, their world-changing feats, place between themselves and the common person an impassable barrier, causing them always to be revered, rarely loved. Epic heroes are not the kind of beings we may cozy up to. We do not come close to them, let alone touch them, with impunity. In this distance and untouchability inheres much of their appeal. Their awesomeness, their venerability, is maintained and amplified by their majestic remoteness.

National idols are always cast in epic proportions, and as Abraham Lincoln came to be so regarded he began to take on a second set of characteristics. Americans continued to appreciate Lincoln's folk qualities: his background of rural poverty, his informality of dress, awkwardness of demeanour and manner, physical homeliness, his story-telling. He remained a kind of second cousin to America's frontier heroes – Davy Crockett and Kit Carson.[10] In the twentieth century, however, Americans began to refashion the man of the people along epic lines. Increasingly, they saw the Christ-like Man of Sorrows. They saw the Saviour of the Union who takes upon himself the pain of his people. They saw the great moralist, the prophet of democracy, the Great Emancipator, the giant who changes the course of history. They saw the man that can never be reached: a man, for sure, but too good, and too big, to be treated as a man.

Lincoln's reconstitution involved demolition as well as construction. Backwoods traits may be just the thing to symbolize a virtuous agricultural nation, but not an urban, industrialized world power. Images of a rustic President uniting quaint stories with neighbourly kindness gradually gave way to an image equally humanitarian, but less sentimental and more dignified. Thus, by 1919, a *Nation* critic observed:

> the homespun mantle which Lincoln originally wore has entirely fallen away. . . . Perhaps the disposition just now to purge him of all weakness

and to make him out a saint and mystic may not last forever, but obviously it is a step in his poetical history analogous to those steps which ennobled Charlemagne and Arthur, and canonized Joan of Arc. (17 May 1919, p. 777)

Correspondingly, Lincoln's humorous side began to lose part of its earlier appeal. Collections of 'Lincoln jokes' were published while he was still President, and continued to sell after his death. Also, many parables attributed to him were brought together in 1901 under the title *Abe Lincoln Yarns and Stories*. But epic heroes are made of more solemn stuff. The popularity of the light-hearted Lincolniana grew, according to Roy Basler, 'until about 1909, when the Lincoln Centennial brought out every stock from the nook. Since then, interest has become more and more fixed in his dignified posture as America's greatest statesman and leader' (1935: 34).

As Lincoln became more dignified, his personality commanded less attention; his achievements and their historical significance, more attention. The people thus made an image from which they deferentially separated themselves. Their own creation became more distant, less familiar. In the words of another *Nation* correspondent:

In America, our veneration of Lincoln is greater, because more intelligent, than it was in 1865. He is a far more commanding figure now than then, a more epic and less intimate hero. His personal character lent itself to a myth-making process. His homely humor led to ransacking of joke-books; his gentleness grew into legends of reprieve, pardons, and consolatory letters. This was a familiarity that bred contempt even with its affection; and it so defeated itself that historians have had a great work to do in restoring Lincoln as he really existed. We now care little for 'Lincoln stories', yet we study his authentic life as that of no other national figure. (*Nation*, 22 April 1915, p. 434)

Equally important in the campaign to dignify Lincoln, this same correspondent tells us, was an emphasis on that one part of his make-up that had been less appreciated than any other, and that was his keen intelligence:

A common conception is that Lincoln came to the presidency as a raw untrained man. The common people like to think this was so, since it fit in so well with their belief, or hope, that mediocre intellectual attributes were sufficient. But we now fully understand that Abraham Lincoln became President with a disciplined and sinewy mind. (*Nation*, 22 April 1915, p. 434)

The *Nation* correspondent's reflections are not unique; they summarize the pronounced dualism in the American people's memory of Lincoln. Unselfconsciously, the people engraved an image that reflected two irreconcilable parts of their social make-up: first, their love of democracy and preference for leaders they can reach, talk to and touch: and secondly, their pride in the power and moral dignity of America, and their wish to embody it in impressively remote men.

This dualism took literally concrete form in the emergence of a national shrine which incorporates both Lincoln's folk and epic qualities. The rude log cabin in which Lincoln was born in Hodgenville, Kentucky is a symbol of his bonds with the common people, and it has come to mean to them as Americans what the humble stable in Bethlehem means to them as Christians. But just as the world's faithful have sanctified the birthplace of Christ by housing it within an impressive Church of the Nativity, so the American people have ennobled the birthplace of Lincoln by housing it within a marble Temple of Fame.

In both conception and accomplishment, the Lincoln Memorial is even less democratic than the imposing Lincoln birthplace shrine. It was for the 1909 Centennial that Congress appropriated the then extraordinary sum of two million dollars to build this monument. Two places in the city of Washington were considered for its location: one near the Capitol building, the other near Union Station. Both places were rejected, and the reasons reveal something of Congress's attitude toward Lincoln. The first location was turned down for fear that the Capitol would diminish the monument by overwhelming it in size; the second, because its location was too peripheral to do Lincoln justice. Most Congressmen believed it necessary to create a new centre for Lincoln's monument, one that would bring it into contact with other symbols of the nation's past without falling under their shadows. John Hay had endorsed precisely that suggestion when he was Secretary of State in 1901. Ten years later, Congress followed. Its rationale, which reiterated that of Hays, provides a concise statement on how monuments transform ordinary men into sacred possessions:

> Lincoln, of all Americans next to Washington, deserves this place of honor. He was of the immortals. You must not approach too close to the immortals. His monument should stand alone, remote from the common habitations of man, apart from the business and turmoil of the city; isolated, distinguished, and serene. (*Outlook*, 12 August, 1911, p. 811)

As a sacred being, Lincoln had to be not only isolated geographically; he also had to be defended against profane contact. For this reason, the Lincoln Memorial designer, Henry Bacon, dismissed the idea of a heroic-size statue of Lincoln placed in an open portico. He invoked the ancient Greek pattern wherein the statues of gods were placed in enclosed temples to secure their separation from common people and their world (*Outlook*, 10 February, 1912, p. 298).

The isolation of the Lincoln shrine expressed the singular

remoteness of the man. The connection of his shrine with others infused that remoteness with democratic content. Planners could imagine the glorious scene: 'From the hills of the District and Virginia the constantly recurring views of a great Lincoln memorial, seen in association with the Washington Monument and the dome of the Capitol, will be impressive in the highest degree' (*Outlook*, 12 August, 1911, p. 812). Impressive, indeed: for such an alignment symbolically joins the memory of Lincoln to that of the Father of his Country, and by this connection to the forum of the people.

VII

Abraham Lincoln stands today alongside George Washington as the most prominent of American historical figures. Yet his status was not always so elevated. Even at the emotional peak of his popularity – the fourteen days when millions turned out to witness his funeral cortege – Lincoln's place in America's collective consciousness was uncertain. Supported at first by the emotional waves that his assassination set in motion, Lincoln's image became more positive and more compelling as time passed, reaching a peak in the first two decades of the twentieth century. Lincoln was not elevated at this time because the people had discovered new facts about him, but because they had discovered new facts about themselves, and regarded him as the perfect vehicle for giving these tangible expression.

According to Peter Karsten, America's increasingly centralized and powerful state is the primary reason for both the growth of Lincoln's reputation and the relative decline of Washington's. Arguing on the basis of contrasting political cultures and presidential performances, Karsten regards Washington as America's paramount 'anti-statist' symbol; Lincoln, the personification of 'statism'. That Lincoln's reputation grew so rapidly during the Progressive Era, a time of significant expansion of governmental power, makes Karsten's argument plausible. Two problems, however, detract from the richness of this argument. First, Karsten underestimates Washington's symbolic role, which, in its celebration of liberty – an anti-statist ideal – remained a salient aspect of American political tradition both during and after the Progressive Era. Secondly, Karsten ignores much of the tension in what Lincoln stood for. Although Lincoln did come to represent the power of the twentieth-century state, he was not commemorated for that reason alone. His embodiment of the virtues and aspirations of the common person – a link that transcends the statist–anti-statist dichotomy – was a necessary element in his extraordinary twentieth-century reputation. Different men of the past and present, including Alexander Hamilton and Theodore Roosevelt, symbolized different aspects of America's new industrial democracy. Lincoln stood above them in the popular imagination not because his life lent itself to becoming a symbol of the majesty of the state but because it had already become a symbol of the majesty of the people. In a society where fear of expanding state power was justified and sustained by a strong libertarian tradition, it was natural that the man who personified the priority of that state and its élites would also be the man who personified the entitlements of the masses.

The reconstruction of Abraham Lincoln during the Progressive Era was the making of a complex figure, one whose contradictory qualities reproduced the contradictions of American society. Love of equality and love of authority, the people's desire for leaders to be at once people they can relate to and people they can look up to, people at once close and remote in relation to them – this dualism had become by the dawn of the twentieth century more salient than it had ever been before, and it insinuated itself into a new appreci- ation of Lincoln. Elevating Lincoln, the Americans affirmed for themselves their commitment to both commonness and greatness.

Although Lincoln's reputation surged during the early years of the twentieth century, it expressed more than the conditions of that particular time. No strict correspondence obtains between the conditions of any era and the objects of its collective memory. Memory-making is an act of enterprise: before any one individual can be regarded as worth remembering, other individuals, like colleagues and family members, political and religious leaders, biographers, artists, editors and writers, must deem that person commemorable and must have the influence to get others to agree with them. Of the many facts stemming from recent studies of reputation and fame, this fact – the dependence of reputation and fame on successful promotion by admirers – is the best established. However, the most prominent of these studies, including Lang and Lang (1988) on the British etchers, Tuchman and Fortin (1984) on women novelists, Thomas Connelly (1977) on Robert E. Lee, Robert Tucker (1973) on Joseph Stalin, focus on only one type of reputational enterprise: that which is either highly visible, tightly organized or state sponsored. In contrast, the extraordinary centennial celebrations of 1909 were decentralized and locally sponsored. Forty volumes of newspaper clippings in the Chicago Public Library describe thousands of local Lincoln Centennial events, but suggest no unifying hand, let alone the hegemonic influence for which the neo-Marxist students of tradition hasten to look (Williams, 1977: 116–17).

The centennial anniversary of Lincoln's birth, the critical point in his canonization, would have been celebrated regardless of contem- porary circumstances, for Lincoln's admirers, although working independently of one another, had made his place in America's collective memory too prominent not to be so recognized. On the other hand, the Centennial's intensity and scope were certainly enlarged by the circumstances in which it took place. Had Lincoln's assumed character and achievements not echoed the concerns of a new society – a stronger and more democratic society – he would have never been recalled so vividly to its memory, let alone become its idol. Thus, it makes sense to assert, with Charles Horton Cooley, that 'fame exists for present use and not to perpetuate a dead past' (1918: 116).

However, Cooley made no less sense in suggesting that 'personal fames are the most active part of the social tradition', and that the famous name must appeal 'not one time only, but again and again, and to many persons, until it has become a tradition' (1918: 112). Cooley never wrote about the past as succinctly as Mead and Durkheim, or as richly as Shils and Lowenthal. He never understood how, through commemorative symbols and ritual, the memory of events and people of the past are preserved. Yet in his commentary on 'Fame' (the 'extended leadership', as he called it), Cooley displayed great sensitivity to the tension that organizes the commemorative process. He recognized the dual need to sustain appreciation of past heroes by keeping their image intact over time, and to sustain them by revising their images to match changing conditions and tastes. Thus, Cooley spoke directly to the present theoretical problem: to distinguish those features of the Lincoln image which are hostage to the needs of the present from those which are indifferent to these needs and resistant to change.

In considering this matter it is necessary to regard the remembering of Lincoln as a constructive process as opposed to a retrieval process. Yet such an understanding is 'presentist'[11] in its outlook, and when pushed too far, as it would be by followers of George Herbert Mead and Maurice Halbwachs, converts Lincoln into a mere screen on which the contemporary society projects its own image. The durability of that screen is always problematic. Although Mead (1929; 1932) believed that the present generation becomes conscious of itself from the standpoint of its own past, he also believed that previously important aspects of the past lose relevance when present conditions change. The transience of the past's hold on the present was also affirmed by Maurice Halbwachs (1951/80: 79, 80). 'How can currents of collective thought whose impetus lies in the past', he asked, 'be re-created, when we can grasp only the present?' The radical element in these formulations is not their *emphasis* on present relevance as a condition for remembering, but rather their assumption that successive generations are essentially foreign to one another, 'like two tree stumps', as Halbwachs put it, 'that touch at their extremities but do not form one plant because they are not otherwise connected'.

To reject assumptions about the cultural autonomy of generations is to appreciate the limits of Lincoln's reconstructability, and of the reconstructability of great people in general. Just as the Church supervises the revelation of Christ to ensure that it remains today and tomorrow what it was yesterday, so the state, through its own archival and commemorative enterprises, seeks to make the appreciation of its great people independent of the different experiences of different generations. Not only states but also regional, local and private organizations sustain definitions of historical greatness by restraining perception. To make a 'good symbol to help us think and feel', Cooley said, we do not start from scratch. Rather, we start 'with an actual personality which more or less meets this need' and we improve it by omitting the inessential and adding 'whatever is necessary to round out the ideal' (1918: 116). The 'actual personality' that we start with, Cooley implies, limits the range of things the collective memory can do.

The endurance of original constructions expresses the endurance of the social realities they symbolize.[12] Early twentieth-century America was vastly different from the America in which Lincoln lived and died, but it was not a different society. It was the same society because it sustained, in the context of dissensus and change, a stable sense of national identity and consensus of values. In this continuity inhere the most decisive limits to the evolution of Lincoln's image. From the initial conception of Lincoln as a man of the people we know that later generations subtracted little; they only superimposed new traits. That this initial image continues to engage society is evidence of the past's effect on contemporary perceptions. When the human mind 'creates types that go beyond nature', as Cooley put it, it does so by 'working through tradition' (1918: 116).[13] The new Lincoln's dignity and remoteness thus subserve rather than undermine the old Lincoln's simpleness and intimacy. Correspondingly, the collective memory comes into view as both a cumulative and an episodic construction of the past.

Notes

This chapter was prepared while the author was a Fellow at the Center for Advanced Studies in the Behavioral Sciences, Stanford, California. The author is grateful for financial support provided by the Andrew W. Mellon Foundation.

1. Another contemporary, George Templeton Strong, filled his diary for years with disparaging comments about Lincoln. In the end, the most he could concede was that 'his weaknesses are on the surface, and his name will be of high account fifty years hence . . .' (Cunliffe, 1988: 16).

2. Many Easter Sunday eulogies were reprinted or paraphrased in the local newspapers (see, for example, *New York Times*, 17 April 1865). For a collection of

Easter eulogies delivered in Boston, see Anon., 1865. See also Atwood, 1865; Boardman, 1865; and Hepworth, 1865. These and other Easter eulogies are reviewed in Stewart, 1963.

3. See Barr, 1865; Cutter, 1865; Garrison, 1865; McClintock, 1865; and Morehouse, 1865. See also Stewart, 1963.

4. See Allen, 1865; Bigham, 1865; Briggs, 1865; Egar, 1865; Gurley, 1865; Harbaugh, 1865; Howlett, 1865; Johnston, 1865; Jordan, 1865; and Krauth, 1865. See also Stewart, 1963.

5. Bancroft's opinion of Lincoln was less certain in the 'eulogy' he delivered on 25 April 1865, as Lincoln's remains were carried from New York City. 'Too few days have passed away since Abraham Lincoln stood in the flush of vigorous manhood to permit any attempt at an analysis of his character or an exposition of his career' (*New York Times*, 26 April 1865: 4).

6. On this point Arthur Vandenberg presented credible statistical evidence. In 1921 he pooled a hundred leading Americans in politics, education, religion and the professions to discover 'The Greatest American'. Forty-nine voters, almost half, named Lincoln; thirty-two named Washington (Adair, 1974: 238).

7. For a discussion of collective memory in the light of late adolescent–early adult political attachments, see Schuman and Scott, 1988.

8. A rich discussion of how Washington and Lincoln have satisfied America's double need for the aristocrat and the commoner is presented by Cunliffe, 1988.

9. The notion of *la vie légère* was introduced by W.S.F. Pickering as a way of amplifying Emile Durkheim's notion of *la vie sérieuse*. The alignment of this dichotomy with folk heroes and epic heroes is altogether consistent with Pickering's analysis (1984: 352–61).

10. For an explicit comparison between Abraham Lincoln and Kit Carson (showing Lincoln the better man), see S.W. Meader's *Longshanks* (cited in Basler, 1935: 141).

11. Alternative conceptions of collective memory within the 'presentist' perspective are described in Schwartz et al., 1986.

12. In contrast, those who believe in the inherent sanctity of national origins assume their memory to be substantially immune to social change. See, for example, Schwartz, 1982; Shils, 1981.

13. Other limits on the past's reconstructability are described in Schudson, 1989.

References

Adair, Douglass (1974) 'Fame and Founding Fathers', in Trevor Colbourn (ed.), *Fame and the Founding Fathers: Essays by Douglass Adair*. New York: W.W. Norton. pp. 109–22.

Allen, Ethan (1865) *A Discourse Prepared for the National Fast Day*. Baltimore: W.K. Doyle.

Anon. (ed.) (1865) *Sermons Preached in Boston on the Death of Abraham Lincoln, With the Funeral Services . . . at Washington*. Boston: J.E. Tilton.

Atwood, Edward S. (1865) *The Nation's Loss: a Discourse*. Salem, MA: Salem Gazette.

Bancroft, George (1866) *Memorial Address on the Life and Character of Abraham Lincoln*. United States Congress, 12 Feb. 1866. Washington DC: Government Printing Office.

Barr, Thomas Hughes (1865) *A Discourse Delivered . . . on the Occasion of the Funeral . . . of our late President, Abraham Lincoln*. Wooster, Ohio: Republican Team Power Press.

Basler, Roy P. (1935) *The Lincoln Legend*. New York: Octagon Books.

Bigham, J.C. (1865) *The Spoiler Spoiled: a Sermon*. Mercer: Office of the Whig and Dispatch.

Boardman, George (1865) *The Death of President Lincoln*. Binghamton, NY: F.N. Chase.

Briggs, George W. (1865) *Eulogy on Abraham Lincoln*. Salem, MA.

Commager, Henry Steele (1950) *The American Mind*. New Haven: Yale University Press.

Connelly, Thomas L. (1977) *The Marble Man: Robert E. Lee and His Image in American Society*. New York: Knopf.

Cooley, Charles Horton (1918) 'Fame,' in *Social Process*. New York: Charles Scribner's Sons. pp. 112–24.

Cunliffe, Marcus (1988)*The Doubled Images of Lincoln and Washington*. Gettysburg, PA: Robert Fortenbaugh Memorial Lecture, Gettysburg College.

Current, Richard N. (1983) 'Bancroft's Lincoln', in *Speaking of Abraham Lincoln: The Man and his Meaning for our Times*. Urbana: University of Illinois Press. pp. 172–86.

Cutter, Edward F. (1865) *Eulogy on Abraham Lincoln*. Boston: D.C. Colesworthy.

de Tocqueville, Alexis (1946) *Democracy in America*. New York: Knopf.

Douglass, Frederick (1962) 'Oration . . . Delivered on the Occasion of the Unveiling of the Freedmen's Monument', in *Life and Times of Frederick Douglass*. New York: Collier. pp. 481–93.

Durkheim, Emile (1912/1965) *The Elementary Forms of the Religious Life*. New York: The Free Press.

Egar, John H. (1865) *The Martyr-President*. Leavenworth, KS: Bulletin Job Printing Establishment.

Ellis, Richard and Wildavsky, Aaron (1989) *Dilemmas of Presidential Leadership: From Washington through Lincoln*. New Brunswick, NJ: Transaction.

Fehrenbacher, Don (1987) *Lincoln in Text and Context*. Stanford, CA: Stanford University Press.

Garrison, Joseph F. (1865) *The Teachings of the Crisis: Address . . . on the Occasion of the Funeral of Abraham Lincoln*. Camden, NJ: S. Chew.

Gurley, P.D. (1865) *The Voice of the Rod: a Sermon*. Washington, DC: William Ballantyne.

Halbwachs, Maurice (1941) *La Topographie légendaire des évangiles*. Paris: Presses Universitaires de France.

Halbwachs, Maurice (1951/80) *The Collective Memory*. New York: Harper & Row.

Harbaugh, H. (1865) *Treason and Law: a Discourse*. Philadelphia: Jas. B. Rogers.

Hepworth, George H. (1865) Sermon, in *Sermons Preached in Boston*. Boston: J.E. Tilton.

Hofstadter, Richard (ed.) (1963) *The Progressive Movement*. Englewood Cliffs, NJ: Prentice-Hall.

Howe, Daniel Walker (1979) *The Political Culture of the American Whigs*. Chicago: University of Chicago Press.

Howlett, T.R. (1865) *Dealings of God with Our Nation: a Discourse . . . on the Day of Humiliation and Prayer*. Washington, DC: Gibson Brothers.

Johnston, Elias S. (1865) *Sermon Delivered on . . . the Day of Humiliation and Prayer*. Harrisburg, PA: Theo. F. Scheffer.

Jordan, E.S. (1865) *A Discourse Delivered on the Day of the National Fast*. Portland, ME: David Tucker.

Karsten, Peter (1978) *Patriot Heroes in England and America*. Madison: University of Wisconsin Press.

Krauth, Charles P. (1865) *Two Pageants: a Discourse*. Pittsburgh: W.S. Haven.

Lang, Gladys and Lang, Kurt (1988) 'Recognition and renown: the survival of artistic reputation', *American Journal of Sociology*, 94: 79–109.

Lowenthal, David (1985) *The Past is a Foreign Country.* Cambridge: Cambridge University Press.

McClintock, John (1865) *Discourse Delivered on the Day of the Funeral of President Lincoln.* New York: J.M. Bradstreet.

Maines, David R., Sugrue, Noreen M. and Katovich, Michael A. (1983) 'The sociological import of G.H. Mead's theory of the past', *American Sociological Review*, 48: 161–73.

Mann, Arthur (1962) 'The Progressive tradition', in John Higham (ed.), *The Reconstruction of American History.* New York: Harper & Row. pp. 157–79.

Mead, George Herbert (1929) 'The nature of the past', in John Coss (ed.), *Essays in Honor of John Dewey.* New York: Henry Holt. pp. 235–42.

Mead, George Herbert (1932) *The Philosophy of the Present.* LaSalle, IL: Open Court Publishing.

Meyers, Marvin (1960) *The Jacksonian Persuasion.* New York: Vintage.

Morehouse, Henry L. (1865) *Evil Its Own Destroyer: A Discourse . . . on the Occasion of the Death of President Abraham Lincoln.* East Saginaw, MI: Enterprise Print.

Nagel, Paul C. (1971) *This Sacred Trust.* New York: Oxford University Press.

Noble, David W. (1970) *The Progressive Mind.* Chicago: Rand McNally.

Oates, Stephen B. (1977) *With Malice toward None.* New York: Harper & Row.

O'Neill, Edward H. (1935) *A History of American Biography, 1800–1935.* New York: A.S. Barnes.

Peterson, Merrill D. (1960) *The Jefferson Image in the American Mind.* New York: Oxford University Press.

Pickering, W.S.F. (1984) *Durkheim's Sociology of Religion: Themes and Theories.* London: Routledge & Kegan Paul.

Roosevelt, Theodore (1961) *The New Nationalism.* Introduction by William E. Leuchtenburg. Englewood Cliffs, NJ: Prentice-Hall.

Schudson, Michael (1989) 'The present in the past versus the past in the present', *Communication*, 11: 105–13.

Schuman, Howard and Scott, Jacqueline (1988) 'Collective memories of events and changes', unpublished manuscript presented at the 1988 Meeting of the American Sociological Association.

Schwartz, Barry (1982) 'The social context of commemoration: a study in collective memory', *Social Forces*, 61: 374–402.

Schwartz, Barry, Zerubavel, Yael and Barnett, Bernice (1986) 'The recovery of Masada', *Sociological Quarterly*, 27: 147–64.

Shils, Edward A. (1981) *Tradition.* Chicago: University of Chicago Press.

Stewart, Charles J. (1963) 'A rhetorical study of the reaction of the Protestant pulpit in the North to Lincoln's assassination', unpublished PhD dissertation, University of Illinois, Urbana.

Stone, Andrew L. (1865) Sermon, in *Sermons Preached in Boston.* Boston: J.E. Tilton and Company.

Tuchman, Gaye and Fortin, Nina E. (1984) 'Fame and misfortune', *American Journal of Sociology*, 90: 72–96.

Tucker, Robert C. (1973) *Stalin as Revolutionary. 1879–1929: a Study in History and Personality.* New York: W.W. Norton.

Weems, Mason Locke (1800) *A History of the Life and Death, Virtues and Exploits, of General George Washington.* Georgetown, DC: Green and English.

Williams, Raymond (1977) *Marxism and Literature.* London: Oxford University Press.

Wilson, Richard G., Pilgrim, Dianne H. and Murray, Richard N. (1979) *The American Renaissance. 1876–1917.* New York: Pantheon.

6
Ronald Reagan Misremembered

Michael Schudson

In the fall of 1986, after the first disclosures of the Iran–Contra scandal, Ronald Reagan's ratings in public opinion polls plummeted. The drop in the *New York Times*/CBS News Poll was from 67 per cent approval of how the President handled his job, at the end of October, to 46 per cent a month later. It was the sharpest and most sudden loss of public support in the history of Presidential polling according to the *New York Times* (7 December, 1986). A *New York Times* editorial noted, 'Until this crisis, Mr Reagan's popularity, like Teflon, deflected wrath and ridicule alike' (7 December, 1986). The editors took for granted that Reagan's 'popularity' had been impregnable from the beginning of his term of office until the Iran–Contra revelations. Two years later, when Reagan left office, the news was full of commentary about how President Reagan left office just as popular as when he came in. Again the assumption was that President Reagan had been unusually popular at the inception of his presidency and generally retained this high level of popularity through his tenure.

In 1986 and 1989, then, the media recalled Ronald Reagan as having been unusually popular from the moment he took office. 'For six years,' another *New York Times* editorial said in the wake of Iran–Contra, 'President Reagan floated in a lofty cloud of public trust' (18 July, 1987). There is no recollection in any of this retrospective media commentary that during his first two years in office Ronald Reagan had the worst standing in public opinon polls of any newly elected president since the Second World War. There is no recognition that early analyses of Reagan's standing in the polls indicated that this representative of the far Right in American political life divided the public more than any other post-war president. In 1983 political scientist Fred Greenstein observed that members of Congress had been persuaded by the White House to regard the 1980 election as a mandate for Reagan's policies and were persuaded further by 'near uniformity in mass media accounts and by partially engineered constituency pressure' that Reagan in 1981 was riding high in popular sentiment – although Greenstein's own analysis of polling data clearly indicated otherwise (Greenstein, 1983: 174). In 1985 George C. Edwards argued in *Public Opinion* that Ronald Reagan was 'the least well-liked' president in three decades, a man who had polarized the polity 'along partisan, racial, and sexual lines'. In an academic study published in 1986, political scientist Martin Wattenberg found Reagan 'the least popular candidate to win election to the presidency since . . . 1952' and found him, far from overwhelmingly popular, an 'extremely polarizing' chief executive. According to Wattenberg, Reagan commanded strong loyalty among a small number of citizens but aroused more intense hostility than any other president since the National Election Studies project, whose polling data he analysed, began (Wattenberg, 1986).

While the news media often reported fairly and accurately that Reagan's poll ratings were low in 1981 and 1982 compared to other presidents in the beginning of their term, there was also an assumption between the lines – sometimes explicitly – that this could not possibly be the case. As early as the summer of 1981, the news media reported on declines in Reagan's standing in the polls as if his standing had been high, or even unusually high, to begin with. In fact, two months into his first term, Reagan's standing in the Gallup poll was lower than that for any president at the same point in his term in post-war America (*The Gallup Poll 1981*). (Harris, Roper and other polling organizations came up with comparable figures. I cite primarily Gallup data because Gallup is the oldest of the polling agencies and provides the best historical data comparing the current president's poll ratings to the ratings of past presidents.)

In contemporary American politics, where polls are regularly treated with extraordinary deference, it is peculiar to find something as centrally important as a president's 'popularity' discussed widely with so little reference to or analysis of poll data. To find this odd is not to imagine the polls to be an infallible guide to 'public opinion'. Critics of polling have made strong arguments that there are problems in even the best of the polls and that their very procedures enact a particular – and highly contestable – concept of what 'public opinion' is (Ginsberg, 1986). I do not even assume polls to be the best guide to 'public opinion', *faute de mieux*. The question is why should polling data not have influenced the social construction of 'popularity' for Ronald Reagan when the norm in American political discourse is that it should? Why was Ronald Reagan's standing with the public perceived and remembered with so little attention to the polls?

The question is puzzling because journalists, politicians and other Washington insiders usually consult a president's standing in the polls as a measure of his likely political effectiveness in office. The view is widely shared among American political élites as well as among students of the presidency that 'popularity' or 'public approval', normally judged by standing in public opinion polls, is an essential political resource for a president in dealing with Congress (Kernell, 1986). While there are other ways to try to ascertain what American citizens think about their president, the data available from standard public opinion polling organizations are particularly convenient to use and have properties that should make them particularly likely to be trusted. First, the data is quantitative; it is reported in simple, easily apprehended figures. The polls are conducted in standard fashion both in the strategies of questioning and sampling procedures, unlike informal opinion sampling (talking to a cab driver, listening to a spouse and children over dinner, reading what news columnists or editorials have to say, gauging opinion from the sample of mail that comes into a Congressional office). Poll data can therefore be taken as *relatively reliable* and *relatively unambiguous*. Secondly, poll data is *recent*, not lost in the fogs of time. Major polling organizations gather information from national samples regarding presidential performance as often as once a month. Thirdly, the information is *public*. It is made widely available through the news media. A strong interest among active political élites in political polling keeps it prominently placed.

Fourthly, polling data about the President is closely *monitored* as part of a continuing public conversation, that is, poll results are not a one-time-only news item, here today and gone tomorrow. Because of continuous attention to the polls, their reporting has taken on a more self-consciously historical flavour than most items in the daily news. Frequently the news stories that report a president's standing in the polls not only discuss how the present reading compares to the polls taken in prior months but also compare it to the poll standing of past presidents at comparable moments in their tenure. Polling services make such information available to the media. Reporters are not required to be inventive or aggressive or enterprising to get it.

Fifthly, the conveyors of poll data – the news media – have no obvious reason intentionally to distort the findings and plenty of reason to report them with accuracy. Journalists' own personal integrity, their professional standards and the very publicness of the poll data that could be used to impeach the media if they reported polls in distorted fashion, all operate to ensure accurate accounts of a president's popular standing as reported in polling data.

Sixthly, and finally, the polls of national standing, especially the polls of the Gallup Organization, have achieved a remarkable legitimacy in American political discourse. The widespread assumption, notwithstanding some scepticism about polling, is that they *should* be consulted. The widespread assumption, to be found throughout the media, is that poll results and 'public opinion' can be regarded as identical, except when otherwise indicated.

In summary, polling data on presidential popularity is relatively reliable, recent, public, legitimate and monitored as part of a continuing political conversation. On that basis, we should expect polls greatly to influence judgements about popularity. Nevertheless, the social construction and collective memory of the popularity of Ronald Reagan by professionals and lay people alike defies the poll data that such constructions are expected to heed. I would like to demonstrate that this has been the case and then try to explain why.[1]

Constructing Ronald Reagan's Popularity

Compared to his elected predecessors, Reagan had the lowest average job-approval rating in the polls for the first two years of his administration. After a month in office, his 'job-approval' rating in the Gallup poll of 55 per cent compared to Carter's 71, Nixon's 61, and Eisenhower's 68. At the end of a year his rating of 47 per cent compared to Carter's 52, Nixon's 46, Kennedy's 77 and Eisenhower's 68. At the end of two years, his 35 per cent rating trailed Carter's at 43, Nixon's 56, Kennedy's 76 and Eisenhower's 69.[2]

Of course, the first two years of the Reagan administration were marked by a serious economic recession. So while Reagan's policies may have been unpopular, the Press regularly reported that his personal popularity remained high. As *Newsweek* put it, the President's tactical problem was one of 'transferring his glow from his person to his policies' (4 May 1981).

This has at least the appearance of truth. Judging from poll data, Reagan was personally more popular than his specific programmes. Twice in 1982 Gallup asked not only the general question, 'Do you approve or disapprove of the way Ronald Reagan is handling his job as president?' but more specific questions about how people regarded him personally ('Apart from whether you approve or disapprove of the way Reagan is handling his job as president, what do you think of Reagan as a person? Would you say you approve or disapprove of him?'); and Reagan's 'personal' ratings came out 25 or 30 points higher than his job-approval ratings. Oddly enough, while news reports tended to provide historical comparisons of job-approval ratings, no report I have encountered did so for personal approval. This is so despite the fact that the Gallup Poll provided such comparisons to its news-media clients. Gallup demonstrated that the disparity in the polls between personal approval and job approval was typical of all presidents and not, as the news media regularly reported, a feature of the unique personal charm of this president (*The Gallup Poll 1982*: 107, 243).

On 18 March, 1981, when President Reagan came up with the lowest Gallup poll rating of any newly elected President ever, not quite two months into his first term, James Reston reported in the *New York Times* that Democratic leaders in Congress 'concede that the President has public opinion on his side'. Even at that early point, then, a strong construction of Reagan's 'popularity' apparently oblivious to contradictory poll data (although that data appeared on page one of the *Los Angeles Times* and page three of the *Washington Post* – page twenty-two of the *New York Times*) had taken hold, at least in Washington. By May, *Newsweek* reported – inaccurately – that Reagan's popularity ratings in some surveys 'are the highest in polling history' (11 May 1981). On 9 August, Hedrick Smith wrote in the *New York Times Magazine* that Reagan 'has enjoyed warm popularity and a successful honeymoon'. When he published those words, the latest polls showed Reagan's standing at 60 per cent approval, 28 per cent disapproval and 12 per cent undecided or with no opinion about how Reagan was conducting himself in office. Jimmy Carter, at the same point in his first term, had a 63 per cent approval rating (and only 18 per cent disapproval), Richard Nixon 63 per cent (and 16 per cent disapproval), John Kennedy 71 per cent (and 14 per cent disapproval) and Dwight Eisenhower 71 per cent (and 15 per cent disapproval). In comparative terms, if the polls are any measure, Reagan did not have a honeymoon at all. If it is not polls to which Smith refers for his knowledge of the President's 'popularity', where does his concept of 'popularity' come from?

By the fall of 1981, Adam Clymer reported in the *New York Times* that 'President Reagan's once solid grip on public support appears to be loosening somewhat . . .' (29 September 1981). The phrase about the 'once solid grip' is a good example of the casual way in which even a distinguished reporter in a distinguished newspaper took for granted Ronald Reagan's enormous popular appeal when that appeal was belied by what could be claimed to be the most reliable, legitimate and accessible evidence. It was the very rare story that noted, as David Broder did in the *Washington Post* in April 1982, that Ronald Reagan 'is the least popular president at this point in his term of any White House occupant since Harry Truman' (4 April 1982, p. 1). (Broder could say 'least popular president' with some assurance because that is what the poll data uniformly showed and that is the standard documentation in American political discourse for claims about 'popularity'.) Why, then, was most of the Press – and the Congress – so quickly convinced of Reagan's high level of popular support without reference to actual poll results?

Oral Culture in Washington

My general view is a simple one: the Washington élite of Congress, the media and others trusted their own gut political judgements much more fully than they trusted the polls, even though it has become customary to defer to the polls. But normally, personal impressions and poll data coincide. Where the abstract, quantitative data the polls provide contradicted a strong, first-hand impression of insiders, the polls were either misreported (as in the *Newsweek* quotation cited above), explained away (as in the effort to tout the importance of a 'personality' rather than a 'job-approval' poll rating) or disregarded.

At the centre of the contemporary American mass-mediated understanding of politics lies the insistently oral culture of Washington. 'Washington', a reporter wrote on the eve of the Second World War, 'is the largest village in the world, and it has but one topic of serious conversation' (Clark, 1941: 11). Washington is a face-to-face society where personal relations orally transmitted are enormously important. The Washington press corps and Washington élites in general liked Ronald Reagan personally, even where they did not agree with his politics. 'Ronald Reagan, whether you like him or not, always comes across as a nice man,' his campaign press secretary said in 1980. 'Carter does not come across as a nice man. And I think that has to have a subconscious effect over reporters' (Robinson and Sheehan, 1983: 137). Carter's close adviser and press secretary, Jody Powell, said of Reagan, 'Most reporters I talk to say they generally like the guy' (*Time*, 11 July 1983). Early in his presidency, Reagan's personal likeability was well established. That the White House press corps liked Reagan personally was reported as early as 2 March, 1981 (*U.S. News and World Report*).

What was true of the press corps was true also of the Congress – so the most likely sources for reporters to hear negative comments about the President, that is, Congressional Democrats, were also disarmed by Reagan's personal affability and stylish good manners. Democratic Speaker of the House Tip O'Neill stated, for instance, 'Generally, I like the fella. He tells a good story' (*Time*, 22 February 1982).

The orality of the Washington press corps is captured very well in

Stephen Hess's study of Washington reporters. Hess notes that Washington reporters rely on the interview as their primary research tool. Reporters in Washington use no documents at all in preparing some three-quarters of the stories they write – apart from routine press releases. Some Washington beats do require more regular use of documents – generally speaking, these are regarded by journalists as less desirable assignments (Hess, 1981: 52). When reporters do use documents, the document to which they refer most often is – the newspaper. Hess observes, 'Given that most copy is produced under deadline conditions and other hardships, research that rests heavily on other newspaper stories bears a high potential for perpetuating error' (1981: 18).

This might also be said of the journalists' absorption in a relatively enclosed social world. Almost half of Washington journalists Hess interviewed report that their closest friends are other journalists. A fair number of Washington journalists believe that Washington journalism is out of touch with the rest of the country – but those who say their three closest friends are journalists are much less likely to worry about being out of touch than those who report that none of their closest friends are journalists. Since the older the Washington journalist, the more likely he or she is to have other journalists as closest friends, it appears that the more powerful and prestigious journalists in Washington are, the more insulated they may turn out to be, or, at any rate, the less self-consciously wary of their own insulation.

In the face-to-face world of Washington journalism, Ronald Reagan was king. The media, the Congress and Washington officialdom in general liked Reagan personally. Reagan took pains to make this 'likeability' work for him. His congressional liaison arranged sixty-nine meetings for key Congressmen in the Oval Office in Reagan's first 100 days. He brought sixty Democrats to the White House the week before the key budget vote in May 1981. Within hours of the vote, the White House delivered thank-you notes signed by the President to all who supported him (*Newsweek*, 18 May 1981). Reagan lavishly used social invitations and small favours like the distribution of presidential cuff-links and signed photographs to members of Congress (Cannon, 1982: 333). Reagan's personal likeability and his insistent attentiveness to pleasing the Congress were reinforced by several other important factors.

First, Reagan's appealing personality and willingness to take media relations and congressional relations seriously contrasted sharply with the Carter administration. Reagan only profited from the contrast. Favourable impressions were especially strong because unfavourable impressions of Carter were so salient.

Secondly, Reagan's respect for congressional and media relations was demonstrated by his employing an excellent staff for media relations and congressional liaison.

Thirdly, the Reagan administration carefully courted favour with Reagan's right-wing constituency. Reagan developed what Hedrick Smith called 'the most potent network of political activists in the nation' and they were effectively mobilized to pressure wavering Congressmen at the time of key votes (Smith, 1981: 17). These stalwarts flooded congressional offices with telegrams, letters and telephone calls when asked to do so. Congressmen were impressed by this readily available indication of public support for the President, and seemed unable or unwilling to contemplate the possibility that it was not representative.

Fourthly, Washington overestimated the power of television and overestimated the impact that Reagan's warm television style would have on the public. In fact, Reagan's television audiences were smaller than those of his predecessors, and declined over his term of office (Foote, 1988: 228). There is no indication from the polls that his personal charm affected the public's evaluation of his handling of his job.

Fifthly, Reagan's early successes – especially with the budget battle he won in May 1981 – helped establish him in Washington circles as an effective president. If one is an effective president, presumably this is because (according to the Washington belief system) one is popular. In a sense, Reagan's victories in Congress helped construct his 'popularity' as much as a construed 'popularity' helped achieve the victories. There were, of course, other elements in his success with the Congress, not least of which was that in the 1980 elections Republicans captured control of the Senate and, if one counts about thirty avowed conservatives numbered among the Democrats, the House. The political situation had dramatically shifted in the Republicans' favour.

Finally, people in Washington, journalist Elizabeth Drew once wrote, deal in 'power and implications' (Drew, 1976: 4). Because they deal in implications, they are busy reading signs. They are particularly eager to read electoral results as articulate statements issued by something called 'the public'. The 1980 election, in which Ronald Reagan received less than 51 per cent of votes cast, was more ambiguous to read than most. In the United States, without a parliamentary system of accountability, the meaning of a presidential election is often difficult to judge under the best of circumstances. The 1980 election, it seems, was particularly difficult to read – and so commentators may have overexerted themselves in attributing meaning to the relatively inarticulate ballot, seeking consensus and

confirmation as much in the opinions expressed by other commentators as in any actual access to the 'meaning' of what voters did.
Thus, for example, just before the election of 1980, *Newsweek*
described President Carter as 'the least popular president to run for
re-election since Hoover' (27 October 1980, p. 15). But within
weeks, the same magazine, whle reporting that four out of five
Reagan voters supported him because of Carter's poor performance
(according to exit polls), also concluded that the election was a
'rousing vote of confidence in Ronald Reagan and his "politics of
nostalgia"' (17 November 1980, pp. 27–32). This was in part a
response to Reagan-administration efforts to 'sell' the 1980 election
as a mandate for conservative policies. But I suspect it was not
simply a matter of White House manipulation of the media; the
media and Washington insiders produced accounts that attempted
to make contradictory or ambiguous aspects of the election make
sense.

At the centre of all this remained the strong working consensus of
the Washington élite that Reagan was a well-meaning, likeable
fellow, although ill-informed about political affairs and ill-equipped
to act as chief executive. The election, Washington assumed,
proved that the public responded to Reagan's likeability but could
not see, or did not care about, his incompetence. Perhaps reserving
for the public a certain level of contempt, the Washington insiders
assumed citizens would be, and indeed had been, won over by
Reagan's charm.

Conclusions

An astute observer of the world of Washington journalism, former
Carter speechwriter James Fallows, has written that Washington
journalists have a 'clear preference to write about politics, rather
than about the history, the substance, or the day-by-day truths of
government's operation'. What is missing, he says, is 'a sense of
history'. 'By history . . . I mean a prudent awareness that others
have walked many of the same paths before and that, by learning
from their errors, we may be spared errors of our own' (Fallows,
1984: 265, 277).

It is routine to criticize the news media for having no sense of
history. Still there were often implicit and frequently explicit comparisons of Reagan's popular support to the popular support for
earlier presidents. Reporting of the polls in historical context was
made possible, no doubt, by the fact that the polling institutions
themselves frequently provided the news media with appropriate
historical comparative data. It was made possible also by a long-

standing tradition of reporting the President and the presidency in historical perspective (Schudson, 1982). In many of the stories on the polls, there is a powerful sense that the current President is one in a series of presidents. Sometimes comparisons are made simply to the preceding president – Carter. But often there are comparisons to Johnson, to Eisenhower, to Roosevelt. (Roosevelt seems to be the beginning of history for presidential reporting – and in many respects, in terms of the point at which the presidency came to be the massive and central agency of the government that it is today, this is a reasonable choice.)[3]

What is missing, I think, was not a sense of history but a sense of the contingency of human cognition. What is absent is an effort to compare disparate data and reports without leaping to some resolution of them. What is wanting is the recognition that even a highly skilled and professional press corps could be making a set of systematic errors. What is certainly missing is the acknowledgement that 'popularity' is a social construction, not an existent 'fact' to be noted in the public ledger.

There is nothing scandalous about this – that is, it suggests nothing of corruption. But it suggests a lot about insularity and the continuing power of face-to-face discussion in an age of electronic media, the continuing salience of the personal, qualitative and anecdotal in an age presumably governed by the statistical and abstract. This should be more than a little deflating to those who believe too fervently in the rationality of actors on the modern political stage. We still live in a world of myth and illusion. We still live in a world in which cultural constructions are treated as rock-solid foundations of existence, belief and action. In politics, no such construct is more central than 'public opinion' and 'the public'. 'What the people want' or 'what the people believe' are phrases that trip off the tongues of politicians and journalists alike. Frequently, political experts refer to public opinion polls to back up their version of 'what the people believe'. More frequently, however, they rely on the same kinds of informal, unsubstantiated, everyday heuristics that lay people do. What their closest acquaintances say, what seems to get taken as the background assumptions in their everyday conversations and everyday reading and viewing, are taken more to heart than the data provided by polling organizations.

In the case of polls regarding Ronald Reagan's popularity, this had severe consequences. It helped propel a president's programme into enactment, over the weak protests of a Democratic Congress cowed by a belief in the President's popularity (and frightened, as well, by an equally pervasive construction of America's 'turn to the right') (Entman and Paletz, 1980). Ronald Reagan's popularity, born in the face-to-face world of Washington society, helped to define an era in American politics. 'Reality', generated in Washington's oral culture, broadcast through the media to the public at large, was a grandiose construction that, according to the norms of legitimate political communication in American culture, must be termed a myth. In retrospect, it reminds us that terms like 'popularity' and 'the public', words that wield enormous authority in politics, are notions socially construed, constructed and recalled. There is, we might say, a rhetorical structure to social institutions, a patterned way in which language comes to be used; once used, referred to; and when referred to, remembered and drawn upon as part of what 'everyone knows'. In Washington, this rhetorical structure is rooted in the face-to-face community of political élites and political journalists whose collective memory (a significant influence on the social memory of the wider public) is strongly shaped by personal encounters and oral communication.

Notes

1. This chapter is based on research conducted jointly with Elliot King. Earlier statements of the research are King and Schudson, 1987; 1988; Schudson and King, 1988.

2. This is Gallup data available from the annual Gallup Poll volumes the organization publishes. Much of this material is compiled in the poll report of 3 Feb. 1983 available in *The Gallup Poll 1983*. It is also conveniently available in 'Reagan and his predecessors', *Public Opinion*, 10 (September/October, 1987): 40.

3. For a discussion of how the American news media present a sense of the past in daily news reporting, see Schudson, 1986.

References

Cannon, Lou (1982) *Reagan*. New York: G.P. Putnam's.

Clark, Delbert (1941) *Washington Dateline*. New York: Frederick A. Stokes.

Drew, Elizabeth (1976) *Washington Journal*. New York: Vintage Books.

Edwards, George C. (1985) 'Comparing chief executives', *Public Opinion*, 9 (June/July): 50–1, 54.

Entman, Robert M. and Paletz, David L. (1980) 'Media and the conservative myth', *Journal of Communication*, 30: 154–65.

Fallows, James (1984) 'The presidency and the press', in Michael Nelson (ed.), *The Presidency and the Political System*. Washington: Congressional Quarterly.

Foote, Joe S. (1988) 'Ratings decline of presidential television', *Journal of Broadcasting and Electronic Media*, 32: 225–30.

The Gallup Poll 1981 (1982) Wilmington, DE: Scholarly Resources.

The Gallup Poll 1982 (1983) Wilmington, DE: Scholarly Resources.

The Gallup Poll 1983 (1984) Wilmington, DE: Scholarly Resources.

Ginsberg, Benjamin (1986) *The Captive Public*. New York: Basic Books.

Greenstein, Fred I. (1983) *The Reagan Presidency: an Early Assessment*. Baltimore: Johns Hopkins University Press.

Hess, Stephen (1981) *The Washington Reporters*. Washington: Brookings Institution.
Kernell, Sam (1986) *Going Public*. Washington: Congressional Quarterly Press.
King, Elliot and Schudson, Michael (1987) 'The myth of the great communicator'. *Columbia Journalism Review*, 25 (November/December): 37–9.
King, Elliot and Schudson, Michael (1988) 'Reagan's mythical popularity', *Psychology Today*, 22 (September): 32–3.
Robinson, Michael and Sheehan, Margaret (1983) *Over the Wire and on TV*. New York: Russell Sage Foundation.
Schudson, Michael (1982) 'The politics of narrative form: the emergence of news conventions in print and television', *Daedalus*, 111 (Fall): 97–112.
Schudson, Michael (1986) 'What time means in a news story', in Robert Manoff and Michael Schudson (eds), *Reading the News*. New York: Pantheon.
Schudson, Michael and King, Elliot (1988) 'By charming the Washington crowd, Reagan put a lock on his "Popularity"', *Los Angeles Times*, 14 September.
Smith, Hedrick (1981) 'Taking charge of Congress', *New York Times Magazine*, 9 August.
Wattenberg, Martin P. (1986) 'The Reagan polarization phenomenon and the continuing downward slide in presidential candidate popularity', *American Politics Quarterly*, 14 (July): 214–45.

7

The Social Construction of Remembering and Forgetting

John Shotter

In this chapter I want to discuss a non-cognitive, social-constructionist approach to forgetting and remembering (Bartlett, 1923; 1932; Gergen, 1982; 1985; Shotter, 1984). It is an approach in which not so much language as such, but our ways of speaking, and in particular their *rhetorical* (and contested) nature (Billig, 1987; De Man, 1979), are our initial (but not necessarily our final) concern. Bartlett's early work (Bartlett, 1923) will occupy a prominent place in the account below. Although Neisser (1967) saw Bartlett's later work (Bartlett, 1932) as inaugurating the current 'cognitive' revolution in psychology – concerned as it is with systematic processes – Bartlett's earlier work is clearly both social constructionist, *and* concerned with practices for dealing with non-systematic, conflicting processes. He said:

> We shall see that the attempt to find the beginning of social customs and institutions in purely individual experience may be essentially a mistaken one. In general terms our problem is to account for a response made by an individual to a given set of circumstances *of which the group itself may always be one*. (Bartlett, 1923: 11, his emphasis)

Bartlett thought of such responses as being initially manifested as *tendencies* to act in certain ways under certain conditions, which are influenced in a *formative* manner in the course of their expression by individuals having to fit them into the circumstances of the group. One such major human tendency is that towards construction itself, and, 'as result, largely, of the operation of the tendencies toward construction and conservation, characteristic institutions arise within in a group and are perpetuated' (Bartlett, 1923: 45). But:

> None of the tendencies which have been considered operates entirely by itself in determining the behaviour of man in society. We must therefore discuss what happens when, in reference to the same situation, more than one tendency is called into activity, and must deal in particular with the conflict of tendencies, and their mutual reinforcement. (1923: 105)

It is towards the recovery, the 'remembering' of this early 1923 stance of Bartlett's – towards the social and institutional determinants not just of remembering, but also of forgetting – that this chapter is directed. For, as we shall see, current *cognitive* accounts of memory, which 'forget' or repress the social processes involved in forgetting, fail, because of that, also properly to account for remembering: the tendencies determining people's behaviour are all conflicting tendencies, in which one is usually dominated and repressed by its polar opposite. In this, ironically, Bartlett proved himself right. As Mary Douglas (1980: 25) puts it, 'The author of the best book on remembering forgot his own first convictions. He became absorbed into the institutional framework of Cambridge University psychology, and restricted by the conditions of the experimental laboratory.' And in such circumstances, he came to treat remembering as that tradition demanded: as wholly an inner process. Both he and others forgot his original emphasis upon social institutions. For instance, although some of Bartlett's work is reviewed in Gleitman (1981: 294–5), not one hint of the social context of remembering is mentioned; and neither in Neisser (1967) is it given any direct attention although he also claims to be following essentially a Bartlettian approach.

The Centrality of our 'Accounting Practices'

In the non-cognitive approach adopted here, our ways of speaking become central, because it is assumed that the primary function of our speech is to 'give shape' to and to co-ordinate diverse social action. We speak in order to create, maintain, reproduce and transform certain modes of social and societal relationships. Such an approach takes it that it is *not* the primary function of all our talk to represent the world; words do not primarily stand for things. If, in our experience, it seems undeniable that at least some words do in fact denote things, they do so only from within a form of social life *already constituted* by ways of talking in which these words are used. Thus, the entities they denote are known, not for what they are in themselves, but in terms of their 'currency' or significance in our different modes of social life – that is, in terms of what it is deemed sensible for us to do with them in the everyday, linguistically structured circumstances of their use.

This approach implies that we cannot take our 'lived' experience as in any way basic. Indeed, from this point of view it becomes a problem as to why, at this moment in history, we account for our experience of ourselves as we do – as if we all existed from birth as separate, isolated individuals, containing wholly within ourselves 'minds' or 'mentalities', set over against a material world itself devoid of any mental processes. This goes for our remembering also: for, although in our experiences of remembering – or at least, in what we talk of as our experiences of remembering – it seems as if we always make reference to something within us such as a picture or impression, like an *object* of some kind. We forget the indefinitely many everyday occasions in which no such experience of referring to an 'inner' image in order to remember occurs. For example, in remembering how to spell and to type the words of this paper, for the most part, no such consultation of memory images occurred. Or did it? . . . One perhaps wants to say: 'I *must* have made such a reference, perhaps unconsciously. How else could the remembering have been done if not by the consultation of a copy, image, trace, or representation of some kind of what one remembers?' What alternative is there?

In Bartlett's (1932) account of remembering, he suggests that, initially, remembering is very largely a matter of feeling or affect; something like a vague, unformulated attitude first emerges: 'Very little of his [a subject's] construction is literally observed and often, as was easily demonstrated experimentally, a lot of it is distorted or wrong so far as the actual facts are concerned. But it is the sort of construction which serves to *justify* his general impression' (1932: 206, my emphasis). Indeed, as will be explored later in more detail, even if it were conceded that reference to some 'inner' already well formed object *must* have occurred, there still remains the problem of how such a reference could exert in any way a formative or informative influence upon our behaviour. Clearly, in remembering, we have the power to 'get in touch with', so to speak, something sensuous, with certain original, unformulated 'feelings of tendency' as William James (1890) called them (what Lakoff and Johnson (1980; Johnson, 1987; Lakoff, 1986) are currently exploring in terms of 'image-schematisms'), and these are what inform our actions and our judgements, not any well formed picture-like 'images'. These are the feelings in terms of which we judge the adequacy of our more explicit formulations and expressions, and, on finding them inadequate, call for their reformulation. And yet we feel driven to forget or ignore this.

Why? What do we remember from our own experience of remembering, and what do we forget, and for what reason? By what warrant do we take certain of our clear experiences as basic – those experiences when it is as if we clearly *do* make reference to an 'inner' picture – and extrapolate from them as models or paradigms to determine the character of those less clear to us? My argument is that it is because our ways of talking about our experiences work, not primarily to represent the nature of those experiences in themselves, but to represent them in such a way as to constitute and sustain one or another kind of social order.[1]

Now although the view of language I am putting forward is very obviously a Wittgensteinian (1953) one, C.W. Mills also put forward a similar view in the following words:

> The major reorientation of recent theory and observation in sociology of language emerged with the overthrow of the Wundtian notion that language has as its function the 'expression' of prior elements within the individual. The postulate underlying modern study of language is the simple one that we must approach linguistic behaviour, not by referring it to private states in individuals, but by observing its social function of co-ordinating diverse actions. Rather than expressing something which is prior and in the person, language is taken by other persons as an indicator of future actions. (1940: 439)

Mills discussed this view of language within the context of people's *accounting practices* – that is, within the context of how people render what is otherwise a puzzling, senseless or indeterminate activity visible as a familiar, sensible, determinate and *justified* commonplace occurrence.

An *account* is not a description, which by the provision of evidence could be proved true or false, but it works as an aid to perception, literally instructing one both in how to see something as a commonplace event, and, in so seeing it, appreciating the opportunities it offers for one's own further action. As Mills put it, in describing the function of 'motive-accounts' in explaining people's conduct: 'Motives are imputed or avowed as answers to questions interrupting acts or programs. Motives are words. Generically, to what do they refer? They do not denote any elements 'in' individuals. They stand for anticipated situational consequences of questioned conduct' (1940: 440). In other words, they serve to keep in good repair and to progress a certain kind of social action, to offer opportunities for one rather than another form of social relationship. And this also is what our talk of memories, of remembering and forgetting, must do. In other words, primarily vague, but not wholly amorphous, tendencies are lin-guistically specified further in this or that particular way, within a medium of communication – according to the particular require-ments of that medium of communication, which is the reproduction of a certain established social order (Shotter, 1984). For example, this can be illustrated in terms of what it is to produce accounts as psychologists. The issue here is not just to do with how we must talk about ourselves as ordinary individuals in everyday life, but also with how as *professional* psychologists we must talk about how, as-ordinary-people, we must talk about ourselves – if, that is, we are to meet the requirements mentioned above. For our talk must be perceived by the other professionals around us as intelligible and legitimate, as authoritative, if they are to find what we say acceptable. It is thus in this way that our talk works to reproduce the professional social order of social scientists.

The Two-sided Rhetorical Nature of Language

The social constructionist privileging of the formative nature of language over its referential aspect (re)emphasizes its primarily rhetorical (and poetic) character – something taken for granted in the past, but gradually forgotten as the scientific revolution took its hold (Ong, 1958; Vico, 1948). There are two aspects to this emphasis, one familiar, the other less so. First, the familiar aspect of rhetoric is to do with the *persuasive* function of language. Billig (1987; and this volume) explores this issue extensively, particularly in relation to people's expression of their attitudes. I want to emphasize here the capacity of speech bodily to 'move' people, its power to affect their behaviour and perceptions in some mysterious (and dangerous), non-cognitive way. It is its capacity to affect people's 'feelings' which we shall find below to be of great importance. Secondly, the other more unfamiliar aspect of rhetoric is to do with the poetic (Gr. *poiesis* – a making, shaping) powers of language to 'give' or to 'lend' a *first form* to what are in fact only vaguely or partially ordered feelings and activities, to give a shared *sense* to already shared circumstances (before one can turn in any Cartesian sense to an intelligible formulation of any doubts about them).

Elsewhere (Shotter, 1986) I have traced discussions of this aspect of rhetoric back to Vico. Current writers on rhetoric, however, often see themselves as influenced by Nietzsche. De Man (1979: 105–6), for instance, in claiming that the figurative (formative) aspect of language is not just one linguistic mode among many, but characterizes all language as such, quotes Nietzsche as follows:

> It is not difficult to demonstrate that what is called 'rhetorical' as the devices of a conscious art, is present as a device of unconscious art in language and its development . . . No such thing as unrhetorical 'natural' language exists that could be used as a point of reference . . . Tropes are not something that can be added or subtracted from a language at will; they are its truest nature. There is no such thing as a proper meaning that can be communicated only in certain particular cases.

Among the many implications of this, as De Man points out, is a whole set of seeming *reversals* (and instabilities) of a surprising kind; a revealing of linguistically created illusions of experience to which we have fallen victim. We have already met one such illusion: The fact that by means of our *immersion* in an intralinguistically constructed reality (which 'has us', so to speak), we come to experience ourselves as possessing our language *within* ourselves (as 'having it'), as if we could exist as who we are, independently of any of our linguistic involvements with others. To this we can add another reversal, one which De Man (1979: 106) notes: linguistically formulated claims gain their authority from being adequate to an already intralinguistically constructed reality, rather than to the nature of an extralinguistic world. But we have already met this reversal too in the claim above that, no matter what else may influence the structure of our ways of talking, they *must* reproduce in their use certain social orders (else they will be considered unintelligible, or illegitimate).

Now my purpose in discussing such 'reversals' is also to make clear their 'instability': the fact that to an extent one *can* say that *both* ways of talking are true. We could say that our ways of talking *depend* upon the world, to the extent that what we say is rooted, or grounded in, what the facts of the world will permit or allow us to say. On the other hand, it is equally true to say that what we take to be the nature of the world *depends* upon our ways of talking about it. In fact, it is not just that one can say that both are true, but that one *must* assert both; for they owe their distinct existences to their *interdependency*. In other words, although one must say about circumstances only what the facts will permit, the nature of the facts above are such that two equal and opposite truths can be asserted. And indeed, this two-sided nature of all such linguistically structured circumstances is general. As Billig (1987: 41) points out (citing Diogenes Laertius), it was Protagoras who was the first person to assert 'that in every question there are two sides to the argument exactly opposite to another'. And also in our interest here, in Bartlett's early 1923 concern with the complexity of the influences determining the formation and development of forms of human expression, we shall find this two-sided nature of the processes involved important.

> A sound psychological treatment must not only recognize and disentangle this multiplicity of influences, but it must at least attempt to find out in what ways they combine, and with what results they conflict. (1923: 107)

Before turning to this task, however, and attempting to discuss both forgetting and remembering as social institutions, we must discuss further the issue mentioned above, which Bartlett raised in his later 1932 work: the justification of memories.

Justifying Memories

Because we have no difficulty in making intelligible use of such ordinary words as 'know', 'think', 'imagine', 'remember' and so on, it is assumed in mainstream cognitive psychology that we all know what such words mean, that we all already know what phenomena these words signify and what states of affairs are described by sentences incorporating them. Hence, our interest must be in the phenomena themselves, in the 'real' nature of thought and memory and so on, the 'inner processes' said to be underlying them. Thus, the right method of investigation is surely the direct experimental study of the real phenomena – the actual 'memory traces', the nature of the actual 'memories' containing them: the 'sensory registers' (the visual icon, the STM and the LTM), the actual 'retrieval processes' and so on. Social constructionists are in total disagreement with such an approach. As they see it, such an interest is both misdirected and mistaken. If C.W. Mills and Wittgenstein are right, there are no such *things* underlying and making remembering possible, and our initial assumption – that we already know what kind of activity remembering is – must be questioned. The fact is, we lack a clear view as to what remembering is – and evidence of that failure is manifested in the puzzles and problems we raise and in the confused manner in which we try to solve them. What Wittgenstein says about thinking is true also about remembering:

> 'Thinking is an enigmatic process, and we are a long way off from complete understanding of it.' And now one starts experimenting. Evidently without realizing *what* it is that makes thinking enigmatic to us . . . (1980: I, no. 1093)

To clarify what is at issue here, let us explore the nature of the question – 'What enables people to 'recall' or 'remember' something from the past? At the moment, instead of probing some of the dubious presuppositions underlying our current answers to this question – (a) that there is some 'thing' or 'trace' of a thing past 'inside' the person to which reference is made, and (b) that there is such a 'how' for every 'doing' (action) a person does – we straightaway embark upon the formulation of theories about the nature of such inner entities, and the search for evidence in their support. We fail to notice the ambiguity of the question; we could be asking either: 'What "in" us enables us to act in such a way?', or 'What socially are the enabling conditions?' The importance of the second way of formulating the question becomes crucial when we realize that, socially, we face a problem when, after having claimed to remember something, someone asks us 'How do you know?'

How do we in fact check that our claim to have remembered something is correct?

One thing is clear: one does not check out whether one is correctly remembering (or imagining) something by referring in one's activity to a copy or an image of what is required. As Wittgenstein (1965: 3) argues, not only is such a process unnecessary, in many instances, it is impossible; he shows this with the example of a person obeying such orders as 'Fetch me a red flower from that meadow.' Wittgenstein says,

> How is he to know what sort of flower to bring, as I have only given him a word? Now the answer one might suggest first is that he went to look for a red flower carrying a red image in his mind, and comparing it with the flowers to see which of them had the colour of the image. Now there is such a way of searching, and it is not at all essential that the image we use be a mental one. In fact the process may be this: I carry a chart coordinating names and coloured squares. When I hear the order 'fetch me etc.' I draw my finger across the chart from the word 'red' to a certain square, and I go and look for a flower which has the same colour as the square. But this is not the only way of searching and it is not the usual way. We go, look about us, walk up to a flower and pick it, without comparing it to anything. To see that the process of obeying an order can be of this kind, consider the order 'imagine a red patch'. You are not tempted in this case to think that before obeying you must have imagined a red patch to serve you as the pattern for the red patch you were ordered to imagine. (1965: 3)

In other words, 'an "inner process" stands in need of outward criteria', as he says elsewhere (Wittgenstein, 1953: no. 580). The correctness of an inner process cannot be tested by comparison with yet another inner process – for how could the correctness of that process be tested? At some point, reference to activities in daily life at large is necessary, for that is where judgements as to what is right and wrong take place. Such judgements as to their own correctness are not made for one by one's biology or neurology; for they operate just as effectively whether one is acting correctly or mistakenly. It is not their job to make correct judgements for one; that is one's own responsibility, and it is a part of the nature of social life that people can take such responsibilities upon themselves. Indeed, as Wittgenstein (1980: II, no. 63) says in his 'Plan for the treatment of psychological concepts': 'Psychological verbs [are] characterized by the fact that the third person of the present [tense] is to be identified by observation, the first person not.' Indeed, the paradigms of observation-knowledge are not applicable to one's knowledge of one's own intentions and actions, nor is it appropriate to think of other people as having this kind of knowledge of their intentions and actions (Gauld and Shotter, 1977: 106). The right to make such unsupported avowals and to have them taken seriously and responded to without being questioned is a part of what it is for human beings to be treated as 'first persons', for them to be accorded their status as competent members of their society. The normal functioning of social life is founded upon such a convention, and could not operate without it.

Remembering and Forgetting as Social Institutions

Let me now turn to a discussion of remembering and forgetting as social institutions. As well as in his early 1923 work, in Part II of his later book *Remembering* (called *Remembering as a Study in Social Psychology*), Bartlett (1932: 296) also makes many such statements as the following: 'Social organization gives a persistent framework into which all detailed recall must fit, and it very powerfully influences both the manner and matter of recall.'

For the early Bartlett – working along with A.C. Haddon, the leader of the famous Cambridge expedition to the Torres Straits – the question was clear. Without the possession of some kind of 'organized setting', as Bartlett (1932) called it, into which to direct one's activities, without a bias or tendency to organize one's experience in one way rather than another, our cognitive lives would be chaotic, quite unmanageable. Memory, like attention and perception, is selective. But what are the principles of selection, and where are they to be located? In 1923, as I have already indicated, Bartlett was quite clear as to the answer. They issue from and are to be located in the social activities of everyday life: remembering is an important part of everyday life and develops so as to meet its demands. This is so because, as Bartlett (1932: 255) later still realized:

> Every social group is organised and held together by some specific psychological tendency or group of tendencies, which give the group a bias in its dealings with external circumstances. The bias constructs the special persistent features of group culture . . . [and this] immediately settle[s] what the individual will observe in his environment and what he will connect from his past life with this direct response. It does this markedly in two ways. First, by providing that setting of interest, excitement, and emotion which favours the development of specific images, and secondly, by providing a persistent framework of institutions and customs which acts as a schematic basis for constructive memory.

Indeed, the persistence of the framework is maintained by those involved in it holding one another responsible for its maintenance.

As I have already indicated above, however, in 1923 what he also noted was that social life is full of conflicting tendencies prone to disrupt it. They have to be dealt with in some way, and one way 'society has of dealing with conflict is', he suggested (Bartlett, 1923: 105) 'that each of the conflicting tendencies is assigned its own characteristic sphere of activity, or its own recognised time of expression' – a strategy, as we shall see, which is not without its difficulties and failures.

As in his 1932 book, Bartlett is also concerned here with the tendencies influencing the formation and the development of folk stories. Such influences differ not only in their source, but in their character and functions also. While some of them work harmoniously together, each reinforcing the others, some are antagonistic. Thus, for example:

> Although fear, alarm, and fright are fairly often depicted in the folk story, they seldom form leading motives, at any rate at a really primitive level. This is because they express tendencies which may conflict with the most important formative influences of the popular tale. Fear, alarm and fright, on the whole tend to destroy comradeship; and are pleasing neither to story-teller nor to his auditors; this leads to their suppression, and, except in an incidental way, to their disappearance from the stories. (1923: 107)

And yet, coping with fear is a central topic in many such stories!

What was true of folk stories was true also of the other aspects of the cultures he studied. To the extent that many things and beings were seen as possessing strange powers, from which may issue both good and ill, the same process of separation and repression could be seen at work; as in the case of 'prophets' and 'witches':

> The prophets are revered, the witches hated. But as in the case of the prophets so in the case of the wizard and sorcerer – the same characteristics occur over and over again. Indeed, in this case the repeated appearance of the same qualities is more striking than ever. For the exploitation of fear produces, alongside the recognized institutions and social groups others that are outside the general life of the community and are consequently looked on with suspicion, so that eventually they may get driven underground. All pathological social developments appear to have a history of this sort. (1923: 116)

Indeed, he points out, if their expression is forcibly opposed, the ultimate result may be not only ill-harmony, but confusion and social disintegration.

The examples given so far have to do with the specialization of the expression of fear, but, as he points out, other two-sided tendencies exhibit the same process – of assigning conflicting tendencies their own spheres and times of expression (with one tendency often privileged over the other).

Take, for example, the instinctive tendency towards conservation and the instinctive tendency of curiosity. These two are clearly in a broad sense opposed. Curiosity prompts exploration of the novel; the basis of conservation rests in blind acceptance of the old. This provides a situation favourable to a delimitation of the field of expression of the two tendencies . . . [But] the history of every primitive group, in fact, reveals certain spheres of activity within which curiosity is not readily to be allowed full sway. (1923: 117–18)

But, as Bartlett points out, attempting to delimit the expression of curiosity in this way is apt, sooner or later, to cause trouble. 'The instinctive curiosity breaks out, not only in its own proper place, but in the realm where conservation holds sway too' (1923: 118) – the return of the repressed!

To read the Bartlett of this period, then, is like reading a Freudian treatise upon the fortunes of conflicting libidinal impulses, where one gains the upper hand at the expense of the other, which later returns to cause trouble. But when one reads such sentences as: 'Maybe the resurgence of old impulses are *deferred* consequences of ways in which antagonistic impulses have been dealt with at a primitive stage, rather than phenomena which have themselves been present at a remote period' (1923: 122, my emphasis), then it is not Freud but Derrida (1977) who Bartlett predates. However, to read the later Bartlett himself on Freud is to read someone who finds what Freud says incredible. There are only two references to Freud in the 1932 book, in one (1932: 15), he accuses Freud of being out of touch with psychological science for suggesting that memory images form a static, lifeless mass instead of being mobile, living and constantly changing. (How, one wonders, would he have viewed current theories of memory in cognitive psychology?) In the other (p. 284), we find someone able, in the course of discussing Jung's notion of the Collective Unconscious, to state the Freudian doctrine of the Unconscious – that it contains 'infantile desires and tendencies which have been repressed because of their incompatibility with the development of the individual character' (p. 284) – but who, instead of relating it to his own earlier accounts of repression, dismisses it with little discussion. And who later, in relation to what he formulates as Jung's claims – that 'stored up somehow in a social structure are ancient images, ideas, formulations and laws which were at one time current interpretations of objective phenomena' (p. 287) – says: 'I have urged already that there is no theoretical or experimental compulsion to accept this view in the general field of remembering' (p. 284).

By 1932, then, Bartlett seems to have forgotten his 1923 claims – that when there are conflicting impulses seeking expression, none 'operates entirely by itself', but they are organized into their own distinct 'spheres of influence' *in relation to one another* – with one sphere, however, usually dominant over the other, with, in particular, anything *fearful* being repressed. But why did he forget? Is there something, perhaps, which is fearful in the theory itself? The answer seems to be 'yes'. As Jacoby (1975) points out in his discussion of Freudian theory: what is repressed are the creative social processes, working non-systematically (or non-mechanically), in terms of apparently contradictory principles (in which both sides cannot possibly be allowed to be true), which are feared and repressed. They are repressed, says Jacoby, by a process of *social amnesia* – the very process of institutionally contrived forgetting or repression of things described by Bartlett in 1923. If events do not fit into the frameworks provided by one's social institutions – into which one has been socialized – then they are not remembered.

Remembering as the Giving of a 'Shared Sense' to Individual 'Feelings'

To turn now to the more 'inner' process of individuals remembering, Bartlett's (1932) view, that the process is a *constructive* one, is well known. What I want to argue below, however, is that the constructive process is not only formally one of a *social* kind, but moreover, that it is also structured as a *rhetorical* (or argumentative) process in all the senses of that term discussed above – especially, in relation to the 'giving', or the 'lending', to an unorganized stream of activity a *first form* of some kind.

If remembering is to be a constructive process of some kind, what is the nature of its 'primitive' origins? Here, I think, Bartlett's views are, seemingly, ambiguous. For at one point he claims that if one's memories are not organized, conventionalized and stabilized by social 'schemas', then the most primitive form of remembering is of the 'rote-recapitulation' type. Indeed, he says, 'all relatively low-level remembering tends, in fact, to be rote remembering, and rote memory is nothing but the repetition of a series of reactions in the order in which they originally occurred' (1932: 203). In such a form of remembering, 'there is no main directing or master tendency at work [in organizing the recall], except the normal "schematic" temporal one' (p. 265). If, however, Bartlett (or his interpreters) take it that this is the actual nature of memory at its most primitive level, then they surely err. There must be a deeper sense in which an organism's past experiences become 'incorporated' into its being, than simply as a linear trace of events. If this were not the case, then there would be no sense in which – as he makes clear in his discussion of making tennis strokes (p. 204) – we could apply what we had learnt in our past experience appropriately to *our* concerns, in our current *circumstances*. In other words, there would be no way in which supposed 'memories' could be accounted *our* memories, and could play a proper part in informing our actions. His account of rote remembering only applies, as a mode of recall, to someone whose psychological capacities have *already been constituted* as those of a self-controlled individual, able because of their participation in a certain set of linguistically mediated developmental practices to indulge in self-conscious acts of recall. It cannot be (and is not, as we shall see) an account of the 'beginnings' of the constructive process. For reasons which will become apparent below, I will call what Bartlett calls rote recapitulation 'Cartesian remembering'.

So, in turning to what must be the nature of such beginnings, let me start simply by pointing out that without the capacity or resources to formulate the flow of one's experiences in some socially intelligible way – thus identifying some as memories, others as fantasies and yet others as indicative of the current circumstances – they would, surely, be as Alfred Schutz (1972: 51), the social phenomenologist, describes them. He suggests that, 'If we simply live immersed in the flow of duration [within the stream of consciousness], we encounter only undifferentiated experiences that melt into one another in a flowing continuum' – a self-cancelling flux, without stopping 'places' to which one can return. Without the skill to direct ourselves to reflect upon and constitute the phases within that flow as objects of attention, as 'commonplaces', there would be nothing in particular, Schutz suggests, to grasp on to, nothing to pay attention to or to remember. While our reactions to our own immediate circumstances would be influenced, of course, by our past experiences, we would not be able – in, as Bartlett (1932: 20) calls them, our self-conscious 'efforts after meaning' – to give names to states of affairs, by fitting them into a 'preformed scheme or setting'. Thus, in such circumstances, without being situated within an organized setting, our behaviour would become pathological: we would be unable to formulate goals, to act from the past towards the future; to remember who we were or what we were about. In short, we would be unable to act as self-determining agents. Disorganized memories, irrelevant to our lives, would come and go wholly undirected by 'us' – our actions would bear no relation to our social identities.

In some way, what we as human beings must be able to do is to take vague and unformulated aspects of such a flow of activity, and to give them a socially intelligible and legitimate formulation (and a formulation which makes them of *use* to us in some way). What the origin of the process is like, says Bartlett, is very hard to describe in more elementary terms. But, he says:

> It is, however, as I have often indicated, very largely a matter of feeling, or affect. We say that it is characterized by doubt, hesitation, surprise, astonishment, confidence, dislike, repulsion and so on. Here is the significance of the fact, often reported in the preceding pages, that when a subject is being asked to remember, very often the first thing that emerges is something of the nature of an attitude. The recall is then a construction, made largely on the basis of this attitude, and its general effect is that of a justification of the attitude. (1932: 206–7)

In other words, while the act of recall 'constructs' the memory, it cannot construct it in just any way; it must be 'grounded' in some way, it can only construct what the initial 'attitude' will permit. Thus, in no way is remembering for Bartlett a matter of 'retrieving' an already well-formed memory trace; indeed, accurate recall is very unusual, as Bartlett continually points out, for as a (re)constructive process, it requires the application of a very detailed set of checks.

So: if the process of remembering is a 'grounded process of (re)construction', what is the nature of the entity or activity within which it is grounded? For, as Bartlett says, it is very hard to describe it in elementary terms. In attempting to describe it, Bartlett turns to Sir Henry Head's (1920) account of 'schemas' – which Head introduced, after discarding (justly, says Bartlett) the notion of individual images or traces, in an attempt to make sense of bodily posture and movement. In our bodily movements, we are aware of *changes*; and:

> Every recognizable (postural) change enters into consciousness already charged with its relation to something that has gone before. . . . For this combined standard, *against which all subsequent changes of posture are measured* before they enter consciousness, we propose the word 'schema'. (Head, 1920, quoted in Bartlett, 1932: 199, my emphasis)

But Head then went on to speak of 'the sensory cortex as a storehouse of past impressions'. But here, Bartlett thought, Head gave 'far too much away to earlier investigators'. For:

> The schemata are, we are told, living, constantly developing, affected by every bit of incoming sensational experience of a given kind. The storehouse notion is as far removed from this as it well could be . . . I strongly dislike the term 'schema' . . . it does not indicate what is very essential to the whole notion, that the organised mass results of past changes . . . are actively doing something all the time; are, so to speak, carried along with us, complete, though developing, from moment to moment . . . I think the term 'organised setting' approximates most

closely and clearly to the notion required. I shall, however, continue to use the term 'schema' when it seems best to do so, but I will attempt to define its application more narrowly. (Bartlett, 1932: 200)

'Schemata', then, for Bartlett are open to different formulations, but function as the *standards* against which the accuracy of a proposed formulation can be judged; indeed, in reassuring ourselves that our claims to be remembering something are true, we can return to the 'schemas' in which they were grounded, to check them further.

But we face a yet further task in our claims to be remembering something, than being able to check the correctness of our formulations 'within ourselves', so to speak; we must also check them for their social function as *accounts* – for verbally recounted 'memories' do not just occur in a social vacuum. Indeed, although Bartlett does not in fact reflexively explore the implications of his own theories for the gathering of his results, it is clear that people are not just providing neutral statements, but feel their conduct 'questioned' in some way. Thus 'the confident subject justifies himself – attains a rationalization, so to speak – by setting down more detail than was actually present; while the cautious, hesitating subject reacts in the opposite manner, and finds his justification by diminishing rather than increasing, the details presented' (1932: 21).

In other words, not only are we working here within a framework of social accountability, such that we have a responsibility to others (and to ourselves) to formulate in our 'efforts after meaning' a justifiable memory-account, but the accounting practice involved has a rhetorical structure of (implied) criticism and justification to it (Billig, 1987). Indeed, we could say, taking into account *both* Bartlett's 1932, *and* his 1923 views, and applying them to the processes of formulation involved in making intelligible statements about 'memories', that such formulations must be argumentatively developed. For it is not just a matter of a social group being 'organised and held together by some specific psychological tendency or group of tendencies, which give the group a bias in its dealings with external circumstances' (1932: 296, to repeat a sentence already quoted above). We also have to take into account the fact that 'none of the tendencies . . . operates entirely by itself in determining the behaviour of man in society' (Bartlett, 1923: 105, to repeat another quote above). The constructive processes involved in remembering have what might be called a two-sided nature to them: everything depends for its nature in some way upon a dynamic involvement with its opposite. This approach to the understanding of remembering is, of course, reflected in the contents of the whole of this volume (but see especially Billig, and Middleton and Edwards, this volume).

Conclusions

The current way of conceptualizing remembering as the 'retrieval' of a 'representation' stems from an outdated (but not outgrown) dualist philosophy, from, as Ryle (1949) has dubbed it, an official doctrine of 'the ghost in the machine': the idea of a private, 'inner' subjectivity, radically separated from an outer, public world of objects, or object-like events – with the relation between inner and outer never having been, of course, adequately formulated. As a consequence, our current conception of memory, although pur-portedly a wholly objective notion is, in fact, a 'brother under the skin' with some of the worst aspects of subjectivism: namely, the fact that apparently 'anything goes!' For the belief that, as private, inner subjectivities, we gain knowledge of our own mental states (as abstract objects) by a form of 'inner observation' (or 'introspection') misses (as Wittgenstein above makes clear) the fact that in our ordinary claims to knowledge, not just in science, we have to assure people (and ourselves) that our claims are *justified*, that we have (or can) institute checks as to their accuracy, their fittedness or appropriateness to the circumstances in question. In other words, as currently conceptualized the retrieval process lacks accountability. In fact, it can be asked, how could a process of checking be formulated and instituted within the process of retrieval to ensure that the processes and principles involved were being applied correctly?

Although the peculiar and special process known as introspection has been discredited as a reliable way of gathering experimental data, cognitive theorists apparently feel no embarrassment in suggesting that, as Anscombe (1957: 57) has put it, we possess 'a very queer and special sort of seeing eye in the middle of the acting' to look at the traces, structures, productions, or whatever which are supposed to represent within us our own past experiences to us. But even if we did possess such a special eye, we would still face many problems. Let me list just a few phenomena which any adequate theory of memory must explain. The fact is that in interaction with other people, or in reading a text, according to the nature of our past experience, we can be 'moved' in certain ways. Some (but not all of us) can appreciate jokes, be moved to tears, laughter, fear, strange experiences of strange worlds. Everyday practical re-membering is not just a matter of self-consciously remembering facts, but of sometimes 're-feeling' certain events, sometimes of being able to reorder by reshaping such feelings to imagine either new relations between well-known things, or completely new worlds. In such practical remembering, our remembering is, so to speak, 'embodied' within us as a part of who we are, rather than 'external' to us and dependent upon signs or representations. And it is not just, as Zajonc (1980) says, that affect is pre- rather than post-cognitive and as such is also present as a 'companion' of thought, but *is* an aspect of our practical, embodied thought.

In discussing precisely this point, in a section called 'The inferiority of the written to the spoken word', Plato tells a tale of the god Theuth, who boasted of his invention of writing to Thamus, the king of Egypt, saying that it would improve both the wisdom and the memory of the Egyptians. But the king was unimpressed:

> Those who acquire it will cease to exercise their memory and become forgetful; they will rely upon writing to bring things to their remembrance by external signs instead of on their own internal resources. What you have discovered is a recipe for recollection, not for memory. And as for wisdom, your pupils will have the reputation for it without the reality. . . . And because they are filled with the conceit of wisdom instead of real wisdom they will be a burden to society. (Plato, 1973: 96–7)

Bartlett, by being in fact true to what he actually observed in his studies (and wrote down clearly for all to read) – that remembering begins in vague feelings, in sensuous rather than conceptual matters – reinforces Plato's distinction here: the distinction between, to repeat, an embodied remembering which is, so to speak, continuous with one's existence as the person one is, and a remembering which is dependent upon 'traces', representations' or other 'external signs' of some kind. And he shows, not only that current doctrine in cognitive psychology – that there *must* be a memory trace somewhere whose structure in some way represents the structure of some past event – is factually unfounded, he also shows (unwittingly) why it is believed so tenaciously. In discussing how in its schematic form the past exerts its influence *en masse*, and how individuals must infer from what *is* present, what probable constituents could have gone into its constitution, he suggests that essentially we say to ourselves, 'This and this *must* have occurred, in order that my present state should be what it is' (Bartlett, 1932: 202). This is why I want to call our current 'cognitivist' version of what remembering is supposed to be 'Cartesian remembering'. For it is a 'story' about the nature of remembering which takes into account not just certain (selected) experimental results, but also a whole theory about the nature of human mentality derived from Descartes – a story which takes it that what is present to self-conscious reflective thought is a basic paradigm for all that informs human action. So that even when it seems there is no 'image', or 'representation' present, to be true to the story we feel driven to say that there *must* be. But if the full implication of what Bartlett wrote is taken into account, then in practical, 'embodied' remembering there isn't!

Note

1. Mary Douglas (1987) has explored precisely this thesis in her recent book, taking Fleck's (1979) account of the growth of a 'thought collective' as central. Fleck's concern is with how *dominant* views are established and maintained, and with how 'cognition modifies the knower so as to adapt him harmoniously to his acquired knowledge' (1979: 86). Douglas's concern is also with institutions as functional, systematic wholes. I have also explored these issues elsewhere, and in particular the way in which we can become 'entrapped' within systems of thought of our own making (Shotter, 1989). Here, however, my concern is with the other side of the coin, with what happens to non-dominant, 'forgotten' or repressed views. And in exploring Bartlett's early views, and in particular his account of how conflicts are dealt with, we shall be concerned with the less systematic aspects of social life. Here, a functionalist approach is quite inappropriate.

References

Anscombe, G.E.M. (1957) *Intention*. Oxford: Blackwell.

Bartlett, Sir F.C. (1923) *Psychology and Primitive Culture*. Cambridge: Cambridge University Press.

Bartlett, Sir F.C. (1932) *Remembering: a Study in Experimental and Social Psychology*. London: Cambridge University Press.

Billig, M. (1987) *Arguing and Thinking: a Rhetorical Approach to Social Psychology*. Cambridge: Cambridge University Press.

De Man, P. (1979) *Allegories of Reading*. New Haven: Yale University Press.

Derrida, J. (1977) *Of Grammatology*, tr. Gayatri Chakravorty Spivak. Baltimore, MD: Johns Hopkins University Press.

Douglas, M. (1980) *Evans-Pritchard*. London: Fontana.

Douglas, M. (1987) *How Institutions Think*. London: Routledge & Kegan Paul.

Fleck, L. (1979) *The Genesis and Development of a Scientific Fact*. Chicago: University of Chicago Press.

Gauld, A. and Shotter, J. (1977) *Human Action and its Psychological Investigation*. London: Routledge & Kegan Paul.

Gergen, K.J. (1982) *Towards Transformation in Social Knowledge*. New York: Springer.

Gergen, K.J. (1985) 'The social constructionist movement in modern psychology', *American Psychologist*, 40: 266–75.

Gleitman, H. (1981) *Psychology*. New York: Norton.

Head, H. (1920) *Studies in Neurology*. Oxford: Clarendon Press.

Jacoby, R. (1975) *Social Amnesia: a Critique of Conformist Psychology from Adler to R.D. Laing*. Sussex: Harvester.

James, W. (1890) *Principles of Psychology*. London: Macmillan.

Johnson, M. (1987) *The Body in the Mind: the Bodily Basis of Memory, Imagination, and Reason*. Chicago: University of Chicago Press.

Lakoff, G. (1986) *Women, Fire, and Other Dangerous Things*. Chicago: University of Chicago Press.

Lakoff, G. and Johnson, M. (1980) *Metaphors We Live By*. Chicago: University of Chicago Press.

Mills, C.W. (1940) 'Situated actions and vocabularies of motive', *American Sociological Review*, 5: 439–52.

Neisser, U. (1967) *Cognitive Psychology*. New York: Appleton-Century-Crofts.

Ong, W.J. (1958) *Ramus: Method and the Decay of Dialogue*. Cambridge, MA: Harvard University Press.

Plato (1973) *Phaedrus and the Seventh and Eight Letters*, tr. with intro. by W. Hamilton. Harmondsworth: Penguin Books.

Ryle, G. (1949) *The Concept of Mind*. London: Heinemann.

Schutz, A. (1972) *The Phenomenology of the Social World*, tr. G. Walsh and F. Lehnert. London: Heinemann.

Shotter, J. (1984) *Social Accountability and Selfhood*. Oxford: Blackwell.

Shotter, J. (1986) 'A sense of place: Vico and the social production of social identities', *British Journal of Social Psychology*, 25: 199–211.

Shotter, J. (1989) 'The unique nature of normal circumstances: contests and illusions', in R. Maier (ed.), *Norms in Argumentation*. Dordrecht: Foris.

Vico, G. (1948) *The New Science of Giambattista Vico*, ed. and tr. by T.G. Bergin and M.H. Fisch. Ithaca, NY: Cornell University Press.

Wittgenstein, L. (1953) *Philosophical Investigations*. Oxford: Blackwell.

Wittgenstein, L. (1965) *The Blue and the Brown Books*. New York: Harper & Row.

Wittgenstein, L. (1980) *Remarks on the Philosophy of Psychology*, vols. I and II. Oxford: Blackwell.

Zajonc, R.B. (1980) 'Feeling and thinking: preferences need no inferences', *American Psychologist*, 35: 151–75.

8

Organizational Forgetting: an Activity-Theoretical Perspective

Yrjö Engeström, Katherine Brown, Ritva Engeström and Kirsi Koistinen

In this chapter, we are looking at collective remembering and collective forgetting from the point of view of activity theory. This approach, often characterized as the cultural-historical school, was founded by three pioneering Soviet psychologists, L.S. Vygotsky, A.N. Leontiev and A.R. Luria (for basic introductory texts, see Vygotsky, 1978; Wertsch, 1981). We shall put forward a conceptual framework for analysing phenomena of organizational remembering and forgetting. This conceptual framework will be applied in analyses of data from two settings of medical work. The first setting is a hospital clinic in California, and the second a health centre in Finland. Three successive sets of qualitative data will be presented.

We shall proceed through the three sets of data using three different modes of analysis. The first one is an ethnographic analysis, based on field observations and interviews carried out in the course of the daily practices of the hospital clinic. The second mode of analysis is that of identifying and constructing ideal-typical explanatory models in interviews given by the physicians of the health centre. The third mode is that of analysing arguments presented in an excerpt of discourse recorded at the health centre. These three modes of analysis yield different, yet essentially complementary and mutually enriching, insights into the phenomena of organizational forgetting. After presenting and discussing the substantive findings, we shall close each section by commenting on the strengths and weaknesses of the mode of analysis employed.

Remembering and Forgetting in an Activity Perspective

In his seminal treatise, P.I. Zinchenko (1939/83: 34) pointed out that involuntary memory is 'characterized by the fact that remembering occurs within an action that has a definite task, goal and motive and a definite significance for the subject, but that is not directly oriented toward the task of remembering'. Correspondingly, voluntary remembering is a special action devoted to remembering: 'the subject is consciously aware of the object of the action as an object of remembering' (p. 78).

Zinchenko's distinction corresponds to the general distinction between action and operation, worked out by Leontiev (1959/81; 1978). For Leontiev, these two were, however, only a part of the hierarchical structure of human activity. His three-level model may be schematically depicted as follows (Table 8.1; see also Engeström, 1987).

Table 8.1   *The hierarchical structure of activity after Leontiev*

Unit	Directing factor	Subject
Activity	Object/motive	Collective
Action	Goal	Individual or group
Operation	Conditions	Non-conscious

The difference between a non-conscious or involuntary memory operation and a conscious, goal-directed memory action carried out by an individual or a group is fairly clear. The level of collective, motive-driven activity is more difficult to grasp (see Harré, Clarke and DeCarlo, 1985). To paraphrase Bronfenbrenner (1979), actions are modular and activities are molar units.

It is helpful to analyse the different time structures involved in actions and in an activity. Actions have a beginning and an end and can be more or less adequately described as stepwise algorithmic procedures (this does not mean that actions are identical with or predetermined by plans; see Suchman, 1987). Action time is basically linear and anticipates a finite termination. An activity does not end when the goal is reached; for example, when a patient is cured – there will be another patient waiting. Activity time is recurrent and cyclic. An activity is systemic and self-organizing rather than finite and discrete. Activities, too, have their beginnings and ends. But the time-scale is large enough to make it difficult to trace the exact moment of beginning and to anticipate the point of termination. It is more appropriate to talk about life cycles and developmental zones of activities.

There are some societally organized collective activities whose objects are traces of the past and whose motive is the *preservation* and *retrieval* of those traces. These may be coined as activities of remembering – the singing of tales, the keeping of records of various kinds, the writing of history, the running of libraries. The list indicates our dissatisfaction with the opposition between collective memory and history. This opposition was championed by Halbwachs: 'General history starts only when tradition ends and the social memory is fading or breaking up. So long as a remembrance continues to exist, it is useless to set it down in writing or otherwise fix it in memory' (1951/80: 78).

From our point of view, history writing differs from the singing of tales in the complexity of the mediating means but not in any fundamentally oppositional way. The notion of a non-mediated, totally 'natural' and direct collective remembrance is a fallacy. Mediating artefacts, both external and internal, are always present in human activity. Even internal actions of remembering are mediated by cultural artefacts. We may try to describe and understand them as social representations, or as mental models. Even a word and an image are cultural artefacts, not reducible to purely individual or biological origins (Wertsch, 1987).

In this chapter, we are not primarily interested in activities of remembering. Our main concern is the role of remembering and forgetting in medical organizations. These are seen as activity systems which have patients as their objects and healing as their motive. Still, remembering is an important aspect of their function-ing, an important type of actions within their contexts. Thus, we shall look into the relationship between the activity of medical care and the subordinated actions of remembering.

In the physician's work, history taking, collecting and storing information concerning the background and development of the patient's problem, is an action of remembering (*preserving*). Examining a patient's records at the beginning of a consultation is another typical action of remembering (*retrieving*). These daily actions have information about an individual patient as their object. Expanding on Hirschhorn's (1984) suggestion, we may call them actions of *primary* remembering within work activity.

There are, however, remembering actions of another kind in work contexts. These are actions of remembering 'how we used to do things in the past', or 'what our work and organization was like in the past' (*retrieving*). They are also actions of writing down an idea or a plan so that it can be recollected, elaborated further and perhaps put into practice in the coming days (*preserving*). These actions have not just an individual patient but the activity system itself as their object. We call them actions of *secondary* remember-ing.

We may depict the dimension of actions of primary and secondary remembering as the vertical axis of remembering in work activity. The *internal* and *external* aspects of remembering actions constitute the horizontal axis. Norman (1988: ch. 3) has a delightful discussion of the relationship between external and internal memory, or 'knowledge in the world' and 'knowledge in the head'. He identifies reminding as a typical action facilitated by external memory aids, from knotted handkerchiefs to alarm clocks. In terms of activity theory, external reminders help transform intentional actions into automatic operations (for example, waking up at the right time).

An external reminder has the signal aspect and the message aspect. In more complex remembering actions, such as checking a patient's records or recollecting how the work was done in the past, the external aids (for example, medical records, memoranda and minutes of meetings) are typically loaded with semantic information while the signal aspect fades into the background.

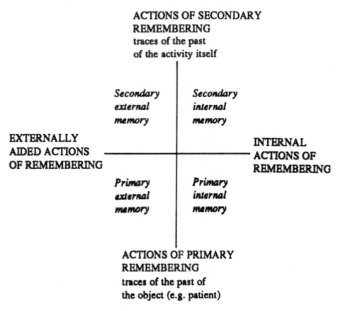

Figure 8.1   *Framework for analysing remembering in work*

The two axes may now be combined to form a framework for an activity-orientated analysis of remembering in work settings (Figure 8.1). The core of the activity system is located around the crossing point of the two axes. Memory events and artefacts located far away from the core are peripheral to the subjects involved in the activity. Remembering is essentially *reciprocal movement between the poles* of the two axes. In other words, remembering is oscillation between using documents and using one's head, or between writing things down and creating internal images of them. Correspondingly, remembering is making connections between primary actions (such as taking a patient's history) and secondary actions (such as reconstructing the way history used to be taken). The latter movement is analogous to Norman's (1988: 70–2) notion of 'memory through explanation'.

In Cartesian and cognitivist terms, forgetting is understood as a technical failure in the storing or retrieval of information into or out of mind. The psychoanalytically inspired alternative view regards forgetting as repression of the unpleasant, as 'social amnesia' (Jacoby, 1975). In the present framework, forgetting is seen differently: as *breaches* or *ruptures* in the movement between the poles of the two axes in Figure 8.1. In graphic form this may be depicted as isolation of memory entities, as missing traffic across the sections of Figure 8.1.

When a doctor cannot construct a connection between her internal image of the patient's history and the patient's external medical record, forgetting ensues. This is much more likely when the patient is treated by a number of different doctors. The external record becomes a crucial collective form of memory. Thus, although the actions of remembering are performed individually or occasionally in pairs and small groups, the external artefacts of memory are truly collective, at least potentially. Through such artefacts, unlimited numbers of individual and group actions are connected. When an individual fails to establish a connection between her internal notion and the external artefact, she fails to establish a connection between herself and her colleagues.

When a doctor fails to establish a connection between his way of taking a history today and the way history used to be taken in the past, he forgets the collective basis of his development. It may well be that he himself never did take a history much differently from what he does today. But forgetting about the collective past makes him unable to see how his actions derive their meaning from the collective activity – and how he may influence the evolution of that activity through his actions.

So ruptures along both axes produce forgetting of a similar type, a type seldom noticed in the literature. We might call it forgetting through silence, or forgetting through solitude, or forgetting through disconnectedness. The obvious counterpart of such forgetting is an inability to relate one's own actions to those of the colleagues, resulting in protective privatism. In terms of time consciousness, this is a breeding ground for an exclusive preoccupation with biography as an individual career or trajectory. Time becomes a chain of individual actions and accomplishments, disconnected from their collective meaning and activity context.

In early forms of remembering actions, physically present other members of the community function as central external mediating 'artefacts'. What would be more natural than to ask your nearest co-worker when you do not remember something. In modern forms of remembering, inanimate objects seem to have gained the central mediating role. However, other human beings are still there, as a very special kind of 'external memory aid'. Other humans are probably the earliest, yet also the most complex external aids of remembering actions. In some cases, all members of the community have equal access to traces of the past. In others, access is strictly limited to specified functionaries. The way the community and its access to the past are organized is actually a third dimension to be mentally added to those depicted in Figure 8.1. To facilitate the mental transformation, Figure 8.2 depicts the access dimension as the horizontal axis.

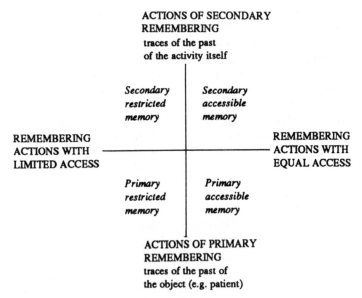

ACTIONS OF SECONDARY
REMEMBERING
traces of the past
of the activity itself

Secondary restricted memory

Secondary accessible memory

REMEMBERING
ACTIONS WITH
LIMITED ACCESS

REMEMBERING
ACTIONS WITH
EQUAL ACCESS

Primary restricted memory

Primary accessible memory

ACTIONS OF PRIMARY
REMEMBERING
traces of the past of
the object (e.g. patient)

Figure 8.2 *Complementary framework for analysing remembering in work*

Again, remembering may be seen as reciprocal movement between equal access and limited access, between specialist responsibility for information and general availability of information. Forgetting, then, occurs when this movement is broken. Information either freezes into a monopoly of some selected individuals, or it becomes so general that it loses all concreteness and distinctiveness. In both cases, there is simply nothing to remember for most members of the activity system.

In the following, we shall analyse three instances of organizational forgetting in medical settings. The first example is from a Urology Clinic of an inner city teaching hospital in Southern California where the second author conducted a six-month field research project in 1988 with the first author as her supervisor. The second and third examples are from a Finnish health centre where the first, third and fourth authors have conducted a long-term project aimed at analysing and developing the work activity of the general practitioners. The data used in the second example are from 1986, the data used in the third example are from 1988.

The Disappearance of the Secondary External Memory in a Hospital Clinic

The Urology Clinic within the southern Californian hospital is the 'business end' of the Division of Urology. The clinic was founded in 1944. The administrative head of the Urology Clinic, or Management Services Officer (hereafter Mr L) is a key figure in the setting. He was the researchers' initial contact and principal informant through the early phases of the study. He had worked in the clinic for 34 years. Four Chiefs of the Division of Urology had served as 'his bosses'. When the researcher asked Mr L to tell her everything that came to mind about the history of the place, he said, 'you're looking at it'.

Outside of Mr L's working knowledge of the growth and development of the clinic itself, the resident teaching programme, the physical management of the facilities, the traditions and assumptions which have set the conditions for the present, the other employees of the clinic were generally unaware of the past of the activity system. Certain names and dates were familiar to nurses and secretaries. When they were asked about 'the past in the clinic', each person knew the name of the people who had their jobs before them. But that was the extent of the frame of reference.

Patients and nurses commented that the two secretaries have been in the clinic 'for a long time'. However, one had been there two years and the other one less than that. It turned out that in this hospital, clinic clerks 'usually last four or five months' in one area. So by comparison, two years is a long time. Patients may return weekly, monthly or tri-monthly for follow-up appointments, and their experience would encourage their continued belief that the secretaries have been there for a long time.

The secretarial role had been previously occupied by one woman,

Mrs J, who had been in the clinic for 15 years. Mrs J is still employed by the hospital. She left the Urology Clinic in 1986 to work in a semi-autonomous treatment centre located in the out-patient centre.

According to Mr L, Mrs J was 'overly curious about other people's work' and would 'stray into areas out of her field of concern'. The researcher also asked two nurses and two secretaries about this woman. The total comments were as follows:

— 'She was really nice to patients, very good with people.'
— 'There were fewer patients then.'
— 'She talked a lot.'
— 'She was here for 15 years.'

Having served in many roles – clerical work, patient preparation, patient scheduling – during her 15 years in the clinic, Mrs J was a potential source of historical insights. In her interview, Mrs J told the researcher straight away that she had differences of opinion with Mr L. Mrs J recounted the following episode concerning a budget meeting in 1980:

> She recollected having made several comments and suggestions which prompted an administrator to remark to Mr L: 'She has some good ideas. You should let her help and learn what you need to do for the budget.' After the meeting, Mrs J asked Mr L about this. He responded with a dismissing remark: 'The budget is sealed and you're not looking at it.'

Mr L is the living cumulative history of the Urology Clinic. But his apparent monopoly of information is not complete. In an interview with the present Chief, Dr N, the researcher expressed her frustration at not being able to find corroborating documents to support or contradict Mr L's oral history. Dr N suggested that she contact a retired urologist, Dr R, who was still involved at the hospital as a visitor or volunteer. This retired physician had not been trained at the hospital but he had been an attending physician there for many years.

When the researcher met Dr R, he brought a scrapbook full of memorabilia – photos, letters, articles from the local Urological Society, minutes from Society meetings, and a 20–30-page paper written by Dr F, the founder of the clinic, entitled 'The organization of a resident teaching program in a non-teaching hospital'. Dr R pointed out that Dr F was a 'charismatic' and 'totally dedicated' authority figure. In his interviews, Mr L gave a similar evaluation of Dr F. These two informants also characterized the subsequent three Chiefs of the Division, their styles of leadership and personal priorities, much in the same way.

The fact that these two versions of the story agree is somehow disturbing. The details are not suspect in themselves. It is the point of view, taken as self-evident. Dr R is interested in the careers of his colleagues and their contributions to techniques of urological surgery. Mr L is interested in the expansion and modernization of the physical facilities of the clinic. Both informants produced their accounts primarily in terms of 'who was the Chief of the Division'. Questions about the broader activity were not well received or easily understood. Descriptions of the daily routines, actions and actors in the clinic – including patients, receptionists, nurses, residents, the three attending physicians – were given without historical context, as if something unchanging, in the information supplied by both Dr R and Mr L. Almost nothing was said about patients, their occupations, their life-styles and attitudes, even their illnesses. The object of the activity is silent in this version of history.

Dr R intimated that he had begun years ago to throw out his old patient records. This went on 'until they told us we had to keep them 'cause it's the law now'. The administrative assistant in the Doctors' Offices expressed frustration that her closets in the office were 'full of stuff' that Dr N said was valuable but that no one ever looked at, and that she did 'not know what to do with it'.

The researcher had several discouraging encounters with librarians and secretaries who could not help her locate documents concerning either urology at the County Hospital or the history of the hospital prior to its university affiliation. The Dean of the Medical School's offices and the Central Campus Library Archives could not help. Microfilms of local newspapers yielded stories of public events. But documents from the inside were missing. The Dean's office secretaries were in an interesting position. They could not let the researcher herself look at the historical records which they still had in the office (in the form of personnel files) because they were 'confidential by law'. They also could not 'spare the manpower' to look through them for the researcher. This information stalemate was repeated several times at other levels.

At the Dean's office, a secretary told the researcher that all of the pertinent documents, the sort she would 'probably want to wade through' were 'in a warehouse somewhere', as far as she knew. The secretary suggested that the researcher get in touch with another more senior secretary who, it was said, knew 'all of that stuff', or where it is. This lead never led to the expected outcome. The warehouse remained a mysterious entity that nobody could locate.

Data and experiences from the field research in the Urology Clinic demonstrate a disappearance of the secondary external memory from the activity system. In terms of the archives, the disappearance is a physical fact, covered with the myth of the distant warehouse. In terms of people in whom the history is embodied, Dr R and Mrs J are already outside or barely marginally in the activity system, while Mr L is still there but not for long. Mr L will in effect 'take it all with him' when he retires, some time in the next four or five years. The secondary external memory is effectively cut off from the internal and primary memories of the bulk of the staff in the clinic. Only Mr L's personal presence creates an illusion of continuity; after all, he has been there 'forever'. The situation is schematically depicted in Figure 8.3. In this and the following figures, the continuous arrows represent connections of influence; the broken arrows represent tendencies of movement.

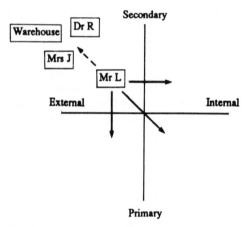

Figure 8.3   *The disappearing secondary external memory in the Urology Clinic*

In terms of access, the rupture is equally obvious. Mr L's knowledge and experience are a part of his personal status as a senior administrative craftsman and patriarch of the clinic. The secretarial employees, care-givers and some long-time patients come to him with problems which he takes it upon himself to solve without 'disclosing the formula' to the person concerned. He has built a network of personal contacts in other hospital departments which he considers his own personal 'domain' as administrator.

Towards the end of the field research period, it became known that the hospital was undertaking a 'marketing campaign' to increase its visibility in the community and to raise the morale of the employees. Part of this project was the presentation of a 'Historical

Wall' which was to be a glass-case display of memorabilia from hospital departments, including log-books of census figures, snap-shots and other artefacts. The whole project was called 'Look Great in '88'.

When the researcher asked the two secretaries about the 'Historical Wall', they pointed at Mr L and said 'That's his thing' and 'He's doing it'. They did not know what was involved or what was being incorporated into the display. It soon turned out that Mr L was in fact the principal co-ordinator of the 'Historical Wall'. Mrs J said in her interview that at one of the planning meetings for the 'Look Great in '88' campaign, she had offered to help Mr L with the data gathering for the 'Historical Wall' and to serve in his committee. According to Mrs J, he had replied 'I don't need a committee'. Once again, 'that was the end of it', said Mrs J.

Apparently Mr L was not delegating any parts of this project. He told the researcher that he had been to the local Historical Society looking for photographs. The researcher asked if anyone else, for instance Dr R, was actively helping him. Mr L replied 'Oh, tangentially, yes . . .', but did not elaborate. Mr L saw the 'Historical Wall' primarily as 'the story of a building'. He told the researcher that although antique medical records and photographs of people would be included, the focus would be on showing the changing size and shape of the physical plant. Aerial photographs, construction plans and blueprints were to be prominently displayed. History is here synonymous with quantitative, physical expansion.

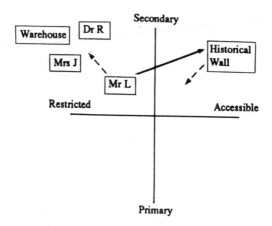

Figure 8.4 *Access to secondary memory in the Urology Clinic*

As Figure 8.4 attempts to show, the 'Historical Wall' was a paradox in terms of access to the secondary memory. The display itself was supposed to be totally accessible and general. It was not supposed to deal concretely with the evolution of any collective activities, only with (a) scattered pieces of memorabilia, and (b) the physical plant. At the same time, the data collection and image construction behind the display were restricted to the point of individual monopoly. History was taking the form of a dual structure of public entertainment and private manoeuvring, with only unidirectional movement in between.

The account presented above has some of the typical strengths and weaknesses of ethnographic analysis. Through extensive field observations, we gained a rather comprehensive, multi-perspective picture of the life at the clinic. Yet it is practically impossible to record systematically and rigorously all the relevant aspects of that life. The danger of impressionistic patchwork is always present. In the following section, we shall demonstrate an attempt at more systematic and constrained analysis of interview data obtained from our second setting, the Finnish health centre.

Historical Vacuum and Surrogate Secondary Memory in a Health Centre

In our analysis of the Urology Clinic, doctors were authority figures, relatively distant from the flow of daily interaction with patients. In our second case analysis, doctors occupy the centre stage.

The Finnish health-centre system was created in 1972. The legislation requires that every municipality offers the primary medical services to all inhabitants free of charge. In a large city, the health centre is typically organized in the form of health stations. A health station offers general practitioners' consultations, supported by nurses, health-centre assistants, X-ray and laboratory services, often also physiotherapy, psychological consultation and other related services. The activity setting in our case consists of two health stations that together form a service district of the health centre of the city of Espoo. In 1986, the city had 153,000 inhabitants and ten health stations. The service district involved in our study had 36,500 inhabitants. The two stations had sixteen full-time general practitioners. During the first six months of 1986, the stations had 33,433 patient visits.

There are certain widely discussed problems in the functioning of health centres. Especially in cities, the waiting times and lines are usually frustratingly long. In Espoo, as in most other cities, the patient could visit any of the doctors (even any of the ten stations), regardless of previous contacts. The continuity of care was very low. Doctors frequently expressed dissatisfaction with the production pressure and bureaucratization they experienced at work. They criticized the city's central bureau of health for an authoritarian style of management. They also criticized patients for visiting general practitioners without medically justifiable cause. In the presence of competition from private medical centres, it was becoming increasingly difficult for health centres to recruit and keep qualified physicians.

Against this background, it is understandable that doctors and politicians are seeking models for the future of primary medical care. The Ministry of Health and Social Services has recently initiated a reform, based on the so-called personal doctor principle. According to this principle, each general practitioner within a health centre gets a population responsibility – that is, a fixed list of his or her own patients. The list is compiled by dividing the population of the municipality into segments according to their addresses or to their already existing doctor–patient relationships. This system should be fully implemented in the early 1990s.

The personal-doctor system will be implemented within the framework of health centres. So far, the system is only a very general administrative frame. It is an open question what the content will be in terms of the physician's daily work and quality of care. The Ministry has left it to the municipalities to experiment and shape their own versions of the general idea.

In this situation, a popular interpretation of the personal doctor principle is to equate it with the system that pre-dated health centres, namely the so-called municipal doctor system. The municipal doctor was a general practitioner formally employed by the municipality but actually gaining his or her income from patient fees. In most municipalities, there was only one municipal doctor. The municipal doctor had a very independent position, being actually his or her own supervisor. The municipal doctor had high prestige among the population. Suffering from a shortage of physicians, the municipalities often offered handsome housing to the doctors. Municipal doctors generally preferred to work alone, seldom having more than one assistant to help with patient appointments and bookkeeping.

The municipal-doctor system seems to avoid some central shortcomings of the present health-centre work. Doctors were not subordinated to bureaucratic control. Patients came mainly to be treated for clear, biomedically identifiable and often fairly serious diseases. The continuity of care was guaranteed, simply because the municipal doctor was often the only alternative. Given these advantages, the obvious question is: Why was the municipal-doctor system replaced with the health-centre system? In other words, why could the old system not be continued and why was the new system created? We presented these very questions to the sixteen general practitioners working at the two stations.

The answers of the doctors can be classified into four distinct types of conceptions. The distribution of the doctors' answers into these categories is presented in Table 8.2.

Table 8.2   *The physicians' conceptions of the transition from the municipal-doctor system to the health-centre system*

Category	Frequency
1 The political and ideological striving for equality as the cause of transition	4
2 Striving for equality plus the excessive amount and unbearable hours of work as the cause of transition	3
3 Transition as a mistake; return to the municipal-doctor system as a necessity	4
– Borderline case between categories 3 and 4	1
4 Transition as a needed move towards preventive and co-operative work	4

In the following, the contents of each conception are described with the help of verbatim excerpts from the physicians' answers.

1   The political and ideological striving for equality as the cause of transition

> *Doctor II*: Well, I don't really know. I am not well informed about the situation before the new legislation, about how the municipal doctors actually worked. I mean, they were municipal doctors, but were they private practitioners, or were they employed by the municipality, I don't really know. I mean, did they get paid by the municipality, in addition to what they got from the patients. I don't really know. I don't know how big an upheaval it actually was. But I think they were more like private practitioners.
>
> *Interviewer*: Why could the municipal-doctor system not be continued?
>
> *Doctor II*: Well, it was politics, obviously, so that they wanted the citizen's basic services to be produced by the municipality. And also so that they are either free of charge, or anyway, so that they are not like . . . They are brought within everybody's reach, so that it's not a matter of money any more. I guess that was the number one issue. I'm not quite sure, but this is my view. Or I suppose that that's how it went.
>
> *Doctor VIII*: Actually it was a consequence of the '60s, surely to a large

extent. And I guess the political support of the Left at that time surely had an impact, so that the system was changed . . .

Interviewer: Why was the municipal-doctor system scrapped? So that they didn't develop it further or could not continue it?

Doctor VIII: Well, now this became a kind of a bureau, the only way to work, compared with the old one, which wasn't . . . Then there was surely a lot of such atmosphere involved. Was it connected to these, those I mentioned, those societal changes. I didn't really follow it at all. It didn't actually affect me much. I didn't have any thoughts at that time, when that discussion was going on, only that I'd get into the Medical School to study. I didn't know what they were talking about. I guess it was a question of, or I don't know, of a health-care system easily accessible to everybody. Though the previous system, too, was easily accessible. But there was a lot of ideology, such were the starting points to a large extent. Then there was the issue of the physician's status, I mean his prestige was pretty high. And generally there was a striving for equality in those days. And when the old system was scrapped, surely they scrapped a lot of physicians' prestige, too.

These doctors attributed the transition to basically external causes, such as the general political atmosphere and striving for equality in the society. They expressed a marked lack of knowledge of the internal conditions in the municipal doctors' work activity.

2 Striving for equality plus the excessive amount and unbearable hours of work as the cause of transition

Interviewer: Why was the health-centre system created?

Doctor XII: To make people equal in their access to services and to facilitate their entrance to care. I guess the idea is that quality services are easy to get for everybody, and of the same quality or along the same lines in the whole nation.

Interviewer: Why could the municipal-doctor system not be continued?

Doctor XII: Could not be continued . . . why was it replaced with a new one? Well, if you think of the doctors, their work was heavy and they were quite tied up in their jobs. But I guess the planning of the organization had a different starting-point, some sort of social policy. Of course people's demands increase and did increase at that time. And this unifies the care quite a lot.

Interviewer: Do you have an idea of why this transition from the municipal-doctor system to the health-centre system took place? Was it needed?

Doctor XIV: It was needed in some sense, because it used to be so that one had to pay. They took quite big fees, it wasn't cheap. People often had to think whether they could afford seeing the doctor. Presumably the idea is now that it will be accessible to people who don't have money. So it was needed . . .

Interviewer: In your opinion, could the municipal-doctor system have been continued? Was there anything besides the fees that required a new system?

Doctor XIV: I can't answer that. I was not so interested at that time. They wanted to get a fixed monthly salary for the physicians. In those days, they had to work as much as they could, and I think they worked around the clock.

These doctors emphasized the external cause but noticed also possible internal factors behind the transition. The internal factors mentioned were the amount and hours of work. However, these factors were present in the municipal-doctor system all through its 90 years of existence. No explanation was offered as to why these factors would have gained decisive importance before the transition to the new system.

3 Transition as a mistake; return to the municipal-doctor system as a necessity

Interviewer: Why was the health-centre system created, what was the purpose of it?

Doctor VI: Well, there are these pretty paragraphs in the law, I have read them. I think this is just a made-up organization. I guess the old one would have worked just as well. I mean the municipal-doctors system, to which we would obviously return in the personal-doctor system. This was made awfully rigid, and the doctors really became civil servants. I don't know if the patients benefit anything from this, surely nothing. The access to the doctor was then just as good as now. The health centre of Espoo is already so big an institution that everything happens awfully slowly and rigidly.

Interviewer: Why could the municipal-doctor system not be continued?

Doctor XIII: As a matter of fact I don't have a clear conception of why they really couldn't do that, so that they would for example develop parallel to each other. We have lost quite a lot. If we are going to develop a personal-doctor system, we must in a way go backwards, to the days of the municipal-doctor system. I think that in those days they had some kind of a personal-doctor system. They did have it. But surely it could have been developed into this system from there on. A general confusion has been created to a large extent, and it makes a lot of obstacles to regaining co-operation and trust among people. So we doctors, too, must kind of search for our identity anew in the personal-doctor system.

These doctors took the municipal-doctor system as a model for the future personal-doctor system. The transition to the health-centre system was regarded as a mistake that created bureaucracy and destroyed the trustful relationship between the doctor and his or her patients. This conception has affinities with conception 1. In both, the health-centre system is seen as a 'made-up organization', created in response to external political interests rather than to practical needs within the activity.

4 Transition as a needed move towards preventive and co-operative work

> *Doctor IV*: Maternal guidance, child health guidance, regular check-ups in schools and with students, occupational health and all environmental and work-place hygienic conditions and such. Knowledge about them has increased and that has created expectations and legislation has created obligations. In those earlier days, with the municipal-doctor resources of the '60s, there is no way that they could have taken care of all these tasks brought about by the two last decades. The changing society, changing housing, changes in people's work, transition from agriculture to industrial and technical occupations, to service occupations. Everything has changed, the picture and structure of the whole society. So such an old-fashioned system of municipal doctors at least in its original form could not have taken care of all these tasks. Not quantitatively and not qualitatively. So there is such a developmental process.

> *Interviewer*: Why wasn't the municipal-doctor system continued?
> *Doctor XI*: Reasons are at least the increase in the whole volume of health services, both in the number of doctors and in the number of consultations, compared with the municipal-doctor system. There are many new things in the activity, too. I think that as such it would perhaps not have been functional. It was so strongly centred around the municipal doctor. In many places the doctor did almost everything himself. Now the laboratory and X-rays and other such functions as their own units exist in a totally different scale. . . . One could hardly conceive of a return to such an earlier system anyhow. If you think of the good aspects people think it had, they are often of such nature that surely even doctors wouldn't consider them good any more. Like being tremendously tied up to the work and having to work alone in most places. Today this is more like consulting and co-operating with different professional groups. And also the volume of services has definitely increased with this law, or with this system.

One doctor gave an answer which can only be classified as a borderline case between conceptions 3 and 4. She criticized the health-centre reform for replacing individual doctor–patient relationships with institutional care and blamed external political interests for a premature solution. She thought that the municipal-doctor system could have been continued. But she did not suggest a return. Instead, she went on to sketch the necessary 'enlargements' that would have been needed in the old system, describing improvements that actually took place as integral parts of the health-centre reform.

> *Doctor X*: But I understand, of course, that in addition to lots of doctors, laboratory and X-ray functions, perhaps nurses and health-guidance nurses needed to be connected somehow to share with the very lonely municipal doctor. Then what was added was health guidance and health education as kind of official parts of primary

health-care work. I mean, the municipal doctors were, after all, more like consultants in health-guidance centres, and the health-guidance nurses ran the activity, as far as I understand. And in this respect the fact that doctors were offered fixed office hours, including a compensation for work in health-guidance centres and schools, this has also been an enlargement.

In the analysis of the Urology Clinic, we set out to identify the more or less collectively accessible external means of remembering (secondary external memory). We found the existing external means drifting away from the core of the activity system, while the attempt to construct a novel external memory (the 'Historical Wall') was designed as a non-interactive display of generalities. In the analysis of the health centre, we set out to identify the conceptions of the individual doctors concerning the transition of their work activity (secondary internal memory). Here the problem is not the disappearance of memory. It is rather a question of an all but total *lack of external secondary means of remembering*. Within the activity system, we found no literature, no documents, no legends or collectively shared stories representing the pre-health centre period in the history of the two stations. Of the sixteen doctors, only two had very brief experiences of working as municipal doctors, neither one from the geographical area where they now worked. We were dealing with a sharp generation gap, probably aggravated by the fact that the last municipal doctor of that area was currently the administrative chief of the city's central bureau of health.

The activity system of the two interconnected stations had

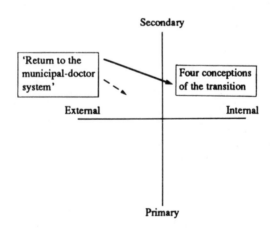

Figure 8.5   *The historical vacuum in the health stations*

actually become a *historical vacuum*. In such a situation, stories and images from public debate and from outside colleagues tended to become – and were promoted as – surrogate entities of the secondary external memory. This is especially clear in conception 3 in the classification presented above. The idea of 'returning' to the municipal-doctor system had nostalgic popular currency in the media. The situation is schematized in Figure 8.5.

Perhaps the most striking feature of the doctors' conceptions is the total absence of the single most powerful explanation to the demise of the municipal-doctor system, offered in any historical treatise concerned with the transition. This explanation is the rapid growth of the hospital system, gaining its full momentum in the latter half of the 1950s in Finland. The very same development in inter-war England has been eloquently characterized by Armstrong (1983: 73–4).

> The growth of hospitals to enclose bodies and the development of laboratory tests to analyse them was accompanied by further specialization as different parts of the body were separately investigated. [. . .] One effect of the strengthening of the panoptic vision in the inter-war years was the undermining of general practice. True, the GP was employed in the examination and investigation of individual bodies but the hospital setting, with its accompanying resources, produced a more efficient and powerful gaze. The GP might have been trained in a panoptic structure (the hospital) and be cognizant with the analytic principles of the panoptic vision, but the conditions of general practice – particularly a widely dispersed patient population – ensured that the gaze was less effective, less penetrating, when compared with hospital practice. The growth in numbers of hospital beds did little therefore to help general practice – indeed, at times, the GP was specifically excluded. [. . .] Access to the new laboratory-based diagnostic techniques remained under the control of hospital specialists; and GPs, until the 1950s and 1960s, were not allowed to use them.

A history of the Finnish municipal doctors (Kauttu, Reinilä and Voutilainen, 1983: 16) puts it in quite similar terms.

> In this technological ecstasy, what had been the strongest aspect of the municipal doctors, familiarity with patients, listening, talking, understanding, seemed obsolete. Along with central hospitals, specialists came even to country districts in the 1950s, and the gleam of new machines began to be reflected not only in doctors' but also in patients' eyes. Like a revolution eats its children, so medical technology disintegrated the municipal doctor service [. . .].

A realization of these irreversible factors behind the transition would reveal the idle nature of ideas of 'return to the municipal-doctor system'. How is it possible that our doctors demonstrated no awareness of these factors?

This brings us to the problem of access to secondary memory. Somehow the historical data on hospital expansion as related to the demise of the municipal-doctor system had become inaccessible to the doctors in the activity system we studied. On the other hand, the popular lore of 'return' was becoming increasingly accessible. This lore typically consists of extremely general claims about the benefits of the municipal-doctor system. It is accessible – and detached from the concrete past of any particular activity system (see Figure 8.6).

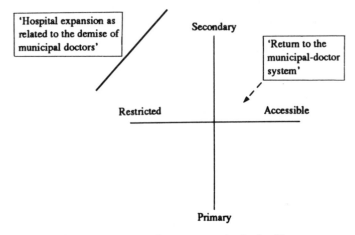

Figure 8.6   *The access to secondary memory in the health stations*

The account presented above is based on an analysis of ideal-typical conceptions found among doctors concerning the past reorganization of their work. Ideal types are sometimes criticized as researchers' typifications that do violence to the situated and dilemmatic nature of people's actual expressions. As Billig et al. (1988: 157) point out, 'somehow, in the process of constructing these ways of looking, the sociologist seems to have become predisposed to treat "ideologies" or "beliefs" as structures which possess remarkable degrees of inner coherence'.

We agree with the critics that people's conceptions have an internally contradictory, dilemmatic and fluid nature. Moving a step further, one could claim that conceptions should only be studied in the form of discourse processes, in constant movement and social interaction. But this is where we object. People's conceptions are not only dilemmatic, situated and processual – they are also remarkably stable, rigid and insensitive to changing situations.

Conceptions do not exist only in the form of ongoing discourse processes – they also exist in the form of fixed external artefacts, canonized rules, relatively stable material, social and mental structures. Stability and change, structure and process, are complementary aspects of human practice and cognition. Thus, we think that it is useful to identify and construct ideal-typical conceptions prevalent within a community, while at the same time acknowledging that no individual in that community fits completely and permanently into any one of the conceptions constructed. Ference Marton (1984: 62–3) formulates this point as follows:

> In empirical investigations, we often find variation in conceptions not only between but also within individuals. Depending on the context, e.g. the question asked, they may exhibit qualitatively different conceptions of the very same phenomenon. The conceptions are thus frequently not characteristics of the individual, rather, they are characteristics of ways of functioning. Instead of seeing the different conceptions as representing different groups of individuals, the intraindividual variation found invites us to think in terms of an abstract system of description, a gigantic space of categories, in which the individuals move – more or less freely – back and forth.

We differ from Marton in the notion of 'an abstract system of description'. For us, an activity system such as the health centre is a very concrete system. Still, one fruitful way of looking at it is to view it as 'a gigantic space of categories'.

Since ideal types have an inherent tendency towards exclusion of contradiction and change, they should be taken as rather restricted transitory tools of analysis. In the account presented above, doctor X is a case in point. Analysis using ideal types can only place her answer in between two categories (3 and 4), as a borderline case. The dilemma in her thinking would be much better understood in terms of an oscillating process of argumentation. In the next section, we shall take a look at data analysable only from such a processual and dilemmatic point of view.

Re-mediating Organizational Remembering

During our research at the health centre, we deliberately organized recurring situations where the staff of the health stations were invited to joint analyses of the history of their activity system. In such meetings, the staff were presented with questions like 'what kinds of means and instruments did the municipal doctors use?', or 'what kinds of patients did they have?', or 'what kind of division of labour did they have?'. We also wrote and circulated among the staff a condensed history of the work of general practitioners in

Finland, drawing heavily on physicians' published autobiographies (Engeström, Engeström, Helenius and Koistinen, 1987). Our aim was to provide and facilitate the generation of alternative external aids of secondary remembering. We may characterize this as an effort to re-mediate secondary remembering. All this was done as groundwork for the challenge the staff of the two stations had taken, namely to plan and design collectively 'from below' a new model for their work activity.

One occasion of re-mediation occurred in the early spring of 1988, in a seminar led by a visiting psychiatrist who had been invited to speak about coping with change. A conversation concerning the transition from the municipal-doctor system ensued. Five different positions were represented: the visiting psychiatrist; a senior administrative doctor from the city's central board of health; three doctors from within the activity system (doctors X, XIII and XVI); a junior collaborator of our research team (a social scientist); and a senior psychiatrist permanently employed as a consultant within the activity system. In the initial interview, doctor XIII had represented category 3 ('return to the municipal-doctor system'), doctor XVI had represented category 4 ('health centre as a necessary move forward') and doctor X had represented a conception between those two. What follows is a verbatim tape-recorded protocol of the sequence of the discussion where the municipal-doctor system is directly taken up.

> *Visiting psychiatrist*: Before this transition, some of you were involved at the time when the old municipal-doctor system was disintegrated, or when mental-health bureaux were formed in the mental-health sector. One of the most essential changes was that the old craftsman's profession was turned into a group practitioner, and definitely from the position of a superior to the role of the group leader. Many experienced it as an overwhelming change and never accepted this new mode. For them, the most important value was that the organization is such that there is me and the patient and nobody else. So that is the simple model. In a way, you are perhaps approaching this old basic pattern again, in which you perhaps regain certain values that are considered important. Well, the message here is that change always entails factors which touch the balance of our self-esteem and they are very difficult. There are offences that cannot be undone, and they leave scars which will always be visible in an organization. They are marks which stay, and they will always be there underneath the surface, easily activated when there is a conflict situation. Do you want to comment or discuss this?
>
> *Senior administrative doctor*: I would most strongly agree with what you said. We who have this historical memory, well not very historical because it was not so long ago, we have perhaps experienced this loss and sorrow in that transition phase. And now we'll return to the good

old days, as they say. But the problem here is that most health-centre physicians are so young, because of this doctor boom, that they of course do not remember this and they can only listen with interest, to hear how things used to be.

Visiting psychiatrist: The same applies very clearly to health-guidance nurses, perhaps in some cases more strongly than to doctors.

Doctor XVI: Well, I would now say that in a certain respect it is a question of returning to craftsman's tradition. But only in a very special sense. To a very essential extent we are facing an altogether different transition. To some degree we can say that it requires increasing the direct responsibility between the personnel and the patients. The health centre actually meant the formation of a working team. It is this that we aim to continue, that is quite central. So it won't change so that doctors will care for their patients as lone wolves in some bureaux. But in a certain sense one can say that the responsibility between the care-giver and the patient increases from the present. I mean, this has been an intermediate stage, where the organization is responsible and the staff are small cogs, so in this respect of course. I must emphasize in this connection that this does not mean a return to working alone or to this old municipal-doctor system.

Doctor X: Then there is the very clear difference here, namely that the old authority of the doctor is not going to exist in the same sense. The doctor is more like a consultant to people, and almost all patients are more emancipated in their reactions. I too have seen some of the municipal-doctor time and lived through the transition and seen those years, how one must learn to speak with people in a quite different way. Not like 'do what I say', you can't manage that way any more.

Senior administrative doctor: The population has changed, too.

Junior researcher: I'd like to continue what the preceding speakers have said and emphasize that we are not returning to the old. We are stepping into a new phase. Quite essential things have changed. Patients are quite different from what they were during the municipal-doctor system. We have new kinds of tools and new ones are continuously developed. We have new kinds of rules that regulate the work, compared to the so-called good old days. We have a different working community and division of labour. So you can say that we are in a transition toward a new way of working. I would definitely not say that we are returning to the old.

Doctor XIII: People's attitudes to interaction with doctors are one example. I have a patient coming to visit me during my spare time, and I realize 'again we ended up talking about illness – see, one cannot talk otherwise with a doctor'. This could be a spot for change. So that the doctor's talk would be understood as a human being talking as such, not only as a role speaking. So this could result in a situation where I as an authority meet a patient on a street and he may ask how my knee is feeling.

Visiting psychiatrist: It is also a question of whether we respond to these role expectations or not. But of course we ought to act in the role of a doctor when we are working as doctors, and then we should carry another role if we are in another role. It is of course the best way to teach and change other people's conceptions.

Permanent consulting psychiatrist: I have one question in my mind, since we are thinking about this transition process, a question that I cannot answer myself. So I ask whether you have any idea. The question is, could we have built the new legislation on the foundation of the patient–doctor relationship, instead of the present patient–health centre relationship? Here we are trying to repair that gap with the help of the population-responsibility principle. Well, in England the primary-care physician is more a private practitioner. That's the way they did it. But even they have these so-called excessive users who go around from one doctor to another, who are a real problem here. I cannot answer this.

Visiting psychiatrist: Surely it would have been quite possible. If one thinks about the old system, its natural continuation would have been this. But one has to remember that health care is a part of the society's welfare policy, and big health-care reforms do not necessarily emerge out of the inner development of health care. They are so-called policy, politics in a broad sense, created in other sectors of the society, at upper levels, although in the last analysis it is the people that creates and decides about them. But in practice they are created in the echelons of chief officials and state administration, not even at the level of municipalities. And if one thinks about the societal development at that time, obviously that phase just had to be passed through. Such were the opinions and the atmosphere at that time.

Permanent consulting psychiatrist: Institutional optimism.

Doctor XVI: Well, I would say that probably there was institutional optimism around, too. But we should of course take into account the quantitative aspect, too. Already in the documents of the early 1970s they talk about closeness and about such small areas and even about continuity of care. On the other hand the situation was such that when the new legislation was implemented, we had about 650 municipal doctors altogether. The planning started with the emphasis on rationalizing physicians' work as far as possible by squeezing out all the capacity and by delegating tasks to other staff. And at that time in the instructions for the construction of health-centre buildings they said that two rooms were required for one doctor, so the doctor would shuttle back and forth while the patients were quickly taking their clothes off. And then they started this division of labour with the health-guidance nurses, which contained principles of popular health care but which actually was based on resource considerations to a large extent. So there was a vision of closeness and familiarity, but at that time it remained invisible. It would have been impossible to realize it in those conditions.

This discussion demonstrates an interesting restructuring in the field of secondary remembering. The lore of 'returning to the municipal-doctor system' gains corporeality as it is brought into the activity system by the visiting psychiatrist, the senior administrative doctor, and the permanent consulting psychiatrist. These three obviously represent seniority and authority. But they – especially the visiting psychiatrist and the administrator – are also outsiders who are marketing a view not born out of concrete experience and evidence from the local activity system. The visiting psychiatrist opens the sequence with an action of secondary remembering which might be depicted as follows (Figure 8.7). The visiting psychiatrist externalizes his notion of 'transition as a mistake' and invokes the external, publicly available lore of 'return to the municipal-doctor system' (move number 1 in Figure 8.7). He offers this explanation to the core members of the activity system in a very personal form, using words like 'self-esteem', 'offences' and 'scars' (move 2 in Figure 8.7).

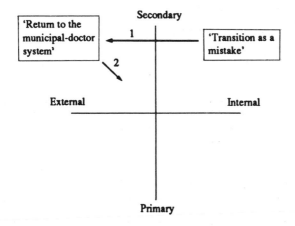

Figure 8.7 *The initial action of secondary remembering by the visiting psychiatrist*

In addition to this analysis, we need a framework to analyse more closely the contents of the arguments presented. In Figure 8.8, we characterize the contents of the initial argument of the visiting psychiatrist and the senior administrative doctor with the help of a simple field structure. The contents of the initial argument of the authorities are clearly dichotomous. The municipal-doctor system is characterized positively. The health-centre system is depicted mainly by negation, as a loss of earlier positive aspects. Group practice is presented in the same light, as a loss of individual autonomy.

	MUNICIPAL-DOCTOR SYSTEM	HEALTH-CENTRE SYSTEM
POSITIVE ARGUMENT	Craftsman profession; superior position; direct personal relationship between doctor and patient	
NEGATIVE ARGUMENT		Group practitioner

Figure 8.8   *Contents of the initial argument of the authorities*

The three doctors from within the activity system reject the argument of the authorities. At first, the three doctors' counter-argument may look like a mirror image, like an exact opposite of the initial argument of the authorities. But there are important differences. One noticeable feature is that, in contradistinction to the visiting psychiatrist, each of the three doctors refers to personal experiences and concrete evidence from the work practice. This perspective is reflected in the use of the personal pronouns 'I' and 'we' in connection with concrete external events and organizational practices. The senior administrative doctor also uses 'we', but only in connection with internal experiences, feelings and projections.

> *Doctor XVI*: The health centre actually meant the formation of a working team. *It is this that we aim to continue*, that is quite central. So it won't change so that doctors will care for their patients as lone wolves in some bureaux. But in a certain sense one can say that the responsibility between the care-giver and the patient increases from the present. I mean, this has been an intermediate stage, where the organization is responsible and the staff are small cogs, so in this respect of course.
>
> *Doctor X*: *I too have seen* some of the municipal-doctor time and lived through the transition and seen those years, how one must learn to speak with people in a quite different way. Not like 'do what I say', you can't manage that way any more.
>
> *Doctor XIII*: *I have a patient coming to visit me* during my spare time, and *I realize* 'again we ended up talking about illness – see, one cannot talk otherwise with a doctor'. This could be a spot for change. So that the doctor's talk would be understood as a human being talking as such, not only as a role speaking. So this could result in a

	MUNICIPAL-DOCTOR SYSTEM	HEALTH-CENTRE SYSTEM
POSITIVE ARGUMENT	Direct responsibility between personnel and patients	Working team; doctor as consultant instead of authority; patients are emancipated
NEGATIVE ARGUMENT	Doctor as lone wolf; doctor as authority	Organization is responsible, staff are small cogs; intermediate stage

Figure 8.9   *Contents of the counter-argument of the health-centre physicians*

situation where I as an authority meet a patient on a street and he may ask how my knee is feeling. (Italics added in the excerpts)

The contents of the counter-argument of the three doctors may be summed as follows (Figure 8.9). The counter-argument is actually a combination of positive and negative aspects in both the old and the present system of general practice. Such a complex argument leads to the conclusion that there is something to be learned from the past, something to be preserved from the present, and most importantly, something new to be created. The counter-argument is constructed jointly. Doctor XVI presents the team aspect of the argument, while doctors X and XIII put forward the aspect of change in patients and in the doctor–patient relationship. In spite of the quite determined tone, especially in the talk of doctor XVI, there is an emergent, searching quality in the counter-argument as a whole. What ensues as a joint argument against returning to the old system and for developing something new instead is obviously not a preconceived standpoint formulated and planned ahead of time. It seems likely that at least for doctors X and XIII the external argumentation takes the lead and paves the way for internal remembering actions.

This kind of personally and concretely argued unity among the doctors seems to be something of a surprise to the senior administrative doctor. He senses the atmosphere and backs up from his initial plea by giving mild support to doctors XVI and X ('The population has changed, too'). Our junior researcher joins the three doctors in a way which might be interpreted as an attempt to manipulate them. However, in the given field of forces, she could hardly dictate anybody's opinion. The three doctors are not relying on her in their standpoints.

In the initial interviews, each of the three doctors expressed a different conception of the transition from the municipal-doctor system to the health-centre system. Having consciously confronted materials concerning the history of general practitioners' work, and having taken the challenge of planning jointly a qualitatively new model for their own work, these doctors exhibit no more nostalgia about the 'good old days'. Paradoxically the senior administrative doctor complains about the lack of secondary memory among these younger doctors. The reactions of the three doctors demonstrate the fundamental difference between an individual's tacit secondary memory (fuelled by the popular lore of 'return to the good old days') and a collective secondary memory re-mediated by examining external aids, such as historical documents.

Towards the end of the excerpt, the permanent consulting psychiatrist asks whether it would have been possible to design the necessary reform on the basis of the old system. The answer of the visiting psychiatrist demonstrates the inner dilemma embedded in his line of argument. He begins affirmatively by stating that 'surely it would have been possible', then he denies that possibility ('obviously that phase just had to be passed through') by resorting to the notion of overwhelming external political forces 'at upper levels' of the society. Doctor XVI breaks this abstract dilemma by providing publicly available concrete data from the time of the transition.

We are here witnessing a reconstruction of an accessible secondary memory in an activity system. This reconstruction takes place in a process of verbal discourse and argumentation. But the reconstruction is not just an outgrowth of an opportune social situation. To interpret it only on the basis of the recorded interaction could indeed lead to a grave misunderstanding. As Cicourel (1987) points out, tape-recorded discourse data require ethnographic context if the researcher wants to go beyond formal analysis. However, in our case, standard ethnography is not enough. To understand how it was possible that the doctors defied authorities and put forward an offensive and optimistic version of history, one needs data on the developmental process that took place between the initial interviews and the actual argumentation – in this case, data on events over a time span of more than one-and-a-half years.

Here we encounter a limitation common to all the three modes of analysis taken up in this chapter. Ethnographic accounts are typically spatially, not temporally, orientated. So are ideal-typical empirical analyses of forms of thought – recall Marton's metaphor of 'a gigantic *space* of categories'. And so are most analyses of discourse, in spite of their processual character. In discourse and conversation analysis, time is a factor that is seldom addressed seriously. Although discourse is seen as emergent interaction, the time slices actually studied are usually very limited.

For the study of developmental processes like the one leading to a reconstruction of the secondary memory among the health-centre staff, a rather specific notion of time is required. It is a notion between macro-historical time and ontogenetic time. We might call it activity-genetic time, indicating our interest in the formation and reconstruction of collective activity systems in time (see Engeström, 1987). The design and implementation of corresponding methods of data collection and analysis constitute a task of increasing importance for investigations in socially shared human cognition and activity.

References

Armstrong, D. (1983) *Political Anatomy of the Body: Medical Knowledge in Britain in the 20th Century*. Cambridge: Cambridge University Press.
Billig, M., Condor, S., Edwards, D., Gane, M., Middleton, D. and Radley A. (1988) *Ideological Dilemmas: a Social Psychology of Everyday Thinking*. London: Sage.
Bronfenbrenner, U. (1979) *The Ecology of Human Development: Experiments by Nature and by Design*. Cambridge, MA: Harvard University Press.
Cicourel, A.V. (1987) 'The interpenetration of communicative contexts: examples from medical encounters', *Social Psychology Quarterly*, 50: 217–26.
Engeström, Y. (1987) *Learning by Expanding: an Activity-theoretical Approach to Developmental Research*. Helsinki: Orienta-Konsultit.
Engeström, Y., Engeström, R., Helenius, J. and Koistinen, K. (1987) 'Developmental study of the work of health-centre physicians' (in Finnish). Technical report. Espoo: Board of Health of the City of Espoo.
Halbwachs, M. (1951/80) *The Collective Memory*. New York: Harper & Row.
Harré, R., Clarke, D. and DeCarlo, N. (1985) *Motives and Mechanisms: an Introduction to the Psychology of Action*. London: Methuen.
Hirschhorn, L. (1984) *Beyond Mechanization: Work and Technology in a Postindustrial Age*. Cambridge, MA: MIT Press.
Jacoby, R. (1975) *Social Amnesia: a Critique of Conformist Psychology from Adler to R.D. Laing*. Sussex: Harvester.
Kauttu, K., Reinilä, A.-M. and Voutilainen, A. (1983) *Kunnanlääkärien työ ja olämä* (The work and life of municipal doctors). Helsinki: Suomen Lääkärillitto.
Leontiev, A.N. (1959/81) *Problems of the Development of the Mind*. Moscow: Progress.

Leontiev, A.N. (1978) *Activity, Consciousness, and Personality*. Englewood Cliffs, NJ: Prentice-Hall.

Marton, F. (1984) 'Towards a psychology beyond the individual', in K.M.J. Lagerspetz and P. Niemi (eds), *Psychology in the 1990s*. Amsterdam: North-Holland.

Norman, D.A. (1988) *The Psychology of Everyday Things*. New York: Basic Books.

Suchman, L.A. (1987) *Plans and Situated Actions: the Problem of Human-Machine Communication*. Cambridge: Cambridge University Press.

Vygotsky, L.S. (1978) *Mind in Society: the Development of Higher Psychological Processes*. Cambridge, MA: Harvard University Press.

Wertsch, J.V. (ed.) (1981) *The Concept of Activity in Soviet Psychology*. Armonk, NY: M.E. Sharpe.

Wertsch, J.V. (1987) 'Collective memory: Issues from a sociohistorical perspective', *Quarterly Newsletter of the Laboratory of Comparative Human Cognition*, 9: 19–22.

Zinchenko, P.I. (1939/83) 'The problem of involuntary memory', *Soviet Psychology*, 22: 55–111.

9
Sharing Knowledge, Celebrating Identity: Community Memory in a Service Culture

Julian E. Orr

Field study of photo-copier repair technicians indicates that community memory is crucially important to the service task. I use the term 'community memory' here to refer to those things known in common by all or most competent members of the technician community, the working set of current knowledge shared among technicians. The social distribution of this knowledge is not perfectly uniform, but members of the community also know who of their number is most likely to know those answers which they do not. The technicians freely exchange information about machines and customers, paying special attention to problems, changes or peculiarities, including both information about new or undocumented machine problems and critical information about the social labyrinths in which the machines are to be found. To understand the importance of community memory for the work, one must first know something of the work and of the social situation, including the machines, in which service occurs.

The task of service is commonly held to be the diagnosis, repair and maintenance of machines, and these are certainly part of the task. However, machine problems may actually be problems in the social relationship between customer and machine, and a large part of service work might better be described as the repair and maintenance of the social setting. Each machine is embedded in the social context of the customer site, and indeed, is placed there by the technicians according to arrangements between the customer and the sales force. The site is the customer's place of business, and those working there, including the machine, are organized to pursue the customer's ends. The customers tend to think and speak of the machine in terms of its participation in their activities, and these terms may differ from those used by the technicians.

Diagnosis of problems may be difficult for both social and technical reasons. The problem may be social, rooted in some mismatch or misunderstanding between machine and customers or in language differences between customers and technicians. The customer may be presumed to know vital information about the behaviour of the machine, having experienced and reported the problem, but this information is only available if the technician and the customer manage to agree on a common set of terms in which to discuss it. Diagnosis may be technically problematic in that the state of the machine itself is often unclear. In all of these cases, definition of the problem, or of the state of the machine, is accomplished through social interaction between technician, customer and machine.

The practice of maintenance and repair is equally problematic. This practice includes the cleaning, adjustment, repair and replacement of mechanical and electro-mechanical components of the machine. The skilled practice of these operations is informed by tacit knowledge (Polanyi, 1958; 1967), which may be thought of both as the ability to do things without being able to explain them completely and also the inability to learn to do them from a theoretical understanding of the task. Collins (1985) discusses the nature of tacit knowledge among scientists building TEA lasers; the critical aspect of this knowledge is the ability to differentiate those details which are important from those which are not in an indefinitely long list of details. Part of the tacit knowledge of TEA-laser construction, for example, is to know when electrical wires have the quality of 'length'. The two ends of a wire are often said to be electrically the same point, but in some electronic circuits and in parts of the TEA laser circuitry wire length becomes critical. Such tacit knowledge, even combined with theoretical knowledge of the domain, does not completely define the domain; one only knows if one knows how to build a TEA laser by having done so, and success cannot necessarily be duplicated. The tacit knowledge of technicians likewise differentiates the mass of available information about a machine into those points which are known to be important and those which are not, with a similar caveat that those which are thought to be unimportant may turn out to be critical in any given case. Neither tacit nor formal knowledge permits the technicians to predict success in all cases; a working machine is the only real demonstration that one's knowledge was sufficient.

Details of practice, including aspects of tacit knowledge, are part of the information circulating in the community memory. The common experience of practice provides the context which makes meaningful those points which could never be explained without the experience. In some cases, they do not become completely meaningful until the technician encounters a comparable situation, but these points at least registered in sufficient detail that the context could be recognized. Accordingly, the technicians' stories are full of previously insignificant details, instructions for practice in the form of short cuts and fixes, and new ways in which the relationship of customer, machine and technician can take paths never anticipated.

According to Akrich and Latour (Akrich, 1987; Latour, 1986; 1988), machines participate in human society. Machines perform social functions and prescribe certain behaviours for human actors. Furthermore, machines must be considered in their social settings; they must be seen simultaneously as products of the social context of their design and production and as participants in the pursuits of the users. From the perspective of the technicians, this reveals the complexity of a service call. It is not simply a matter of finding out what is wrong with the machine; there may be nothing wrong with the machine as a thing, in and of itself. The problem may rather lie in the interaction of the machine as it is, the uses its designers anticipated for it, and the uses and methods desired, understood and chosen by the customers. The designers' interpretation of how one would use the machine cannot preclude other interpretations, but the others, because unanticipated, may be unsuccessful. This may appear to be a problem to the customer whose interpretation of how to use the machine fails.

Should there actually be something wrong with the machine as a thing, another complication arises. The service documentation is commonly thought to be a source of information to use when the machine's behaviour is problematic. However, the documentation is not a pure or complete representation of the machine and its prescriptions, but must be regarded as a mechanism in and of itself. It is a device by which someone attempts to provide information to the technicians, but the information is selected and arranged according to the documentation designers' interpretation of what is necessary for the tasks which they wish the technicians to perform. Thus, its repertoire depends heavily upon the designers' understanding of the tasks involved in service and upon their choice of what it is that the technician is to do.

Some current documentation, known as directive documentation, is designed not to enable deduction but to direct the technician to the solution through a minimal decision tree. That is, the technician is directed to perform a series of actions and tests, and the results of tests cause the sequence to branch in different directions, until the results of a final test dictate a repair procedure. The premiss is that the most efficient diagnostic sequence can be determined in advance and provided for the technician to use. This directive documentation may omit information which would contribute to understanding the problem. The success of this scheme clearly depends on the success of the documentation designer in correctly anticipating and providing for the troubles which occur in the field, and this success has proved elusive.

There are many reasons why it is difficult if not impossible to create such documentation. The machine changes, both through use and through modification, and the problems experienced with the machine change accordingly. Although there are procedures for incorporating lessons from the field into the documentation, it cannot happen until after the problem appears, so for some period new problems must be solved by the technicians without the documentation. More importantly, the premiss of such documentation is false. First, it presumes that machines can be known in some complete sense, and so far that has not proved to be true. Secondly, it presumes that problems with the machines themselves are the only problems in the service world, and I have tried to suggest above that this is not so. Finally, it presumes that comprehensive instructions are possible, and there is a body of work in ethnomethodology which suggests that this presumption is equally false (Garfinkel 1967; Suchman, 1987). Instructions must ultimately be interpreted in the context of their application, and this context will differ in ways that cannot be anticipated from that imagined by the person writing the instructions. Beyond these objections, even if documentation designers could successfully predict the myriad possible problems and design appropriate diagnostic strategies, success of such documentation would also depend on the users, the technicians, making the anticipated use of the documentation.

The technicians, however, use the documents in pursuit of their own goals, and these are only somewhat the same as those of the designers of the documentation. A technician's primary goal is to keep the customer happy, which includes, but is not limited to, fixing the machine as necessary. Customers normally lease machines and may cancel those leases at any time; this may happen due to dissatisfaction with service as well as dissatisfaction with the machine itself. Under these circumstances, customer satisfaction is of primary importance to the corporation; through the use of customer satisfaction surveys to rate technician performance, the corporation makes customer satisfaction equally important to the technicians.

'Don't fix the machine; fix the customer!' is a slogan which I heard from several technicians. Technicians with no service calls to do perform 'courtesy calls', visiting their accounts both to check on the machines and to converse with those responsible for the machines to see if any problems are developing. Part of keeping the customer happy is keeping the customer assured that the situation is under control, and most technicians observed are quite diligent about finding the person responsible for the machine and explaining its problem and repairs. This is particularly true for difficult problems which occur intermittently; in such circumstances the fact that the machine is working cannot be taken as a sure sign that the problem is solved. The point of telling the customer what has happened is to establish that the problem was addressed in a professional manner, and this requires being able to tell what the machine is doing and being able to say what was done to fix it. Directive documentation might solve a problem, but if the information is not there which would allow the technician to explain the problem and its fix to the customer, neither technician nor customer could feel particularly confident that future problems would be solved. Consequently, directive documentation may be used by the technicians, but in doing so they try to determine the purpose of the various tests, to understand what the documentation is testing, to know what they are doing.

This is not done just so one can impress the customer. The commonest machine failures, which are the ones most likely to be correctly anticipated by documentation designers, quickly become routine for the experienced technician and no longer require documentation. The unusual, rare, exotic failure modes are much harder to anticipate and may not occur with sufficient frequency to justify more efforts to anticipate them. However, for the customer whose valued machine is not functioning, the rarity of the failure is small consolation. The technician who is responsible for the machine must still fix it in order to preserve the social contract with the customer,[1] who expects the technician to be able to fix the machine, and possibly to preserve the legal contract between the two corporations. Accordingly, the technicians' work life includes the necessity to prepare to solve completely unanticipated problems, and this requires learning everything one can about the machine, not in any expectation of complete understanding but rather with an awareness that any point may turn out to be crucial for some future problem. This need to know reveals another problem with the directive documentation: the technicians expect to learn from each other's experience, but the absence of information about the tests in the documentation makes it impossible for the technicians to talk to each other about what they have done. This creates another reason to interpret the documentation as they use it, to try to learn from the actions which it directs.

Thus, there are social and technical reasons why the technicians require a good verbal understanding of the machines and both technical and policy reasons why the documentation may not provide all the information they need. Some technicians develop contacts elsewhere in the corporation who may be able to supply needed information; other information is developed experimentally in the course of fixing machines with new problems. This results in a tentative association of symptom and repair strategy which may or may not be confirmed by later experience. Information from whatever source is shared freely among the technicians, and this communal understanding or community memory is sufficiently important that one may think of the technicians as a community of knowledge.

One significant factor in the functioning of this community is that there appears to be every incentive to share information and virtually none to keep it private. Personal animosity motivates the few known instances of withholding information from another technician. This may be between individuals, or a group may decide to withhold information from a team-mate in an attempt to force that person to leave. There are no other reasons because information kept private cannot contribute to a technician's reputation. There is no way to solve a difficult problem and have it known without telling the story. Fixing the machine does not contribute to reputation because that is what one is expected to do. Problems are not permitted to continue long enough to acquire a reputation such that solving one would be heroic. Problems which do persist are usually addressed in collaborative trouble-shooting sessions such that the solution would be known anyway. The characteristics of the work are such that the only way for one's work to be known to one's peers is to tell them, and the only way to make it interesting is to have a difficult problem and present it so as to be recognized as such by other competent practitioners.

There are practical reasons for sharing information with one's colleagues as well. Technicians have assigned territories, collections of machines in some degree of geographic contiguity, but machine failures are irregular and unpredictable. Consequently, they cannot work only on their own machines, nor can they be the only ones to work on their machines. Machines are thus serviced collectively, although some degree of responsibility remains with the assigned technician. For each technician, then, sharing information enables the other technicians to work as efficiently as possible. For each technician this means that when out of territory the machine will have been well serviced, reducing the work to be done on each call, and ensures that other technicians will do a competent job when servicing one's own machines, reducing potential conflict with one's customers.

The utility of sharing information is recognized and encouraged, both informally and, to some extent, officially. I have argued elsewhere (Orr, 1986; 1987) that war stories, anecdotes of experience, serve as a vehicle of community memory for the technicians, to share information gained in diagnosis with those members of the community who were not there. The war stories told in this community are particularly apt for this purpose because of their situated quality. This derives from Suchman's definition of situated action: 'That term underscores the view that every course of action depends in essential ways upon its material and social circumstances' (1987: 50). The war stories are situated in that they combine facts about the machine with the context of specific situations. The contextual information demonstrates the claimed validity of the facts of the story, guiding the integration of those facts to the hearer's model of the machine. The context also constrains the application of that augmented model by defining the situation in which those facts are known to be true. War stories may actually be told during difficult diagnoses, as technicians search for inspiration to integrate the recalcitrant facts before them. Such war stories are doubly situated, first in the context of their origin and then in that of their telling and possible application, and the comparison of the two situations has much to do with the degree of their usefulness. However, utilitarian sharing of information does not seem to be the primary motivation for telling stories. Technicians talk about machines and customers, talk about their current problems and tell stories about situations they have seen not because to do so is useful but because it is interesting. They have a deep and abiding interest in the characters and social dramas of their world, and their stories both make sense of events and make *something* of their world, presenting their actions as an achievement to notice.

The literature on stories seems to be divided between that which seeks to define stories and specify their structure and grammar, and that which discusses their multiple roles in social interaction. I shall briefly consider some points from the latter camp. Renato Rosaldo (1986) finds Ilongot hunting stories particularly revealing of Ilongot culture in that they emphasize the portions of hunting experience which Ilongot find interesting, omit those portions which every culturally competent listener knows and finally celebrate the hunter's prowess, marking culturally valued behaviour in the process. Turner (1980) tells us that narratives make explicit the meanings inherent in the social dramas which they portray or to which they even belong. In doing so, they make sense out of what has happened in a way which provides a model for things to happen in the future. Early (1982) also sounds the sense-making theme, as her informants, traditional residents of Cairo, use narratives to set illness in context, evaluate options and make sense of the situation. An important point to this use of narrative is the role of finding or creating meaning in an inherently ambiguous situation. The use of narrative as a response to ambiguity appears in the court-room analysis of Bennett and Feldman (1981), which suggests the value of viewing trials as competing narratives interpreting approximately the same set of facts. They note that cultural differences between the jury and participants in the trial may make some stories incomprehensible to the jury and therefore unlikely to be judged true. Successful stories, then, require a certain degree of culture in common between teller and listeners. Smith (1980) notes that stories must in fact be seen as social transactions between teller and audience, that the words of a story are determined by the context in which it is told as well as by the subject.

There are three principal points here which one should bear in mind. First, the idea of using stories to make sense of ambiguous situations; secondly, the fact that the details told are those important to the natives; and thirdly, the idea that the telling is as situated as the incident recounted. We shall consider three versions of a single story, two versions occurring in a single antiphonal recitation and one told under rather different circumstances.[2] The first two versions were told during the last of a series of prolonged trouble-shooting episodes. The machine had recently been installed in a new building and had never worked reliably. Failure consistently produced definite error messages of a specific type; however, changing the indicated components did not change the behaviour of the machine. This particular customer had many machines and even an assigned technician; should the customer have become unhappy enough to cancel the contract, the cost of failure to solve this problem would have been greater than normal. The team's technical specialist, whose job combines roles as trouble-shooting consultant, supervisor and occasional instructor in technical matters for the team of technicians, had joined the technician responsible for the machine in addressing the latest appearance of this problem. A dozen stories were told during this session, as the two searched their memories for possible culprits, looking for the key perspective which would integrate their random facts. This story appeared early in the session.

There are some technical terms which appear in the story; their exact meaning is irrelevant here, but it may be useful to differentiate the categories of interest. The first is components; those mentioned are dicorotrons (or dicors for short), the shield, which is part of the dicorotron, and the XER board, one of the machine's circuit boards. The 24-volt Interlock Power Supply is not exactly a component but is an output from a power supply controlled by numerous safety interlocks. It is only present when all of the interlocks are closed, so the observation that the relay switching it has opened is significant. Another pertinent category is error codes, such as E053 and F066; these are diagnostic error codes, and the documentation contains procedures to track down the causes of each error code. The problem is that some error codes can be produced by problems other than those anticipated by the documentation. The final category of interest here is what is referred to as the 'dC20 error log', a record, maintained by the machine, of various events in its history. Accumulation of entries in this log is very useful in diagnosis.

This story was triggered by the observation that the characteristic failure of the machine includes opening the 24-Volt Interlock Relay. The curious point about this recitation is that the two are telling the same story, they are talking about their personal encounters with the same problem, but the two versions are significantly different:

The False E053 Error[3]

> *Technical specialist*: See, this runs along with the problems we've run into when you have a dead shorted dicorotron. It blows the circuit breaker and you get a 24-volt interlock problem. And you can chase that thing forever, and you will NEVER, NEVER find out what that is.
>
> *Technician*: Yes, I know, E053, try four new dicors . . .
>
> *Technical specialist*: But, if you went in . . . OK, you won't . . . You lose your 24, that's what it is: you're losing your 24-volt out of the power supply, but that's not what it's caused by. Now the key there, though, is when you pull up your dC20 log, you get hits in the XER board.
>
> *Technician*: Yeah. The other thing is as you're going on and on and getting E053s, you get, yeah, . . . F066 . . . in the sequence . . .
>
> *Technical specialist*: If you're lucky enough for it to run long enough, you'll get an F066 problem which leads you back into the dicorotrons – you check them – yeah, I've got one that's a dead short. You change it and everything's fine, but if you don't . . . if you're not lucky enough to get that F066 or don't look at the dC20 log; it's really a grey area . . .
>
> *Technician*: Well, dC20 logs . . . when I ran into that I had hits in the XER a few times previously, so I was tending to ignore it until I was cascading through after an E053 which is primary, I'm cascading to see what else I've got – F066 – what the hell's this? Noise?
>
> *Technical specialist*: E053, which one's that?
>
> *Technician*: Well, that's a . . . that's a 24 . . . lock. . . .
>
> *Technical specialist*: 24 Interlock failure? Yeah. We did . . . I did that not knowing when they changed the circuitry in the XER board, normally if you had a shorted dicorotron, it'd fry the XER board – just cook it. Now they've changed the circuitry to prevent frying of that, but now it creates a different problem.

Ethnographer: This is with your dicor shorted to ground or . . . ?
Technical specialist: Probably shorted to DC shield.
Ethnographer: Ah hah, yeah . . . yuck.
Technician: Mm. I see.
Technical specialist: OK, and then that goes [*snaps his fingers*], you know. That's where it's popping the breaker, and when it does that, that's when you end up with . . . through the boards, it pops it, before it pops the breaker, because you don't have any DC boards . . . you'll get a DC Interlock, . . . 24-volt DC interlock failure. Now that came about after these boards came out and I've gotten burned twice on that same problem. I guess I . . . that four hours of sticking my head in the machine and tracing 24-volt interlock problem the first time didn't do it. The second time, it took me a long time, and it finally dawned on me – what the hell am I doing – get in there and that's what it was. Now I've had very intermittent dicorotron problem – same thing – guy sits there, and he says 'I've got . . .', he says it's intermittent, once, maybe twice a day; you shut it off, turn it on, and it will run . . . just a 24-volt interlock failure problem. So I asked him about the dC20 log and he said 'Yeah, I had XER failure' – I says OK – he says, I checked all the dicorotrons – I said, you're going to have to stress test 'em for a long period – 4 to 5 minutes in the high . . . you know, in your dicorotron check-out where you really, you've got the currents boosted up on 'em . . . and yeah, after about 4 minutes one of them [*snaps his fingers*] glitched.

The gist of the story, then, is that there is, first, a red herring, an E053 error code which is not to be believed, which may be followed by a second error code, F066, indicating the true culprit, a shorted dicorotron. Failure to remember the connection between the E053 which is not a problem and a shorted dicorotron could mean a long, frustrating, futile attempt to diagnose the problem. In my previous work (Orr, 1986; 1987), I found that the use of story-telling both to preserve knowledge and to consider it in subsequent diagnoses coincides with the narrative character of diagnosis. That is, the key element of diagnosis is the situated production of understanding through narration, in that the integration of the various facts of the situation is accomplished through a verbal consideration of those facts with a primary criterion of coherence. The process is situated, in Suchman's terms, in that both the damaged machine and the social context of the user site are essential resources for both the definition of the problem and its resolution. The telling of the first two versions of this story happens in such a diagnostic situation as the two technicians consider their experience and examine it for applicability to their present problem. They are faced with a failing machine displaying diagnostic information which has previously proved worthless and in which no one has any particular confidence this time. They do not know where they are going to find the information they need to understand and solve this problem. In their search for inspiration, they tell stories.

The progress of the responses in this dual recitation underscores Smith's point that story-telling must be seen as an interaction between teller and hearer and suggests that these stories can only function as the community memory because of the situated nature of their telling (Smith, 1980). Although both versions are based on personal experience with the problem, they reflect significantly different views of the problem and apparently different approaches to the task of understanding the machine. The technician's version tells of a pattern-matching diagnosis, which associates a solution with the first error code: 'Yes, I know, E053, try four new dicors . . .' The appearance of the secondary, more important error code is not seen as problematic: 'The other thing is as you're going on and on and getting E053s, you get, yeah . . . F066 . . . in the sequence . . .' In the technical specialist's version, the appearance of the second error code is very doubtful: 'If you're lucky enough for it to run long enough, you'll get an F066 problem which leads you back into the dicorotrons.' For him, the problem is more reliably indicated by apparently random and insignificant entries in a particular part of the error log: 'Now the key there, though, is when you pull up your dC20 log, you get hits [logged events] in the XER board.' He suggests that even testing for the true fault may be problematic, requiring longer than usual periods of testing to provoke the fault under some circumstances: '. . . he says, I checked all the dicorotrons . . . I said, you're going to have to stress test 'em for a long period . . . 4 to 5 minutes in the high . . . you know, in your dicorotron check-out where you really, you've got the currents boosted up on 'em . . .' His version includes both the evolution of the problem, that it is the result of a fix preventing the same fault from destroying parts of the control system, and evolution of the understanding of the problem through his own history of performing the diagnosis. It is worth noting that the technical specialist's version associates the problem with a system, the 24-Volt Interlock, while the technician associates it with an error code. In fact, the specialist does not immediately recognize the error code when it occurs in the technician's version.

The misunderstanding about the error codes may be indicative of the difference in their approaches. The technical specialist begins thinking about the 24-Volt Interlock system and uses that as the entry point for this story about the same system. He does not make the connection to the error code, but then it is not obviously relevant because that is not the error code facing them. The senior technician recognizes the story, perhaps by the reference to a shorted dicorotron, but his pattern-matching version is based on the error codes. The link to the present situation is less obvious because the link of the error code to the 24-Volt Interlock system is hidden, and he stumbles when asked what the error code indicates.

There is a curious alternation in voice to be observed in the telling of the two versions of the story. Both tellers initially favour a generic second-person presentation: 'See, this runs along with the problems we've run into when you have a dead shorted dicorotron.' In this utterance one finds both a 'we' for the community experience and a 'you' for the abstracted technician encountering the problem. At this point the story concerns a class of problems that occur on this class of machine; there is no direct reference to personal experience. The two continue with this impersonal second person until the technical specialist says: '. . . if you're not lucky enough to get that F066 or don't look at the dC20 log; it's really a grey area . . .' This prompts the technician to change voice and tell his personal experience: 'Well, dC20 logs . . . when I ran into that I had hits in the XER a few times previously, so I was tending to ignore it until I was cascading through after an E053 which is primary, I'm cascading to see what else I've got – F066 – what the hell's this? Noise?' He had fallen for the trap described by the technical specialist but had been sufficiently lucky to have the secondary error code which indicates the true problem. The last long utterance by the technical specialist begins in the second person and switches to the first to recount his experience with the difficulty of remembering the association, a point he had been making earlier and probably his point in telling this particular story. Thus, the second person appears to be used to describe a specific problem in a somewhat abstracted way, while the first person is used for their personal experiences with this problem. This alternation of voice is also a movement here from the less-situated second person in no particular context to the situated first person account, and it seems to be the situated experience which gives credibility to the more general accounts.

There is a curious distribution of ellipsis and detail to observe in this story. The ellipsis leaves out so much that the story is only marginally recognizable as such to those outside the community of technicians. This ellipsis is common among the technicians: since every service call has essentially the same pattern, stories told among technicians need only discuss the interesting parts of this particular social drama. Like Rosaldo's Ilongot hunters, much of the story is uninteresting, because routine, and so omitted. There are differences in individual understanding among the technicians, but misunderstandings through excessive ellipsis can be adjusted in the conversation. It is clear that the technical specialist's tale relates two encounters with the problem, both successful, but there is nothing to indicate where or when they occurred, or how the first encounter was solved. Solution to the second occurred through the grace of a reluctant memory, reminding the technical specialist that this had happened before. Some of this detail is restored in the next version, so one must consider the importance of the selection in this telling and then consider the difference between the two occurrences to understand the different selections.

The principal theme of the technical specialist's version in this telling is that the problem as perceived is insoluble because the report is wrong. This also describes the problem confronting them. The lack of logical connection between the reported problem and the real problem makes the connection extremely fragile, as attested in the last utterance here, describing a second period of trouble-shooting the false problem until memory intervened. This recognition of tenuous and arbitrarily recovered connections between symptom and problem might be either inspiration or warning to them as they search for the real problem whose link to the present false symptom is either forgotten or undiscovered. The additional information about the origin of the problem and its known variant provides context for the tale which may prove valuable in considering its relevance to the new context.

Before continuing the discussion, there is a shorter version of this story I acquired three months later.[3] This is told during lunch at the branch office; the technical specialist encountered in the previous dialogue is playing cribbage and talking with various passers-by. One of the technicians on his team, who is not the same technician as in the previous episode, is going to have another researcher observing him the following day:

Technician: It'd be nice if I get an E053, . . . put in a short somewhere in the machine, that'd be good trouble-shooting. Sam [*the technical specialist*], why don't you go to High Tech [*a customer site*], Friday evening, and put in an E053 code, so I could find it, show this guy some trouble-shooting.
Technical specialist: You don't want me to do that.
Technician: I know, 'cause you'd probably make sure I couldn't find the damn thing and ruin my whole week.
Anonymous other technician: A short somewhere is kind of vague.
Technical specialist: No, it's not, not when you understand wiring.
Ethnographer: Oh. Well, there was that one that we had [*the technician, when I was observing him*], over at that first place you and I went, where there was the short because the RDH harness was in the wrong. . . .
Technician: Right.

Ethnographer: That's what you had in mind?
Technical specialist: No. [*Pause, deals.*] The common one is when you
have a shorted dicorotron . . . Can't even get the machine to run, it'll
cycle about twice and then shut down, and give you an E053.
Ethnographer: Oh, well, that's too easy. [*Pattern-matching . . .*]
Technical specialist: Well, it wasn't the first time I had that. [. . . *when
the pattern is not yet known.*]
Ethnographer: Where does the dicorotron short, to the shield?
Technical specialist: Direct arc. [*Pause for cribbage.*]
Ethnographer: From foreign matter or just, ah . . .
Technical specialist: . . . bad glass on the wire or something, a direct arc
. . . [*but he doesn't say where to. Long pause for cribbage.*] First time
with the new boards, the new XER board configuration, it wouldn't
cook the board if you had an arcing dicorotron. Instead, now it trips
the 24-volt Interlock in the low-voltage power supply, and when it
comes back . . . the machine will crash and when it comes back up
it'll give you an E053. It may or may not give you an F066 that tells
you the short is in, you know, check the xerographics. That's exactly
what I had down here, at the end of the hall, and Weber and I ran for
four hours trying to chase that thing. All it was was a bad dicorotron.
We finally got it, . . . run it long enough so that we got an E053 with
an F066, and the minute we checked the dicorotrons we had one that
was totally dead. Put a new dicorotron in it and it ran fine. [*Long
pause for cribbage.*] Yeah, that was a fun one. That's . . . the first
time . . . you know usually, if you have a real bad dicorotron, you
used to cook the boards, generally more than one. So, saved us
buying a lot of boards.

In the version the technical specialist tells here, the understandings seen in the previous two versions have converged, and the story
has become somewhat more concise and didactic. It is clear from
the start of this exchange that both the technician and the technical
specialist know they are discussing the same problem, and the
association of error codes with the problem is accepted by both. The
most dramatic difference is in the situation of its telling; and, while
the convergence may be due primarily to the passage of time, it
seems probable that the other qualitative differences stem from that
situation.

To begin, the scene is not one of crisis but occurs during a time of
relaxation; furthermore, this exchange occurs backstage at the
branch, away from customers and other non-initiates (with the
partial exception of the author)[4] nor is there any particular machine
involved. In this context, the technician feels free to express his
desire to demonstrate serious trouble-shooting prowess while being
observed by an outsider the following day. It should be noted that
such a display is only possible for an outsider; to another technician
he would merely be doing a competent job. Given the inherently
unpredictable nature of technicians' work, nothing interesting may

happen, and a planted problem could liven things up considerably for the visitor. Such planted problems are used in school as part of the technicians' training. However, the technicians have a saying, 'If it ain't broke, don't fix it', and this certainly extends to not breaking those things not yet broken. Their agreement on this recognizes both that there may be unforeseen consequences to perturbing a working machine and that the social situation is not that of school, where such consequences could be tolerated and used for learning. The working environment has the machines placed with customers for the customers' purposes; the social contract with the customer is based on the customers' need for outside expertise to keep the machine running and the technicians' possession of that expertise. The machines are sufficiently complex, and causality sufficiently vague, that one cannot be entirely sure of the consequences of doing things to them; even repair actions may change machine behaviour in unpredictable ways. This is an entirely acceptable risk when repairing a broken machine, but, given these considerations, planting a shorted dicorotron in a working machine to produce The False E053 Bug would be foolhardy in the extreme.

The story does not appear in this preliminary exchange between the technician and the technical specialist because both know whereof they speak, so elaboration would be pointless and uninteresting. The story is triggered by the fact that both an unidentified other technician and the ethnographer reveal their failure to understand the significance of the short which causes E053s. We were not privy to the community understanding of this problem which permits the two to speak in such elliptical terms. Part of the technical specialist's job is to see that the technicians keep their skill and information current, and he wanted me to understand what was going on, so the technical specialist responds with this rather didactic telling of the False E053 story. This version should perhaps be viewed as how the community ought to understand the problem.

Initially the technical specialist attempted to resolve our confusion with a short summary of cause and false error code: 'The common one is when you have a shorted dicorotron . . . Can't even get the machine to run, it'll cycle about twice and then shut down, and give you an E053.' Further questions produce the whole story, beginning with its appearance as the result of a fix to another problem, so that shorted dicorotrons now trip the 24-Volt Interlock Relay instead of destroying the XER board. Tripping the relay produces the E053 even though the problem is not really in the 24-Volt Interlock system. He mentions that the true error code, F066, might appear.

He then concludes with a first-person account of how hard it was to find this problem the first time he encountered it. The point of this is to emphasize to his listeners the importance of associating false E053 error codes with shorted dicorotrons; the use of the first person with so much situated detail, who else was with him and which specific machine it was, lends authenticity to the rest of the account. Some of the detail about the origin of the problem (and the disappearance of the 'cooked-board' problem) may appear extraneous, but it does enrich the hearer's understanding of the machine, and one never knows which piece of information will prove crucial as new problems continually appear. The apparent object is to keep all knowledge as closely connected as possible, so that if a new problem connects to any known facts at all, it connects to an understanding of the system with known failures and solutions on which to base a diagnostic strategy.

This in fact may be the key to the importance of community memory for the technicians. Diagnosing machines may be seen as *bricolage*, borrowing the concept from Lévi-Strauss. He wrote of the *bricoleur*.

> His universe of instruments is closed and the rules of his game are always to make do with 'whatever is at hand', that is to say with a set of tools and materials which is always finite and is also heterogeneous because what it contains bears no relation to the current project, or indeed to any particular project, but is the contingent result of all the occasions there have been to renew or enrich the stock . . . Consider him at work and excited by his project. His first practical step is retrospective. He has to turn back to an already existent set made up of tools and materials, to consider or reconsider what it contains and, finally and above all, to engage in a sort of dialogue with it and, before choosing between them, to index the possible answers which the whole set can offer to his problem. (1966: 17–19)

For my purposes, the significant aspect of *bricolage* is the reflective manipulation of a set of resources accumulated through experience, with the range of manipulation neither totally free nor constrained to the original manifestation of any element. Like the *bricoleur*, the technician has a closed set of information resources which do not necessarily provide definitive answers. The facts which are known about the particular machine must be examined in the light of experience to see which combination provides the most reasonable interpretation of the problematic situation. In the trouble-shooting episode in which the first two versions of the False E053 story appear, the two technicians examined a total of twelve stories from their collective experience, to see whether there was some way they could be applied to the present situation or whether there were constraining elements which ruled them out. The False E053 was told as a possible analogue to the problem situation; the fact that it involved the 24-Volt Interlock system suggested possible parallels, but the fact that the error code displayed was not E053 or in any way related to it ruled it out of serious consideration.

The technicians, then, are piecing together an understanding from bits of experience, their own or others', in the absence of definitive information. The documentation they have is not and cannot be a definitive resource. Each story, each fragment of community memory, is examined both for possible direct application and for what it could be, what it might suggest for further investigation. The stories combine facts about the machine with details of the context in which they are relevant, presenting both a fragment of theory about how the machine works with an illustrative example which both guides and constrains the application of the information about the machine. In this way, stories are well suited to this diagnostic *bricolage*, and the technicians display a fine *bricoleur*'s instinct in telling their stories, preserving the event in all its detail against the future chance to make something of it.

This one story in three versions on two occasions is a very small part of the community memory of the technicians, and yet it shows clearly two great themes of technician culture, the fragility of understanding and the fragility of control. Machines continually break, problems masquerade as other problems and the best resource the technicians have is to remember these connections between appearance and reality when they find them. The variation in the three versions shows something of the working of the community of knowledge. In the trouble-shooting session, the technical specialist is thinking of the different systems involved and of the evolution of the machine, while the technician makes an instant association between the shorted dicorotron and the false E053 code without apparently thinking of the systems involved at all. During lunch at the branch, we see the same experience and the same association being put into circulation, increasing the community memory as it is passed on to someone who has not yet heard.

Problems and solutions are only part of the information circulating in the community memory. The technicians circulate large amounts of quite mundane information through their conversations, tracking all the players in their world, the machines, their customers and themselves, but the machines hold the greatest interest. The machines have as much individuality as the humans, made unique by history and social setting. Technicians know each machine in their flock, their problems and their updates, and a technician who services another's machine will take the next opportunity to tell the responsible technician what was done and what is likely to develop.

In fact, the machines are both perverse and fascinating, and this is reflected in the technicians' stories. Earlier models featured both fires and explosions, and the stories describing the labour involved in recovering from such disasters are imbued with an affectionate pride. Catastrophes resulting from oversight are described with the same fond pride as part of the process of becoming a 'real technician'. The machines can be merely difficult, but the technical specialist's first version of the False E053 has no tinge of malice as he describes first the hours of trouble-shooting necessary to make the elusive connection between the inconclusive behaviour of the machine and the crucial failure and then the hours of retracing his steps another time until he remembers the first occasion. Indeed, how could he bear malice, for such a machine is a worthy opponent, partner, other. It is in terms of these machines and their situations that the technicians construct their own selves, both hero and fool, both in pride in coping with this perversity and in humility in acknowledging their failures.

'Why are we huddling about the campfire? Why do we tell tales, or tales about tales —? . . . Is it because we are so organized as to take actions that prevent our dissolution into the surroundings?' (Le Guin, 1980: 198).

So why do we tell stories? – or, more to the point, why do technicians tell stories about their encounters with customers and machines? I have suggested several reasons why the technicians invest so much energy in keeping each other informed. It is clear that the community memory preserves and circulates needed information, and yet this somewhat functionalist interpretation does not seem to be the whole story. Stories may be seen as products of diagnosis, in that the hardest part of diagnosis is making sense out of a fundamentally ambiguous set of facts, and this is done through a narrative process to produce a coherent account. In this view, the stories in the community memory are produced in the real work of diagnosis and are further useful because their form prepares them for use in the next narrative creation of sense out of facts. The first two versions of the story discussed above were told as part of this process of making sense of an ambiguous situation and are themselves the products of earlier struggles to make sense of ambiguity. The third telling is clearly circulating information, feeding the community memory. However, there still seems to be more going on in and around these stories. At the beginning of the scene in which the third story is told, the technician hopes for a problem which will permit him to display some good trouble-shooting to an outside observer; that is, he hopes for an opportunity to demonstrate that he is a technician, and being a technician can only be done through dealing with serious problems in machines at customer sites. One may come out of such an encounter as hero or as fool, and their stories recognize both possibilities, but it is the only way to be a technician. Their community memory is about being a technician, and it helps them to be technicians.

This construction of their identity as technicians occurs both in doing the work and in their stories, and their stories of themselves fixing machines show their world in what they consider the appropriate perspective. It is in telling stories of their encounters with machines and customers that they have the opportunity to show their work as the interesting and even heroic enterprise that it is. Myerhoff tells us:

> One of the most persistent but elusive ways that people make sense of themselves is to show themselves to themselves . . . by telling themselves stories. . . . More than merely self-recognition, self-definition is made possible by means of such showings, for their content may state not only what people think they are but what they should have been or may yet be. (1986: 261)

Indeed, in telling stories of how they solved difficult problems, the technicians are showing themselves as competent practitioners and are being competent practitioners through the preservation and circulation of knowledge. Telling stories of others' fixes shows that they have learned in a competent manner from the resources of the community. At the beginning of this essay I suggested that service work is only partially about the maintenance and repair of machines, and this is so. Service work really occurs in a triangular relationship of technicians, customers and machines. However, the definition of a technician is pinned to the relationship between technician and machine; and, of the three, information about the machine is the most problematic. The identity of technicians, then, is defined by the ability to do technical things to a machine. The skill that they demonstrate in fixing machine problems creates and proves this identity, and their stories celebrate this identity to themselves and others, while creating another part of the identity: member of the community, contributor to the community memory.

Notes

1. I use the term 'social contract' to refer to the understanding between technician and customers through which a potentially disruptive outsider, the technician, is allowed into the customers' work-place on the strength of the technician's claim to technical competence which offers solution to the customers' problems with their machine. It is actually a set of expectations and allowances which defines normal

behaviour between the two parties. It does require technical competence on the part of the technician.

2. I consider these different tellings to be the same story much as different versions of a folk-tale are considered to be the same story. The problem is the same, as is the path to solution, so the plot is constant. The protagonists are categorically identical, a machine and a technician; changing the name of the technician does not really change the story any more than changing the name of Cinderella. Finally, the technicians focus on the fact that the problem is the same, not that different people have experienced it.

3. This is a verbatim transcription from audio tape; however, no attempt was made to get accurate timing information. Ellipsis does indicate a pause, but of no particular duration. The technical terms remain for verisimilitude, but they are better thought of as Widget 1, Widget 2 and so on, since their exact nature is irrelevant here. Proper names have all been changed.

4. The author worked nine years as a technician, although not in field service. In preparation for this research, I took the course in which these technicians are trained to fix these machines. This was done in order to understand better what they were doing while I was observing them. Serendipitously, the combination of school and experience also seemed to qualify me partially as one of them.

References

Akrich, Madeleine (1987) 'How can technical objects be described?', Working Paper, Centre for the Sociology of Innovation, Paris, published as 'Comment décrire les objets techniques', *Technique et Culture*, 5: 49–63.

Bennett, W. Lance and Feldman, Martha S. (1981) *Reconstructing Reality in the Courtroom*. New Brunswick, NJ: Rutgers University Press.

Collins, H.M. (1985) *Changing Order: Replication and Induction in Scientific Practice*. London: Sage.

Early, Evelyn (1982) 'The logic of well being: therapeutic narratives in Cairo, Egypt', *Science and Medicine*, 16: 1491–7.

Garfinkel, Harold (1967) *Studies in Ethnomethodology*. Englewood Cliffs, NJ: Prentice-Hall.

Latour, Bruno (1986) 'How to write "The Prince" for machines as well as for machinations', a working paper for the seminar on Technology and Social Change, Edinburgh, 12–13 June.

Latour, Bruno (1988) 'Sociology of a Door', *Social Problems*, 35 (3): 298–310. [Pseudonymously attributed to Jim Johnsons, Columbus Ohio School of Mines.]

Le Guin, Ursula K. (1980) 'It was a dark and stormy night; or, why are we huddling about the campfire?' in *On Narrative*, 1980.

Lévi-Strauss, Claude (1966) *The Savage Mind*. Chicago: University of Chicago Press.

Myerhoff, Barbara (1986) ' "Life Not Death in Venice": Its Second Life', in V.W. Turner and E.M. Bruner (eds), *The Anthropology of Experience*. Urbana and Chicago: University of Illinois Press.

On Narrative (1980) Special issue of *Critical Inquiry*, 7 (1). Chicago: University of Chicago Press.

Orr, J.E. (1986) 'Narratives at work: story telling as cooperative diagnostic activity', proceedings of the conference on Computer-Supported Cooperative Work, Austin, Texas, December. Reprinted in *Field Service Manager: The Journal of the Association of Field Service Managers International*, June 1987: 47–60.

Orr, J.E. (1987) 'Talking about machines: social aspects of expertise', in *The ARI Project: Section III: Research in Modeling, Reasoning, and Expertise: Four Papers from Research into the Semantics of Procedures*, a final report to the Army Research Institute, Contract MDA903–83–C–0189, July.

Polanyi, Michael (1958) *Personal Knowledge*. Chicago: University of Chicago Press.

Polanyi, Michael (1967) *The Tacit Dimension*. New York: Anchor.

Rosaldo, Renato (1986) 'Ilongot hunting as story and experience', in V.W. Turner and E.M. Bruner (eds), *The Anthropology of Experience*. Urbana and Chicago: University of Illinois Press.

Smith, Barbara Herrnstein (1980) 'Narrative versions, narrative theories', in *On Narrative*, 1980.

Suchman, Lucy (1987) *Plans and Situated Actions: the Problem of Human–machine Communication*. Cambridge: Cambridge University Press.

Turner, Victor (1980) 'Social dramas and stories about them', in *On Narrative*, 1980.

Turner, Victor W. and Bruner, Edward M. (eds) (1986) *The Anthropology of Experience*. Urbana and Chicago: University of Illinois Press.

10
Folk Explanation in Language Survival

Carol A. Padden

In very fundamental ways, languages are collective memories. We need only look at cases of language death, when languages are replaced by a more dominant language, to remind us that living languages are those in which the speakers agree to remember them. Dyirbal, a collection of dialects spoken in the north-eastern corner of Australia, is a particularly instructive example of language loss through organized forgetting. Citing a disinterest in Dyirbal and its irrelevance to their increasingly modern life-styles, younger members of the Dyirbal community not only avoid using Dyirbal with whites and among each other, but they avoid using it with Dyirbal elders. They complain that older speakers further contribute to their disinterest in Dyirbal by correcting or ridiculing the little Dyirbal they do use. For these speakers, English has become the language of choice, representing the generation's shift away from the traditional life of their elders. After a single generation, only older speakers remain committed to the use of Dyirbal and the 'collective memory' for that language may be lost to future generations (Schmidt, 1985).

Other languages have been dying less dramatically, although in much the same pattern. The replacement of Scottish Gaelic by English has been taking place for hundreds of years. Various disruptions through the history of the Scottish Highlands, from land clearances carried out in the 1800s to introduce sheep farming to the deterioration of the indigenous fishing industry, have all slowly but inexorably diminished Gaelic in favour of English (Dorian, 1981; 1985). As familiar contexts for Gaelic embedded in traditional fishing communities were replaced by contexts in which English was required, each new generation of children failed to learn more of the language: they failed to contribute to the collective memory of the language for future generations. Today there are very few complete speakers of Scottish Gaelic; most of those who now speak it are 'semi-speakers' and can only use it interspersed with English (Dorian, 1977; 1981).

Dramatic change and disruption are not necessarily fatal to

languages, as illustrated by the large influx of Latin vocabulary into Old English in the sixth century. The infiltration of Latin brought new possibilities, including concepts ideal for the rise of Christianity throughout Europe (McCrum, Cran and MacNeil, 1986). But what seems to characterize dying languages is loss without replacement or expansion. Instead of the two-term tense system used by older speakers of Dyirbal, in which there is a marked form for future and an unmarked for all other references to time, younger speakers of Dyirbal have lost the future tense marking, leaving only an unmarked form for all tenses (Schmidt, 1985). Modern speakers of Gaelic have lost the masculine gender marking in the language, further reducing the class of gender distinctions.

Crucially, in the case of language death, almost as dramatic as the disappearance of structures is the disappearance of an explanation for why speakers of a language should continue to use and remember the language. As the following report of an English–Gaelic bilingual shows, speakers of dying languages find that the contexts in which they can use the language are shrinking, leaving what Dennison (1977) finds to be the demise of dying languages: the realization that 'there is nothing left for them appropriately to be used about'.

> See, when you go to the shops, here, or when you meet people on the road, and they don't understand, well, you've got to speak the language they understand and that's the English. There's more English in the parish now than there is of Gaelic, and before we were born it was more Gaelic than English. See, times have changed. People's changed with it. (Dorian, 1981: 104)

Speakers need a tradition of explanation about the language that helps them organize social forces for remembering it. The Gaelic speaker offers an entirely reasonable explanation, perhaps overly reasonable, of pressures that justify non-use of Gaelic. In the case of Dyirbal, not only have younger speakers replaced their parents' language with English, but they seem to have replaced their parents' mythology about the place of Dyirbal in their lives. Today, when younger speakers of Dyirbal and Gaelic talk about their use of their ancestors' language, they do not repeat their parents' references to tribal and language identity; instead they use themes of resignation and dismissal, of futility in face of the dominant language, as in this comment by a Dyirbal speaker about his language: 'Talking Duwal [everyday Dyirbal] to a waybala [white man] – it's like singing and you're ashamed of your voice . . .' (Schmidt, 1985: 18). Use of Dyirbal is associated with 'backwardness' and a traditional life that is increasingly at odds with their modern practices. In Nahuatl, an Aztecan language being replaced by Spanish, younger speakers do not show shame, but their association of Nahuatl with the ways of the past achieves much of the same ends: in their explanations about Nahuatl, they position the language remotely from the circumstances of their everyday lives (Hill and Hill, 1977).

American Sign Language (ASL), a natural sign language used by communities of Deaf people in the United States and Canada, has many of the social features of languages under threat like Dyirbal, but unlike Dyirbal, it seems to be thriving.[1] A primary feature in the memory of ASL, one that is perhaps absent in younger-generation Dyirbal and Gaelic, is the community's collective explanation about the central place of the language in their everyday lives. In stories and anecdotes that the group tell about their language, themes of regeneration, preservation and transmission are common currency. Such collectively held explanations can be seen as ways of collectively reminding each new generation of the special circumstances of becoming a native speaker of the language.

As in Dyirbal, there are dislocations across generations of ASL users. Young deaf children, more often than not, do not learn ASL at birth. Only about 10 per cent of all deaf children are born to parents who are also deaf. Of this number, most, but not all, have deaf parents who use ASL. This leaves the large majority of other deaf children without access to ASL until later in life, if at all. The ages at which deaf children learn ASL vary widely, from the small number of deaf children who learn at birth to the larger numbers who learn by age six, when they attend school with other ASL users, and there are sizeable numbers of teenage and adult learners of ASL. Like Dyirbal, ASL must also co-exist with a powerful dominant language, English. ASL is very rarely the official language of social institutions that govern the early lives of deaf children, notably the school.

But from all indications, ASL has managed to sustain its vitality over nearly two centuries of tenuous transmission, with each new generation learning mostly from non-relatives rather than the family. There are no reliable official counts of primary users of ASL in North America, but based on the number of users known to social-service agencies, a conservative estimate is about 200,000 (Padden and Humphries, 1988).

There may be a good explanation as to why ASL remains tenacious in face of strong pressures from the more dominant English-speaking community. English is a spoken language, communicated primarily by speech. For Deaf people who do not hear, the inability to access speech would appear to make English a difficult, if not impossible, alternative to ASL. However, there have been, over the years, alternatives to ASL for Deaf people. A powerful alternative has been the signed English systems in which ASL is reconfigured in forms which are putatively more reminiscent of English structure (see Ramsey, 1988). Additionally, there are orally based forms of communication among deaf people where sign language is used in a sharply reduced form. While these form of communication exist, they have not replaced, nor have they displayed a dominance equal to that of, ASL in the North American Deaf community.

Very little has changed over the years in terms of how ASL is learned by new generations of signers; it is still unusually hard to learn. Yet ASL has remained surprisingly durable despite the lack of a strong institutional base for maintenance of the language throughout its history. ASL continues to have currency among Deaf communities in the United States and Canada and is slowly gaining ground in official institutions outside of the Deaf community. One measure of its growing recognition is the number of colleges and universities which now allow ASL to be used to meet hearing students' language requirements (*San Diego Tribune*, 27 January 1989).

Certainly one of the most interesting stories about the survival of ASL has been the community's flexibly changing explanation over time about why the language needs to be remembered. To understand the history of explanations about ASL, a brief history of the mythological roots of such explanations is necessary. Many 'stories' about ASL are framed as stories about the uniqueness of the language and how Deaf people came to use it in place of speech. Stories about the earliest use of ASL can ultimately be traced back to a folk tale told in deaf clubs in France about the founder of a public school for deaf children in Paris: the Abbé de l'Epée. Epée, a priest in search of a calling in the late years of his life, was introduced to the deaf daughters of a widow, and decided to organize a small school for deaf children. His initial success with the children attracted funds from the city and a distinguished benefactor, Louis XVI; his school grew to serve seventy-two deaf children by 1785. At the time of his death in 1789, Epée was a minor celebrity and left behind a legacy of several students and disciples who went on to establish additional schools, including a deaf man, Laurent Clerc. With Clerc, the American story of origins begins. In 1816, Clerc travelled to America with an Episcopalian priest, Thomas Hopkins Gallaudet, to help establish the first public school for deaf children in America. Clerc introduced his native French Sign Language as the first language of the school. Nearly two centuries later, ASL and FSL are no longer mutually intelligible, although they share a common base (Lane, 1984).

The popular version of how Epée came to his calling is still told in dramatic form in deaf clubs throughout France. Described in an account of a trip taken throughout France by myself and my husband (Padden and Humphries, 1988), 'the story of the Abbé de l'Epée' is almost always a preface to an official deaf-club event, to remind visitors such as ourselves of the significance of Epée to Deaf people in France. When these stories are told, it is clear that they are not merely anecdotes, but variations on a stylized folk-tale, to be rendered in heightened, lyrical form. One version, recorded by us at one such event, appears below:

> The Abbé de l'Epée had been walking for a long time through a dark night. He wanted to stop and rest overnight, but he could not find a place to stay, until at a distance he saw a house with a light. He stopped at the house, knocked at the door, but no one answered. He saw that the door was open, so he entered the house and found two young women seated by the fire sewing. He spoke to them, but they still did not respond. He walked closer and spoke to them again, but they failed again to respond. The Abbé was perplexed, but seated himself beside them. They looked up at him and did not speak. At that point, their mother entered the room. Did the Abbé not know that her daughters were deaf? He did not, but now he understood why they had not responded. As he contemplated the young women, the Abbé realized his vocation.

The theme of the tale is essentially religious as it draws on motifs of a light at the end of a dark road and a warm fire. At the light, Epée is introduced to two deaf women and undergoes a transformation. His transformation was perhaps the most powerful motif of all, one which would acknowledge his role in the formation of a national community of deaf people in France. Officially, Epée founded a school for deaf children but he had also created a community of deaf children who were housed together for most of their formative years, children who would later form a secondary community of adults around the core of the school. In some versions of this tale, Epée is proclaimed the father of sign language, the inventor of the language of deaf people. Although the credit is misplaced – no individual can create a language, only generations of speakers can – Epée is symbolically the catalyst for the formation of a community of deaf people that continues to this day (Lane, 1984; Padden and Humphries, 1988).

The Epée tale is 'reincarnated' in various forms in the United States in the person of his student, Laurent Clerc. Each year, deaf children at the American School for the Deaf in Hartford, Connecticut perform celebrations of the day Clerc and Gallaudet founded their school, the first school for deaf children in the United States. In much the same style of Founding Fathers' mythology, deaf children at the American School for the Deaf in Hartford,

Connecticut re-enact how Clerc met Gallaudet and agreed to leave his homeland to sail with him across the Atlantic.

Increasingly, however, this kind of story-telling is being supplanted by a modern variation, one that is much less religious, much less centred around persons such as Epée or Clerc and Gallaudet. The new explanation for the place of ASL in the everyday lives of Deaf people is essentially 'scientific', not because it exhibits features of academic or scientific discourse, but because it is self-reflective and driven by references to features of 'language' and 'culture', vocabulary which until very recently did not belong to the group.

This transition from the religious or the mythical in stories about ASL to the 'scientific' mirrors a profound change in the community itself, best summarized in terms of the emergence of a deaf middle-class, a professional class of deaf people who now dominate myth-making in the community, including explanations about their language. The new folk explanation about ASL, if we examine it closely, has not lost its mythical roots, but it has taken on new vocabulary and new kinds of representations that cast it in a decidedly modern light. These new representations form the basis for ways of talking about the place of the language in Deaf people's lives, ways that reflect replacements to earlier explanations without loss.

The crucial role of the middle class in myth-making about ASL underscores the relationship between control of social resources and opportunities for remembering. Survival of minority languages is, as Dorian (1981) notes, dependent not on the numbers of speakers but on *who* is using the language. Catalan is a classic example of a stable minority language thriving in what would otherwise be a hostile situation. Used by the political élite in the Catalonian region of Spain (Woolard, 1983), Catalan has maintained its integrity in the face of pressures from the larger nation-state in which Castilian is spoken. Each new generation of Catalan speakers, including the children of merchants and power brokers of the state, are expected to learn the language. By dominating myth-making about their language, the economically established class maintains resources for remembering the language.

The thematic shift in the folk explanation about ASL can best be illustrated by comparing selections taken from two popular Deaf news magazines, one in 1950 and the second in 1989. In 1950, a few issues after the inauguration of a new magazine for Deaf people, the *Silent Worker*, the editor's page featured a stern editorial on the subject of 'The Sign Language'. The theme was a familiar one to Deaf people: the sign language was in serious danger of deterioration owing to pressures surrounding it. There were 'oralists' who demanded elimination of the sign language from schools for deaf children in favour of teaching speech. Readers were exhorted to join forces and work to preserve the language. The vocabulary features the popular explanation for the language of the Deaf community in America: it is known simply as 'the sign language', it is characterized by the fact that it is not speech. The editor could not use the word 'grammar' in reference to sign language; he instead uses the word 'standard' which he argues derives from 'custom'. And in recognition of good signing, the editor refers to it as 'art' because it is carefully constructed and pleasing to see.

> Anyone who has been observant can detect a vast difference between the sign language in use today and that of a quarter of a century or so ago . . . What has happened will be considered by some as changes due to the passing of time, while others will call it plain and simple deterioration. At any rate, the sign language is in danger of becoming a lost art unless something is done by the deaf to keep it at a standard where it can be considered the medium of conversation of a cultured people.
>
> There is no grammar in the sign language. There is no standard authority by which it is determined that one sign is correct and another is incorrect, but custom has given us a fairly good standard, and we recognize a correct and incorrect form of usage. . . . (*Silent Worker*, February 1950, p. 2)

The themes in this editorial are solidly rooted in older worries about sign language. In a filmed lecture made by the National Association of the Deaf in 1913, the president of the organization gives an emotional and rousing speech on 'The preservation of the Sign Language', resounding much of the same themes that appear in this editorial. Users of the sign language must always 'protect and guard their language' against larger forces that conspire to eliminate the language. These malevolent forces seek to 'trap and imprison' Deaf people against their will by forcing them to abandon sign language for speech. In his powerful closing, the president invokes the deity as he acknowledges the sign language as 'the noblest gift God has given to Deaf people'.

In a recent issue of the *Silent News*, a popular Deaf newspaper published monthly, 'the sign language' has taken on a new name: it is now called 'American Sign Language', popularly referred to in its abbreviated form, ASL. The following article, reporting on a development in a Deaf community in Canada, is filled with quasi-scientific references:

> On the evening of December 6, 1988, a private member's resolution was passed unanimously which recognizes the cultural uniqueness of the deaf community and ASL as a distinctive language with its own grammar

and rules of usage. It is now recognized as the true and complete first language of Deaf Manitobans.
The resolution received the unanimous support of all the parties. . . . Gary Doer, leader of the New Democratic Party, concluded the debate by congratulating the Deaf Community for bringing forward this resolution and spoke of his party's pride in being able to 'support their resolution to have their distinct society and distinct culture with their language, the [*sic*] American Sign Language [recognized]'.
Lawrence Zimmer, president of the Winnipeg Community Center of the Deaf, said 'This resolution marks the first time a government in Canada has officially recognized ASL and Manitoba leads the other provinces as a model in recognizing ASL.' Several American states have also recognized ASL as the language of deaf people, including California, Michigan and Texas. (*Silent News*, February 1989)

As these two selections illustrate, the popular explanation about ASL has changed dramatically, over time as short as a single generation. In 1950, the *Silent Worker* used 'the sign language'; in 1965, a book on the structure of the language (Stokoe, Croneberg and Casterline, 1965) added a qualifier and called it 'the American sign language' to distinguish it from other distinct, unrelated sign languages of the world, thus broadening the world pertinent to Deaf people to include other nations and other languages. In 1980, at the centennial celebration of the founding of the National Association of the Deaf, their national convention featured public workshops in 'the structure of American Sign Language'. Not only was the article dropped, but the language achieved final autonomy as all three words were capitalized. The transition from the lower-case to the capitalized, from the generic to the specialized, is but a single example of a profound shift in how Deaf people in the United States refer to their primary language.

What precipitated such a profound change in vocabulary and ways of talking about ASL? Numerous factors have been cited: the popularization of the civil-rights language extending to not only ethnic groups but disabled groups as well and new paradigms for research in deaf children and signed language which draw from disciplines of linguistics and anthropology. But these are frames of explanation which come from outside of the community; what changes took place within the community to cause such a wide scale appropriation of this vocabulary? What is often overlooked in this critical transformation beginning in the early 1970s is the emergence of new patterns of work life in Deaf communities in the United States and Canada, one that would demand a new vocabulary for their language, one to match the new social contexts in their everyday lives.

Until about the middle 1960s, the primary occupations for deaf people in the United States were either the 'solitary' trades (shoe repair, upholstery, printing or factory assembly) or as school teachers or dormitory supervisors (Braly and Hall, 1935; Crammatte, 1987; Cronenberg and Blake, 1966). Teaching at that time had little of the trappings of 'professional' life: there were few requirements on type of training other than a college degree, and sometimes not even this was required. Deaf people were insulated from the ranks of management; nearly none were elevated to principals or supervisors in their schools. The working-class standard within the community was so predominant that it was entirely appropriate and common for deaf teachers to moonlight as printers or upholsterers to supplement their small teaching incomes.

Perhaps an important signal of changes in the economic lives of Deaf people was the formation of a National Theatre of the Deaf (NTD) in 1967. Funded initially by a grant from the Department of Health, Education and Welfare, the NTD was awarded enough money to form a permanent theatre. They assembled a repertory of deaf actors and accepted national and international bookings for performances featuring deaf actors in revues they had never before performed – in college theatres, city halls and mainstream auditoriums. These actors had long been community performers; they were well known to the community for the folk entertainment they provided at deaf clubs, picnics and conventions, but the novelty of the NTD was the promise of full-time employment as actors. Many left their jobs as school teachers or printers to be thrust in the public light as actors. The popular entertainment they had provided for the small community of Deaf people was now transformed into an expensive spectacle for the hearing public (Miles, 1974). As they travelled to Deaf communities throughout the United States and Canada, the NTD presented an image of the specialized Deaf professional, one who could earn a living at something other than the traditional trades.

The 1970s were remarkable for another change: the professionalization of teachers of deaf children. The expansion of the access mandate for the handicapped (section 504 of the Civil Rights Act, passed in 1974) and the rapid increase in public funding made it economically lucrative for public schools and universities to offer 'mainstreamed' programmes for deaf children. Colleges and universities began to provide disabled students with support services, including Deaf students with sign-language interpreting. The general trend towards professionalization in teaching extended to teachers working with deaf children. Certificates and master's degrees were required for new positions. New specializations were offered: 'counsellors for the deaf', 'elementary education', 'post-secondary education, etc.' highlighting the burgeoning industry of special education in the 1970s and 1980s.

The 1970s also marked the appearance of another profession: the ASL teacher. As public interest in ethnic diversity increased, the demand for adult classes in ASL exploded, to an estimated 50,000 new students each year in the language (*San Diego Tribune*, 27 January 1989), with classes in colleges and universities and in increasing numbers, in high schools. The professionalization of ASL teaching has probably more than any other field contributed to the introduction of the disciplines of linguistics and anthropology into mainstream Deaf life. Teachers of sign language became, within a few short years, newly recast as teachers of a language, ASL.

There were several consequences of the emergence of professionalization within the deaf community, the most significant of which was new social tensions between the middle class and the working class within the community. Teachers now no longer moonlighted as printers; they lost interest in the traditional social organizations of the community, especially the segregated deaf clubs, and sought out new affiliations outside of the community. Deaf clubs in the United States today have nowhere near the popularity they once enjoyed in the 1940s and 1950s when the clubs were packed every weekend night. After the Second World War, the Los Angeles Club of the Deaf was at the height of its strength; it owned a building in the centre of town and was the political and social centre of the deaf community. It is now defunct, its social and political functions distributed elsewhere in the community (DeBee, 1985).

The flight of Deaf people from the traditional club has variously been blamed on television, the video-cassette recorder and the telephone. As the argument goes, Deaf people turn to more private pursuits and they lose interest in the traditional group activities. But again, the new interest in this technology was not uniform within the community, but promoted most heavily by the new middle class. Along with their new economic lives came a desire for the trappings of middle-class life: to conduct one's business by telephone instead of the traditional face-to-face encounter and to participate in the consumption of televised goods.

Their new economic status brought about new types of political agendas, ones that promoted technological expansion in the community. In 1964, Robert Weitbrecht adapted surplus Western Union tele-typewriter machines for use across telephone lines, and a small group of Deaf people purchased for the first time a telephone in their homes which allowed them to use these machines for typed communication with each other. By 1988, Deaf organizations in the States of California, New York and Minnesota had successfully lobbied for free distribution of these machines to any Deaf person subscribing to the telephone service (Telecommunications for the Deaf, Inc., 1988). Bowing to intense political pressure from Deaf social-service agencies, in 1987 the public-utilities commission in California began providing free 'relay' services using operators to link calls between a user of a tele-typewriter device with those who did not have one. After six months, the volume of calls rose to approximately 40,000 calls per *week* made to the relay service in the State of Calfornia alone (California Public Utilities Commission, 1987). There are now continuing efforts to persuade the federal government to expand this service nation-wide. In 1981, a federally funded private organization began providing 'closed captions' on network television which appear only on televisions equipped with a specially purchased decoder. These English subtitles appeared on regularly scheduled network- and cable-television programming. In 1989 an estimated 375 hours of closed captioning per week were featured on network, cable and pay channels provided by at least four independent captioning companies (National Captioning Institute, 1988).

These social and political changes are accompanied by new ways of talking about their language. Deaf people began using a vocabulary that reflected the specialization of their work lives, a vocabulary that included special names for not only ASL but other varieties of signing. What was formerly referred to as 'the sign language' was now divided into several different categories, each with distinct labels, reflecting new cultural sensibilities about appropriate and inappropriate language behaviour. Forms of signing which depart from ASL and mimic some structural features of English are called 'Sign English'; individuals who use this form of signing run the risk of being judged as overly compliant to the dominant language. Another form of signing, called 'SEE', an acronym for a pedagogically developed system, Signing Exact English, has much more drastic departures from ASL where many forms are judged as 'odd' and ungrammatical. Signing in SEE is highly stigmatized in the community, drawing suspicion and ridicule. With each new label are new types of tensions, new ways of collectively evaluating the language behaviour of the group. These tensions are played out in a number of rich ways, reflecting rapid cross-generational change (see Padden and Humphries, 1988 for further discussion).

Deaf people's contexts for learning and living, formerly called 'custom', are renamed, as the *Silent News* segment illustrates, as instances of 'cultural uniqueness' and 'distinctiveness'. While the community has always promoted a theme of uniqueness organized around their unusual language, these new ways of referring to the group as a 'culture' and a 'society' are new ways of acknowledging the group's minority status in the face of pressures to assimilate. Instead of the deity, the traditions of science and pluralist humanism have become the new standards for themes about self-justification.

These thematic shifts are not specific to the Deaf community; other minority languages, notably Navajo (National Education Association, 1987) and Athabaskan (Paul, 1980; Scollon and Scollon, 1979) have also turned to self-conscious enterprises such as linguistic analyses of their languages in an attempt to maintain survival, with varying results. Perhaps this self-conscious appropriation of scientific vocabulary has been successful in the case of ASL because of how it is thematically intertwined with the changing economic and social lives of Deaf people. As the *Silent News* article illustrates, unlike in Dyirbal, younger Deaf people see ASL as a key emblem of their own future, one which lays claim to cultural uniqueness and to co-existence with English.

The survival and maintenance of a language is typically thought of in terms of maintaining access to that language. The argument presented here is that 'living' languages also depend on sharing folk explanations that remind speakers of the language's central position in everyday life. Folk explanations are fundamentally ways of collectively remembering the significance of what a language is to a particular culture, of privileging certain explanations above others. The collective memory for a language is embodied in the collective memory that is formed in justifications, explanations, the rhetorical organization of accounting for the necessity of the survival of a language such as ASL. In this way, the 'folklore' of a language contributes to the organization of social resources for maintaining the language in the face of pressures from the outside.

Notes

An earlier version of this essay was presented at the Center for Language, Politics and Culture, University of Chicago, May 1989. I thank David Laitin, David Middleton and Tom Humphries for instrumental suggestions.

1. Lower-case 'deaf' is used when referring to the audiological condition of not hearing, and upper-case 'Deaf' when referring to a particular group of deaf people who share a sign language such as American Sign Language (ASL) – and a culture.

References

Braly, Kenneth and Hall, Percival (1935) 'Types of occupations followed', in *The

Federal Survey of the Deaf and Hard of Hearing. Gallaudet College Normal Department in collaboration with the Office of Education.

California Public Utilities Commission (1987) *Report on Funding Problems Involving Deaf and Disabled Telecommunications Services*. San Francisco, CA: California Public Utilities Commission.

Crammatte, Alan (1987) *Meeting the Challenge: Hearing Impaired Professionals in the Workplace*. Washington, DC: Gallaudet University Press.

Cronenberg, Henry and Blake, Gary (1966) *Young Deaf Adults: an Occupational Survey*. Arkansas Rehabilitation Service.

DeBee, James (1985) *The LACD Story*. Film distributed by Beyond Sound, Los Angeles, CA.

Dennison, Norman (1977) 'Language death or language suicide?', in W. Dressler and R. Wodak-Leodolter (eds), *Language Death*, special issue of *International Journal of the Sociology of Language*, 12: 13–22.

Dorian, Nancy (1977) 'The problem of the semi-speaker in language death', in W. Dressler and R. Wodak-Leodolter (eds), *Language Death*, special issue of *International Journal of the Sociology of Language*, 12: 23–32.

Dorian, Nancy (1981) *Language Death: the Life Cycle of a Scottish Gaelic Dialect*. Philadelphia: University of Pennsylvania Press.

Dorian, Nancy (1985) *The Tyranny of Tide*. Ann Arbor, MI: Karoma Press.

Hill, Jane and Hill, Kenneth (1977) 'Language death and relexification in Tlaxalan Nahuatl', in W. Dressler and R. Wodak-Leodolter (eds), *Language Death*, special issue of *International Journal of the Sociology of Language*, 12: 55–70.

Lane, Harlan (1984) *When the Mind Hears*. New York: Random House.

McCrum, Robert, Cran, William and MacNeil, Robert (1986) *The Story of English*. New York: Viking Press.

Miles, Dorothy (1974) 'A history of theatre activities in the deaf community of the United States', Master's thesis, Connecticut College, New London.

National Captioning Institute (1988) *Captioned Newsletter*. (Falls Church, VA: National Captioning Institute), Fall.

National Education Association (1987) *Navajos: a Source Booklet for Teachers and Students*. Washington, DC: National Education Association Human and Civil Rights.

Padden, Carol and Humphries, Tom (1988) *Deaf in America: Voices from a Culture*. Cambridge, MA: Harvard University Press.

Paul, Gaither (1980) *Stories for My Grandchildren*, transcribed and ed. by R. Scollon. Fairbanks, Alaska: Alaska Native Language Center.

Ramsey, Claire (1988) 'Signing Exact English: the meaning of English in deaf education', mimeograph, University of California, Berkeley.

San Diego Tribune (1989) 'Educators in debate on language', 27 January.

Schmidt, Annette (1985) *Young People's Dyirbal: an Example of Language Death from Australia*. Cambridge: Cambridge University Press.

Scollon, Ronald and Scollon, Suzanne (1979) *Linguistic Convergence; an Ethnography of Speaking at Fort Chipewyan, Alberta*. New York: Academic Press.

Stokoe, William, Croneberg, Carl and Casterline, Dorothy (1965) *A Dictionary of American Sign Language on Linguistic Principles*. Washington, DC: Gallaudet College Press.

Telecommunications for the Deaf, Inc. (TDI) (1988) *International Telephone Directory for TDD Users*. Silver Spring, MD: TDI.

Woolard, Kathryn (1983) 'The politics of language and ethnicity in Barcelona, Spain', dissertation, University of Pennsylvania.

11
Social Memory in Soviet Thought

David Bakhurst

Remembering Soviet Conceptions of Memory

The recent literature on collective or social memory contains two principal themes. The first emphasizes the significance of 'group remembering', of those social practices by which the members of a community preserve a conception of their past (see, for example, the chapters by Orr, Padden and Engeström et al. in this volume). Such practices, it is argued, must be brought from the periphery to the centre of social theory, for within them a community's very identity is sustained and the continuity of social life made possible. The second theme is the social constitution of individual memory. Here we find a radical challenge to the orthodox view that memory is located solely within the head, a challenge which suggests that the nature of individual memory cannot be analysed without essential reference to notions such as 'society', 'community' and 'history'.

This chapter is devoted primarily to the second of these themes. Any argument that memory is an essentially social phenomenon flies in the face of the individualist conceptions of mind dominant in Western philosophy and psychology and provokes a range of predictable, yet worrisome, objections. Thus, for example, it will be argued that memories are undeniably states of the brain, or at least of 'the mind', and to admit this is surely to locate memories in the individual head. Moreover, since 'remembering' is just an operation on memories, it is natural to hold that it too goes on in the head. Of course, the objection continues, we are certainly often caused to (mis)remember events by 'social interaction', but that is no more grounds to believe that memory is essentially social than my Siamese cat's reminding me of days spent in Toronto is grounds to believe that memory is essentially feline!

I propose to examine whether such objections can be met by arguments in the writings of certain Soviet thinkers, in particular the psychologist Vygotsky (1896–1934). Vygotsky is well known to have advanced a theory of the social genesis of the mental, and work on memory was central to the development of his position. Vygotsky's legacy is thus an obvious place to look for an argument that memory, at least in its 'higher', human manifestations, is a capacity of social origin. Furthermore, other like-minded Soviet thinkers seem to offer ways to strengthen and develop Vygotsky's position. In the work of his contemporary, V.N. Voloshinov (1895–1936), for example, we find the suggestion that, since remembering involves giving a *reading* of the past, our memories are the products of interpretative skills that are social in both nature and origin. In addition, the philosopher Evald Ilyenkov (1924–79) offers a vision of how human social activity serves to preserve the past in the present, thereby constituting a form of memory irreducible to happenings in any individual mind. The Soviet tradition, then, seems rich in resources for defending a strong reading of the social foundation of individual memory, and one which represents a marked departure from the prevailing orthodoxy in the West.

However, as we construct the argument we shall find ourselves drawn inexorably into a discussion of the first of the two themes, into cultural issues of collective remembering and forgetting. The writings of these Soviet thinkers are often complex and inaccessible; to use them as a resource requires much interpretative work. In this, the socio-political context in which they were produced is inescapable. It determines both the agenda and the mode of expression of these thinkers' contributions. Especially significant is that social and political circumstances have greatly determined how this Soviet work has been remembered, commemorated and (in some cases) forgotten by subsequent generations. The way in which it is read today is the outcome of a long and sometimes mysterious process of collective remembering.

Consider Vygotsky, a thinker with an explicit political commitment to founding a 'Marxist psychology', whose views took shape in the lively intellectual milieu of the Soviet Union in the 1920s. He was immediately recognized as a leading figure within Soviet psychology, a discipline charged with making a significant contribution to the success of the new regime. Accordingly, Vygotsky often addressed questions with immediate consequences for Soviet educational, clinical and academic policy, and spoke on them to audiences with established political commitments. This role must have called for considerable sensitivity to the political situation, and as the climate darkened with the rise of Stalinism, he and his group moved the base of their activities from Moscow to the Ukraine. Nonetheless, soon after his premature death in 1934 his works were banned and erased from the history of Soviet psychology. For twenty years his thought was preserved by his former collaborators, largely within an oral culture which itself was influenced greatly by changing social and political circumstances. Since Vygotsky's rehabilitation in 1956, his works have been gradually republished in the USSR, where he is celebrated (in some circles) as the founder of Soviet psychology, though the issues to which his views are read as contributions have changed since the time he was writing. Vygotsky's brilliance has also been recognized in the West, though many who cite him know his work only from a small number of translations, some highly edited.

This history makes clear that the path leading from Vygotsky's contribution to our present ways of representing it is an extremely tortuous one. It is therefore significant that the political context of his work is virtually ignored by modern scholars concerned to recover it. Vygotsky is portrayed not so much as a Marxist theorist who negotiated a tense political environment and whose work was a victim of Stalin's purges, but as a thinker whose genius 'transcend[s] historical, social and cultural barriers' (Wertsch, 1985: 231; also Levitin, 1982: ch. 1; and Luria, 1979: ch. 3). It is easy to understand why this is so. The very political climate that has so influenced how Vygotsky has been remembered has also served to inhibit discussion of its influence. There is therefore no tradition in the USSR of scholars writing serious histories of their disciplines. The situation has been scarcely easier for the few Western scholars in the area, for those who have mastered the Soviet tradition have done so by entering the oral culture which sustains it, and have found themselves subject to the constraints and responsibilities such participation entails.[1]

Vygotsky has been our example, though similar stories could be told about Voloshinov (see pp. 216–21 below) and Ilyenkov (see Bakhurst, in press). It is clear that anyone who would seek to draw on their insights must be aware that their work has been preserved in a collective memory under extraordinary constraints and pressures, paramount among which is that the nature of the process of remembering must never be explicit in the memories it yields. The memory of their tradition suffers from amnesia about its own history. This cannot be irrelevant to the interpretation of the substance of their theories.

Thus, issues from both the themes identified above will be interwoven in what follows. We shall explore how a strong reading of the social nature of memory can be defended by appeal to these Soviet thinkers, but we shall do so in a way which reveals the collective memory of their contributions to be an exceedingly relevant factor in the construction of that defence.

Vygotsky's Conception of Mind and Memory

I begin with an exposition of Vygotsky's basic theoretical stance –

faithful, I hope, to the way it is usually remembered. I shall then present Vygotsky's account of memory.[2]

Vygotsky made his entrance on the Soviet psychological stage in 1924, when he presented his 'Methods of reflexological and psychological investigation' to the 2nd All-Russian Psychoneurological Congress in Leningrad. In this and other early works, his main concern was to identify what he called the 'crisis in contemporary psychology'. Vygotsky argued that, like most young disciplines, psychology was a battleground of warring schools. Gestalt psychology, psychoanalysis, behaviourism and Stern's personalism, for example, all seemed to offer insightful suggestions for a theory of mind. Yet since each school employed an explanatory framework incommensurable with the others, it was impossible to integrate their separate findings. It therefore seemed that psychology would become a unified science only if one of the competing schools defeated its rivals. But, Vygotsky argued, none of the existing frameworks had sufficient explanatory power to ground a science embracing all psychological phenomena. Each offered insights in its own limited domain but threatened to become vacuous when its principles were applied more widely.

The weakness of the prevailing schools was clearest in their failure to make good sense of *consciousness*, the phenomenon Vygotsky saw as the principal subject of psychological enquiry. Psychologists, he argued, adopted either one of two strategies to its analysis: either (a) a subjectivism which treated consciousness as a sui generis, non-physical phenomenon occurring in a self-contained, 'inner' world of thought and accessible to the investigator only through 'non-scientific' modes of enquiry (for example, through the introspective reports of the subject or phenomenological analysis); or (b) an objectivism which held that consciousness is reducible to a set of objectively observable physical happenings governed by a specifiable set of physical laws (of which laws relating 'stimuli' to 'responses' seemed the most likely candidates).[3]

For Vygotsky, the debate between these positions was structured by two widely held beliefs: first, that the two strategies exhausted the possible alternatives for a theory of consciousness; and secondly, that psychology could be scientific only by adopting a reductionist approach. Neither belief could be true, Vygotsky argued, since both subjectivism and objectivism were untenable. While the former transformed the mind into an occult entity beyond the reach of scientific investigation, the latter brought the mental into the ambit of science only by doing violence to the higher forms of human psychological functioning. Thus, if the Soviets were to establish a scientific psychology, their task was to carve a path between subjectivism and objectivism.

Vygotsky's proposals for this project invoked a sharp distinction (drawn from Marx and German classical philosophy) between 'elementary' and 'higher' mental functions. The elementary functions are said to be characteristic of purely animal, in contrast to human, psychological functioning. They include non-verbal thought (simple problem-solving activity), involuntary memory and primitive forms of attention, perception and desire. Vygotsky held that an organism possesses such elementary functions purely in virtue of its physical organization, and that they develop and mature as the organism develops physically. The character of a creature's elementary mental functioning is thus determined exclusively by natural or biological considerations, and *can* therefore be explained in reductionist terms.

In the case of the human child, however, psychological development is not limited to the natural evolution of the elementary mental functions with which it is endowed by nature. On the contrary, the child comes to develop 'higher' mental functions which are distinctively human in kind. These include verbal thought, intellectual speech, voluntary or 'logical' memory and attention, and rational volition. The higher mental functions form a system or totality of psychological capacities said to be 'interfunctionally' related; that is, the character of each is determined by the developing relations it bears to the others. On a Vygotskian perspective, consciousness is portrayed not as one among other higher mental functions, but as the system of interrelated functions itself. As the child develops this system, so its innate, elementary functions are totally restructured or cease to exist altogether.

Crucial to Vygotsky's position is the claim that higher mental functions are qualitatively distinct from, and hence irreducible to, their primitive antecedents. This is so, he argues, because higher mental functions represent *mediated* forms of psychological activity.

Vygotsky's elusive notion of mediation underwent significant development as his work progressed. It first emerged as a response to stimulus–response (S–R) theory. Vygotsky held that in analysing psychological states in terms of behavioural responses caused by specific stimuli, the S–R model was unduly unidirectional. It concerned itself with the effect of the world on the psychological subject without considering the subject's effect upon the world. Vygotsky demanded that psychology be concerned with the consequences of human action as well as its causes, arguing that the distinguishing feature of human behaviour is that human beings actively change their environment so as to create new stimuli. We fashion special artefacts, tools, solely for the purpose of manipulating the world and, thereby, the behaviour the world elicits from us. And we create signs, a class of artificial stimuli that act as means to control behaviour (by tying a knot in a handkerchief we create the cause of our own later remembering). Hence the relation between world and subject is never simply unidirectional, but is constantly mediated by tool and sign. The linear connection between stimulus and response is replaced by a triangular inter-relation between stimulus, response and 'mediational means'.

From the outset, Vygotsky stressed how the creation of the sign vastly broadens the horizons of the human mind. Just as the tool helps us master nature, so the sign enables us to master our own psychological functioning (hence Vygotsky calls signs 'psychological tools'). We employ signs to draw attention, to aid recall, to represent problems in a way that facilitates their solution and so on. Hence, Vygotsky concluded, the key to the nature of higher psychological functioning lies in the mediating role of the sign.

As Vygotsky explored this role, so he became fascinated with the notion of *meaning* and, with this, his account of mediation underwent an important change. While earlier he had portrayed signs as a class of special, artificial stimuli, operating alongside other 'natural' stimuli, he now came to focus on our ability to create elaborate symbolic systems, such as natural language and math-ematics, which mediate our relation to the world through the power of representation. For the later Vygotsky, the introduction of such semiotic systems of mediation completely transforms our psycho-logical relation with reality. We now stand in relation not just to a brute, physical world, but to an *interpreted* environment, an environment conceived as being *of a certain kind*. This being so, our behaviour can never be simply 'called forth' by the world in itself. Rather, we act in the light of some reading of reality, a reading that renders our behaviour an appropriate response to the perceived situation. On this view, our actions are more like conclusions to arguments than effects of physical causes. Such a position places the semiotic at the very heart of the relation between psychological subject and reality; the world is an environment endowed with significance, and the trajectory of the subject's behaviour is determined by the meaning he or she takes from the world.

While Vygotsky's early account of mediation may seem a variation on the stimulus–response theme, the later 'semiotic' approach represents a radical departure from that framework. The attraction of the S–R model derived from its promise to establish law-like relations between stimuli and responses described in purely physical terms. However, on this Vygotskian position, the subject's acts, and the situation in which they are undertaken, are described not in a purely physical vocabulary, but in words which render those actions meaningful in the light of the subject's interpretation of the situation. Moreover, the project of establishing laws which relate world and action described in such meaning-laden terms is hopeless. Thus, when Vygotsky recognized semiotic analysis to be 'the only adequate method for analysing human consciousness' (quoted in Wertsch, 1985: 79), he strengthened his conviction that a scientific psychology cannot be achieved by treating human mental capacities on the model of physical phenomena governed by natural laws.

Thus, for Vygotsky, for psychology to be scientific it must employ, not a reductionist method, but one adequate to the specific character of semiotic mediation. To this end, he urged that psychology become a 'socio-historical' discipline. The systems of mediation which form the fundamental basis of human mental functioning are, he argued, cultural creations. They are products of social history and are preserved in human activity, in what might be called the 'interpretative practices' of the community. The development of the child's higher mental functions must therefore be seen, not as the outcome of some process of natural evolution, but as the consequence of the child's appropriation, or 'internalization', of such interpretative practices, in particular, natural language. Psychology must therefore make systematic sense of the child's assimilation into its culture and of the qualitative transformations in mental functioning that this precipitates. These transformations will be captured, Vygotsky believed, only by a 'genetic' account which reveals the history of the developing system.

The Vygotskian model, then, is this. The human child enters the world endowed by nature with only elementary mental capacities. The higher mental functions constitutive of human consciousness are, however, embodied in the social practices of the child's community. Just as the child's physical functions are at first maintained only through connection with an autonomous system beyond the child, so his or her psychological life is created only through inauguration into a set of external practices. Only as the child internalizes or masters those practices is he or she transformed into a conscious subject of thought and experience.

The distinction between 'elementary' and 'higher' mental functioning is central to Vygotsky's research on memory. Vygotsky describes 'natural' memory as 'mechanistic' or 'instinctive'. This is purely involuntary recall, evoked spontaneously by some state of affairs in the world. The infant may be caused to remember his or her last meal by the smell of the next, or that it is bath time by the sound of water running, but these are cases of remembering over which he or she exercises no control. In contrast, the higher mental function of memory permits us to search at will for an image or an account of the past. In such voluntary or 'logical' memory, it is not

that the mind is just prompted to 'go and get' an image by some
encounter in the present; rather, the past is deliberately recalled for
a determinate reason. Vygotsky argues that logical memory is made
possible by the mediating power of signs. By using signs as aids to
memory human beings are able deliberately to control the conditions of their future remembering. He writes:

> The very essence of human memory is that human beings actively
> remember with the help of signs. It is a general truth that the special
> character of human behaviour is that human beings actively manipulate
> their relation to the environment, and through the environment they
> change their own behaviour, subjugating it to their control. As one
> psychologist has said [Dewey], the very essence of civilization consists in
> the fact that we deliberately build monuments so as not to forget. In the
> knotted handkerchief and the monument we see the most profound,
> most characteristic and most important feature which distinguishes
> human from animal memory. (Vygotsky, 1931a: 86; 1978: 51)

In the late 1920s and early 1930s, Vygotsky and his colleagues
designed a series of experiments to explore the influence of
mediational means on children's remembering. These experiments
used cases of simple memorization and recall. Children were asked
to remember lists of words, the members of which bore no special
relation to one another. Vygotsky compared the children's performance in cases (a) where they were required to recall the list 'by
heart', and (b) where they were offered symbolic devices in
conjunction with the list as an aid to recall. (From the various
accounts of these experiments, it seems that these symbolic aids
were usually schematic representations, pictographs, of objects
which, when suitably interpreted, could be linked with the word to
be recalled; thus a picture of a jug of milk might be employed to
help remember 'cat', and so on.) Vygotsky found that, after the age
of four, children were able actively to employ the pictographs as
memory aids and that their performance was significantly improved
as a result. Conducting similar experiments with adolescents and
adults, however, revealed that for these groups the availability of
symbolic aids caused a less significant improvement in their ability
to remember, and sometimes even inhibited their performance.
Vygotsky concluded that the adolescents and adults were indeed
employing symbolic devices as aids to memory, only now their
techniques had become *internalized*; they worked with various
mnemonic systems which they had silently invented in thought, and
which could easily be disrupted if they were forced to use external
aids.

   Vygotsky consistently maintained that these findings confirmed
his general theory of the mind. His interpretation of their

significance, however, altered in a way which reflects the shift in his understanding of mediation. At first, Vygotsky argued that the use of signs as memory aids can be understood on the stimulus–response framework: signs figure as artificial stimuli which we consciously employ to cause ourselves to respond in the desired way. Thus in 1929 he wrote that mediated memory can 'be divided without remainder into the same conditional reflexes as natural memorizing' (1929: 420). However, as he began to consider exactly how signs facilitate remembering, Vygotsky came to recognize that the character of semiotic mediation could not be explained by extending the S–R model.

In some versions of the experiment, the children had been allowed to choose which pictures to use as memory aids. The experimenters noticed some unexpected choices and asked the children to explain how these signs had helped them remember. Thus, for example, one child who had chosen a sketch of a camel to remember the word 'death' explained that the camel was in a desert where its rider was dying of thirst. Another, who had taken a picture of a crab on the beach to remind him of the word 'theatre', replied that the crab spends all day looking at a beautiful stone (also represented in the picture) as if it were at the theatre (Vygotsky, 1931a: 242). Faced with such accounts, Vygotsky moved to the position that the sign could not be represented as simply an extra, artificial link in a causal chain. Rather, it seemed that the sign facilitated remembering as part of an argument in which the word to be recalled figured as the conclusion. It was as if the child used the picture to construct a story which led to the required word as its punchline. This suggests that the structure of mediated memory must be seen as *narrative*, delivering its results in virtue of the meaning of the employed mediational means, and not as straight-forwardly causal. We remember by constructing narratives which require the recall of past events for their intelligible completion.

I believe that as Vygotsky came to appreciate this insight, he began to regret that the memory research he and his collaborators had so far conducted had not explored in more depth the semiotic dimension of mediation. In 1932, he wrote that while their research had successfully set the debate on memory into motion, it had not produced definitive conclusions. 'Moreover', he continued, 'I am inclined to think that it represents a colossal oversimplification, even though at first it was often criticised as unduly complex [because of its rejection of a linear S–R model]' (Vygotsky, 1932: 392 (the passage is mistranslated in Vygotsky, 1987); see also Leontiev and Luria, 1968: 345). Sadly, Vygotsky's life was cut short before he could take this work further.

What, then, does this work contribute to our understanding of the claim that individual memory is a social phenomenon? Vygotsky, it appears, would endorse a very strong reading of that claim. Throughout his career he held that the distinctive character of human memory is that it is mediated by symbolic means which are cultural phenomena; the human child thus only acquires the higher mental function of memory in so far as he or she is led to appropriate those cultural means by adult members of the community. Moreover, towards the end of his life Vygotsky began to develop a distinctive view of symbolic mediation which introduced a yet richer conception of the social basis of memory. On this view, to possess 'logical memory' involves more than a sensitivity to the instrumental use of cultural artefacts; it requires the ability to engage in the specific practice, social in origin, of the production and interpretation of narrative forms constructed in that most powerful of socially forged symbol systems, natural language. Furthermore, Vygotsky holds that the genesis of logical memory entails the complete reorganization of the elementary forms of memory the child is given by nature. Thus, it seems that, for Vygotsky, no form of adult memory can be rendered intelligible without essential reference to the concepts of 'society', 'community' and 'culture'.

Yet, however attractive Vygotsky's conclusions may be, his writings fail to provide arguments which would make them truly compelling. The experimental research, though often novel and ingenious, remains underdeveloped, relying heavily on Vygotsky's theoretical framework for its interpretation. In turn, while I have argued elsewhere that Vygotsky's theoretical vision can be developed and defended (for example, Bakhurst, 1986), it remains that much of it consists of pregnant insights in need of further elaboration. This is particularly true of his later ideas about semiotic mediation, the development of which would appear so central to the defence of his mature position.

Thus, if Vygotsky's legacy is to provide the basis for a theory of social memory we must find ways to strengthen and develop his insights. A natural place to look is the work of his students and followers, Soviet and Western, who see themselves as members of a 'socio-historical' school of psychology with its roots in Vygotsky's thought. Such a project, however, draws us inevitably into a discussion of how Vygotsky's thought has been preserved in the complex collective memory of the Soviet psychological tradition.

Vygotsky Remembered

Two crucial elements of Vygotsky's insights about memory which need further clarification are, first, his conception of the relation of 'the cultural' and 'the natural' which lies behind his distinction between 'higher' and 'elementary' mental functions; and secondly, his understanding of the nature of semiotic mediation. I want to argue now that the way these features of Vygotsky's thought are presently remembered has been significantly influenced by events largely forgotten in accounts of his contribution – namely, the suppression of his writings in the 1930s. This will prove relevant to how Vygotsky's position should be defended and strengthened.

The Soviet intellectual climate at the beginning of the 1930s was dominated by the 'Great Break', a period of massive cultural revolution in which groups of young Party activists in several fields called for the 'bolshevization' of their disciplines and accused the first generation of Soviet scholars of a multitude of sins. These included 'formalism', a failure to produce theories responding to the practical needs of the Soviet state, inadequate 'party spirit' and a betrayal of the 'Leninist stage' in Soviet thought. Although these criticisms were mostly without substance, they were forcefully endorsed by the Party leadership and precipitated a wave of persecution throughout the Soviet academic world.

Little has been written about the bolshevization of Soviet psychology in 1931 (see Joravsky, 1978; Kozulin, 1984: 20–3; Valsiner, 1988: 95–8). It seems, however, to have drawn inspiration from the assault on philosophy of the previous year (see, for example, Bakhurst, 1985; and in press: ch. 2; Joravsky, 1961; Valsiner, 1988: 89–95). In this, Abram Deborin's school of Hegelian Marxism, which had dominated Soviet philosophy for several years, was accused of 'menshevizing idealism', an epithet apparently coined by Stalin himself. The same heresy was soon detected among psychologists, including Konstantin Kornilov, the influential 'reactologist' who directed the institute where Vygotsky and his collaborators pursued their research. Menshevizing idealism in psychology, it was asserted, was 'rotten at its roots [and] contributed nothing to the practice of socialism, but rather slowed down socialist development with the help of its objectively reactionary, pessimistic theories' (Zalkind, 1931: 19). The currency of such dangerous nonsense in the capital must, at least in part, explain the Vygotsky group's decision to move the base of their activities from Moscow to Kharkov in 1931. As the mythology around menshevizing idealism grew, to remain under Kornilov's patronage was to risk not only the preservation of the group's research, but the very lives of its members. Several philosophers perished in the prison camps, and there was no reason to believe that psychologists guilty of 'ideological deviation' would not suffer a similar fate.

Although the move to the Ukraine secured the survival of the group's research, Vygotsky's legacy remained under threat. After his death in 1934, his work suffered a barrage of criticisms. First, he was attacked for 'cosmopolitanism'; that is, for showing respect for the work of 'bourgeois' authors. Secondly, despite his well-known critique of conventional intelligence tests, his interest in psychological testing was dismissed as reactionary. Such testing, it was argued, always serves to preserve the status quo, representing the less educated as the intellectually inferior. Finally, a third criticism zeroed in on just those elements of his work we have found central to his views on memory. He was argued to have emphasized semiotic and cultural phenomena at the expense of practical activity in his account of the development of consciousness, thereby implying that the mind is formed not in 'material production' (that is, in the process of object-orientated activity with material objects), but through interpersonal relations (that is, participation in communicative and representational practices). He was thus held to have misrepresented the relation between the 'natural' and 'cultural' forces in development, overemphasizing the significance of enculturation, while ignoring the (purportedly) natural process of the child's material interaction with the physical environment.

The second of these criticisms is usually cited as most significant. When the Central Committee's 1936 decree outlawed 'paedology', a form of child psychology which emphasized testing, his work was withdrawn from public consumption for the remainder of the Stalin era. However, the effect of the third criticism's assault on Vygotsky's semiotic and cultural emphasis should not be underestimated. With Vygotsky's writings banned, his legacy could only be preserved in an oral culture sustained by his followers. I shall argue that this third criticism significantly shaped how his disciples came to represent and remember his contribution.

Despite its more scholarly tone, the third criticism is no less ideologically motivated than the others. In this period, Soviet polemicists would typically seek to discredit their opponents by associating their work with some form of philosophical idealism. This is precisely the criticism's implication: Vygotsky's recognition of the fundamental explanatory importance of 'ideal' phenomena such as meaning and communication is perceived as an idealist departure from the orthodox dialectical materialism of the founders of Marxism, with its emphasis on human beings' material transformation of nature. In the Stalin period, no one would have made such a critique without realizing its implications; the third criticism is certainly a charge of ideological heresy in academic guise. It is therefore interesting that those who raised this criticism included members of the Kharkov group itself, such as Alexei Leontiev, and

Peter Zinchenko, who explicitly attacked Vygotsky's account of memory.

To be fair, the Kharkovites may initially have made this criticism in self-defence. With Vygotsky in disgrace, they surely had little choice but to distance themselves from his views. Since they could not avoid an ideological pronouncement, it would have made sense to produce a critique with some theoretical content, for this at least required them to give voice to Vygotsky's position in the course of 'refuting' it. Nonetheless, whatever the Kharkovites' intentions, the criticism quickly became a habitual feature of their presentation of Vygotsky's work. Indeed, they began to define their research programmes in response to these supposed weaknesses of their teacher's contribution. A good illustration is Leontiev's 'activity theory' (see Leontiev, 1975), an approach which has proved very influential in both the USSR and the West. The initial rationale for this theory, which identifies object-orientated activity (*predmetnaya deyatel'nost'*) as the developmental root of human consciousness, was precisely to replace Vygotsky's cultural-semiotic orientation with an account on which psychological operations 'are determined by the actual [that is, physical, material] relations between child and reality' (Leontiev, 1935: 14). Thus, it seems that the scholars responsible for keeping Vygotsky's thought alive through the Stalin period internalized an image of his work which, paradoxically, had its origins in the Stalinist attempts to suppress it.

This image endured long after Vygotsky's rehabilitation. In 1968, for example, in an article introducing Vygotsky's work to a Western audience, Leontiev and Luria still maintain that his 'cultural-historical' theory of the mind 'has serious shortcomings related to an insufficient regard for the formative role of man's practical activity in the evolution of his own consciousness. Thus it counterposed too sharply the various forms of conscious activity of social origin with "naturally formed" mental processes' (1968: 342). These remarks reproduce almost exactly the case Peter Zinchenko made against Vygotsky some thirty years earlier (P.I. Zinchenko, 1936; see Kozulin, 1986: xlv–lii).

Since the Kharkov school was the guardian of the oral culture which preserved Vygotsky's memory, it is natural that its representation of his contribution should have had enormous influence on how it is presently interpreted and assessed. An excellent example of this influence is found in James Wertsch's exposition of Vygotsky's views in his recent *Vygotsky and the Social Formation of Mind* (1985). Wertsch's text is the finest book-length treatment of its subject, Western or Soviet. One of the reasons for its excellence is its author's ability to speak with the authority of a participant in the debate; Wertsch absorbed himself in the Soviet tradition and arrived at his interpretation through discussions with many of Vygotsky's former collaborators (Wertsch, 1985: xiii). A consequence of this, however, is that Wertsch's presentation reproduces the Kharkovites' critique. Despite his admiration for many of Vygotsky's ideas on meaning, Wertsch argues that Vygotsky was wrong to take a semiotic category, 'word meaning', as the basic unit of analysis of consciousness in his classic *Thought and Language*. Wertsch proposes the notion of 'tool-mediated action' as an alternative unit, which he draws from the work of Vladimir Zinchenko (Peter Zinchenko's son) (V.P. Zinchenko, 1985; see Wertsch, 1985: 196–7, 205–8). Moreover, like the Kharkovites, Wertsch maintains that Vygotsky's work is flawed for its opposition of the natural and the cultural, which, he suggests, is so radical that it precludes a proper explanation of their interaction (1985: 197–8). Again like the Kharkovites, Wertsch argues that this weakness is 'directly tied' to Vygotsky's account of meaning (1985: 197). Thus, we find that our contemporary reading of Vygotsky bears the mark of a critique forged in the political machinations of the Stalin era.

At the opening of this section, two elements of Vygotsky's thought were identified that need further elaboration if his suggestions about the social essence of memory are to be developed into a theory: namely, his conception of semiotic mediation and his view of the relation between the natural and the cultural. We now know it is unlikely we shall find the inspiration for this project in the work of those psychologists to whom we owe the preservation of Vygotsky's legacy. On the contrary, since the Stalinist attempt to suppress Vygotsky, the collective memory of his thought has consistently marginalized its semiotic orientation and sought to reshape his view of the natural and the cultural.

We have no choice, then, but to look beyond the mainstream of Soviet psychology. We turn first to a theorist of language also working in the 1920s, V.N. Voloshinov, whose ideas have been argued to complement Vygotsky's (Emerson, 1983; Wertsch, 1985: 224–6). In Voloshinov, I believe, we find the means to develop the semiotic dimension of Vygotsky's stance. As expected, the result is a radical view of the cultural constitution of mind in general, and memory in particular.

Voloshinov and the Textuality of the Mental

Our present understanding of Voloshinov's work is a legacy of collective remembering every bit as intriguing as the processes which have preserved Vygotsky's thought. Little is known of

Voloshinov's life. He was born in 1895 or 1896 in St Petersburg, where he began studying law some twenty years later. By 1918 he had moved to the provincial town of Nevel where he became a member of the circle of thinkers surrounding the now famous scholar Mikhail Bakhtin. He followed Bakhtin to Vitebsk and eventually back to Leningrad in 1924, where he re-enrolled at the University. His interests included not only philosophy of language and psychology, but also musicology and composition. He died in 1936 from tuberculosis. During his life, he published two books, a critique of Freud, *Freudism* (1927), and his seminal work on language, *Marxism and the Philosophy of Language* (1929). He also produced several scholarly articles.

The controversy around Voloshinov's legacy began when, at the commemoration of Bakhtin's 75th birthday in 1970, the Soviet linguist Vyacheslav Ivanov declared that Bakhtin was the author of the major works published under Voloshinov's name. Ivanov's claim was neither confirmed nor denied by Bakhtin himself and, as the evidence remains inconclusive, scholars have taken contrasting views of its authenticity. In the West, Bakhtin's biographers, Katerina Clark and Michael Holquist, are adamant that he is the true creator of these works, while Voloshinov's translator, I.R. Titunik, maintains that Voloshinov should be regarded as their sole author. Still others, such as Tzvetan Todorov, treat Voloshinov's writings as one voice among many in a Bakhtinian discourse and call their author 'Voloshinov/Bakhtin' (Todorov, 1984: 11).

This puzzle is significant because the different solutions invite different readings of the Voloshinov texts. Those who treat Bakhtin as their author must somehow account for the Marxist idiom, conspicuously absent in Bakhtin's other writings. Clark and Holquist, for example, suggest that references to Marxism were added to the already completed texts to get them past the censor (see, for example, 1984: 159). From such a perspective, the Voloshinov texts are read primarily as stages in the development of Bakhtin's theory of language, 'ventriloquated' through the persona of an orthodox Marxist (Holquist, 1983: 6).

However, once Voloshinov is restored as author, it becomes possible to treat the professed Marxism of these writings as central to their concerns. We can read Voloshinov as setting out, like Vygotsky, to re-establish his discipline on a Marxist foundation. Indeed, there are many interesting parallels between the way in which Voloshinov and Vygotsky conceived their respective projects. For example, Voloshinov shares Vygotsky's conviction that a Marxist approach must carve a path between subjectivism and objectivism. Hence, in the philosophy of language, Voloshinov seeks an account which neither treats the individual mind as the sole source of meaning, nor construes meaning as a property of language conceived as a purely formal system (see 1929: II, ch. 1). Moreover, also like Vygotsky, Voloshinov argues that an alternative to subjectivism and objectivism is possible only by recognizing the essentially social nature of the phenomenon under study. For Voloshinov, the linguistic act (the utterance) 'is born, lives, and dies in the process of social interaction . . . Its form and meaning are determined basically by the form and character of this interaction' (1926: 105). Finally, despite his emphatic appeal to the social, Voloshinov is as anxious as Vygotsky to avoid a crude social reductionism. He denies the claim of some Soviet Marxists that the content and character of a discourse is exhaustively explained merely by citing the socio-economic situation of its participants. Rather, he advances a more subtle position where the voices we may choose to speak in, and the ways in which we shall be understood, can be rendered intelligible only in light of the specific character of the communicative practices of our culture, which, in turn, cannot be explained without essential reference to socio-economic factors.

On this reading, Voloshinov's texts appear as part of a developing Soviet Marxism, rather than as a contribution to another intellectual tradition dressed up in Marxist attire. I find such an interpretation more plausible than that of Clark and Holquist. The parallels with Vygotsky – whose professions of Marxism are now generally regarded as sincere – are only one example of how Voloshinov's work is indeed characteristic of (good) Soviet Marxist writing in the 1920s. Although Bakhtin was certainly clever enough to write in this idiom, had he done so he would in fact have been making a contribution to Soviet Marxism. Thus, in so far as the argument for Bakhtin's authorship of the Voloshinov texts falsely implies that their Marxism is a deceit (or alternatively that Bakhtin was a Marxist), we should continue to consider Voloshinov to be their author.

Voloshinov offers an argument to strengthen Vygotsky's account of the social nature of memory. The first step is Voloshinov's claim that conscious psychological states are essentially semiotic phenomena. They are all forms of *utterance* (or 'verbal reaction'). This is true, he argues, not only of those mental states which are clearly propositional in content (such as beliefs, desires, intentions and so on), but also of the human subject's conscious experiences. 'Experience exists', he writes, 'even for the person undergoing it only in the material of signs' (1929: 28). Hence, for Voloshinov, there is no pure experience of reality to which we later give words;

rather, the world we confront is one already organized by our modes of representation. There is no access to reality which is not an interpretation or reading, and hence the world our minds encounter is always a read or interpreted world (1929: 26). Hence, he concludes, '*consciousness itself can arise and become viable only in the material embodiment of signs*' (1929: 11; his emphasis); if we deprive consciousness of its semiotic content, there would be 'absolutely nothing left' (1929: 13).

It follows that the content of our mental states is determined by the meaning of the signs which comprise them. However, Voloshinov maintains that signs do not possess meaning in virtue of their intrinsic properties, but take on meaning only in the context of communicative practices in which they are interpreted. And as we have seen, Voloshinov argues that these practices are essentially social in nature. Thus, just as the author's intentions do not fix the meaning of his or her work, so the individual subject does not occupy a logically privileged position in the interpretation of their own thoughts. He writes:

> The verbal component of behaviour is determined in all fundamentals and essentials of its content by objective-social factors. The social environment is what has given a person words and what has joined words with specific meanings and value judgements; the same environment continues ceaselessly to determine and control a person's verbal reactions throughout his entire life.
>
> Therefore, nothing verbal in human behaviour (inner and outward equally) can under any circumstances be reckoned to the account of the individual subject in isolation; the verbal is not his property but the property of his *social group*. (Voloshinov, 1927: 86; his emphasis)

Thus, if 'the reality of the inner psyche is the same reality as that of the sign', and the sign derives its meaning from the interpretative practices of the speech community rather than the fiat of the individual (Voloshinov, 1926: 105; 1927: 79; 1929: 86), then psychological states are, in a very strong sense, socially constituted phenomena. 'The logic of consciousness', it transpires, 'is the logic of ideological communication, of the semiotic interaction of the social group' (1929: 13).

What, then, of memory? For Voloshinov, the social essence of individual memory follows simply from the social constitution of all mental states. On this position, to remember is always to give a reading of the past, a reading which requires linguistic skills derived from the traditions of explanation and story-telling within a culture, and which issues in a narrative that owes its meaning ultimately to the interpretative practices of a community of speakers. This is true even when what is remembered is one's own past experience

(Voloshinov, 1927: 87). For Voloshinov, memory can never be understood as an immediate relation between the thinking subject and some private mental image of the past. The image, he argues, becomes a phenomenon of consciousness only when clothed with words, and these owe their meaning to social practices of communication.

Voloshinov's argument greatly strengthens Vygotsky's position. First, while Vygotsky's studies focus narrowly on a specific species of remembering (recall of lists mediated by the use of mnemonic devices), Voloshinov's conclusions are quite general in kind, stressing the social constitution of all forms of individual memory. Secondly, Voloshinov's account is consonant with Vygotsky's account of higher mental functioning in general and of the role of semiotic mediation in particular. Moreover, Voloshinov's writings contain material that suggests how a Vygotskian theory of semiotic mediation might be developed; they are a rich resource for any theory which represents consciousness as a developmental achievement precipitated by the internalization of communicative practices broadly understood.

Significantly, if we enrich Vygotsky's account of semiotic mediation by appeal to Voloshinov, we find further support for the former's radical opposition of the 'cultural' and the 'natural'. Like Vygotsky, Voloshinov insists that the human mind cannot be treated as a natural phenomenon intelligible by appeal to natural laws. Mind is 'a socioideological fact and, as such, beyond the scope of physiological methods or the methods of any other of the natural sciences' (Voloshinov, 1929: 25). We are not born conscious persons, but *become* them after 'a second birth, a *social* birth' when we 'enter into history' (Voloshinov, 1927: 15; his emphasis). Such Vygotskian thoughts abound in Voloshinov's writings. However, Voloshinov's position suggests a way to defend them not articulated by Vygotsky himself. For Voloshinov the relation between the contents of consciousness and the physical states of the thinking subject's body or brain is analogous to the relation between the meaning of a text and the physical form in which it is inscribed, or (to use a more dynamic model) between the content of a drama and the physical states of the medium (for example, television) in which it is presented. Just as it would be hopeless to look for law-like relations between the physical states of a television and the semantic content of the programmes it transmits, so the search for laws relating the states of mind and brain is, for Voloshinov, equally in vain.

As the Kharkovites would have predicted, taking the notion of semiotic mediation seriously leads to a very radical opposition between 'the natural' and 'the cultural', and to the view that human psychological phenomena are essentially cultural, and hence non-natural, phenomena. Such a view was too radical for many of the Kharkov group, and may be too much for Vygotsky's Western followers. If Vygotsky's thought is developed in this way, there seems little prospect of reconstructing him as an 'emergent interactionist' (Wertsch, 1985: 43–7), where the mental development is traced as the outcome of an interplay between biological and cultural forces. For while Vygotsky and Voloshinov hold that mind emerges in the transformation of the child's biological being through the appropriation of culture, they both invoke quite different principles of explanation for the natural and cultural realms. It thus seems unclear how there could be a systematic *theory* of their interaction.

Ilyenkov, Ideality and Memory

Now that we have used Voloshinov's writings to strengthen Vygotsky's position we should briefly return to the Kharkovites' critique of it. We observed that, since the 1930s, the mainstream of Soviet psychology has tended to marginalize the semiotic dimension of Vygotsky's legacy. The theories of his best known followers (Leontiev, Luria, Zaporozhets, Galperin, Meshcheryakov, V. Zinchenko and Davydov) have all taken 'object-orientated activity', rather than a semiotic category, as the basis of the genesis of consciousness. It would seem that there are two conflicting trends within Soviet Marxist philosophy of mind; one, seen in the contributions of Vygotsky and Voloshinov, which treats semiotic mediation as the foundation of consciousness, and another, dominant since the 1930s, which adopts the 'activity approach'.

It would be wrong, however, to take the conflict between the two camps at face value. The judgement that there is a genuine theoretical incompatibility between them, itself a product of the 1930s, may owe more to the political shadow-boxing of orthodoxy and heresy than to genuine argument.

This can be seen, I think, if we consider the work of Evald Ilyenkov, one of the most interesting Soviet philosophers of the modern period. In his work of the early 1960s Ilyenkov sought to revitalize Soviet philosophy after the stagnant years of Stalinism. Though he never referred to the thinkers of the 1920s, he reintroduced many issues and ideas which had been prominent in their debates. It is interesting, therefore, that despite his constant emphasis on activity as the foundation of the mental (which endeared him to Leontiev), Ilyenkov seems to share Vygotsky's and

Voloshinov's presupposition that there need be no grand opposition between the practical and the semiotic in a Marxist theory of the mind.

Consider, for example, Ilyenkov's theory of 'the ideal' (see Ilyenkov, 1962; 1977; a fuller exposition is given in Bakhurst, 1988; and in press: ch. 6). This theory is an attempt to explain the nature and possibility of ideal (that is, non-material) phenomena (for example, values, reasons, psychological processes and states) in the material world. Ilyenkov turns to the concept of activity for his explanation. A Marxist form of materialism, he argues, must hold that ideal phenomena are genuine constituents of objective reality that ultimately have their source in human activity. On this view, the natural world comes to embody non-material properties as objectified forms of social activity. Ilyenkov's argument pre-supposes, however, that the act of transforming nature is itself a semiotic act: by acting on the world, human beings endow their natural environment with meaning, with the significance which is its 'ideal form'. This is illustrated by appeal to a concept important to Vygotsky: the tool. An inanimate lump of matter is elevated into a tool through the significance with which it is invested by activity. It stands as an embodiment of human purpose in virtue of the way it is fashioned and employed by human agents. And the artefact created through the manipulation of matter by tools is, Ilyenkov argues, more than merely material because of the meaning it derives from incorporation into human practice.

Ilyenkov takes his theory of the idealization of the natural world very seriously, arguing that his account of the ideality of the tool and the artefact may be generalized into a wholesale theory of the relation of culture and mind. For Ilyenkov, 'humanity's spiritual culture', the total structure of normative demands objectively confronting each individual member of the community (including the demands of logic, language and morality), must be conceived not as a realm of super-material phenomena, but as patterns of meaning embodied in the form of our material environment through the influence of our activity. In turn, Ilyenkov argues that the capacity to think is just the ability to inhabit such a meaning-laden environment. For him, the higher mental functions must be seen primarily as capacities to engage in a certain species of activity: the negotiation of ideal properties and relations.

Like Vygotsky and Voloshinov, Ilyenkov argues that the human child does not possess the capacity to inhabit an idealized environment from birth, but is inaugurated into the relevant species of activity by adult members of the community. As the child masters or 'internalizes' these activities, so he or she becomes a thinking subject. Ilyenkov, again like Vygotsky, conceives of internalization as the appropriation of patterns of social meaning, as the assimilation of a culture, and he would accord language learning a special place in this process. But Ilyenkov would certainly not claim that the internalization of these patterns of meaning should be contrasted with engaging in 'real, practical activity', since, for him, to assimiliate a culture is to appropriate the forms of social activity which sustain it. To learn a language, for example, is to learn to manipulate a special class of artefacts, words.

Thus, for Ilyenkov, activity is the root of consciousness. It is so, however, only because in activity the natural world is invested with enduring patterns of meaning, the negotiation of which constitutes thought. In Ilyenkov's work, the practical and semiotic orientations in Soviet theory live in harmony.

Ilyenkov's contribution, however, offers more to the present discussion than the suggestion that there need not be a theoretical impasse between those trends of Soviet thought which take semiotic mediation as the unit of analysis of consciousness and those which adopt an 'activity approach'. His theory of the ideal offers another dimension to our account of social memory. Ilyenkov holds that the socially significant practices of the community represent thought made objective. Each human child enters the world to find the forms of activity which constitute thinking embodied in the community's activities and expressed in the shape impressed upon the physical environment by human labour. Just as our status as conscious subjects requires that we master these activities, so the continuity of our mental lives over time depends on the preservation of the world of shared significance the activities sustain. Thus, this idealized world of 'humanity's spiritual culture' can itself be seen as a form of memory, and one which is essentially collective in kind.

Conclusion

I have argued that a distinctive theory of the social nature of memory may be drawn from the work of three distinguished Soviet thinkers, Vygotsky, Voloshinov and Ilyenkov. This theory holds, first, that memory is a psychological function which is essentially social in origin; secondly, that memories are socially constituted states; and thirdly, that certain forms of collective activity represent a form of social memory, irreducible to the happenings in any individual mind, yet essential to the continuity of the mental life of each individual.

Our discussion revealed that the contributions on which we sought to draw have themselves been preserved by complex processes of collective remembering that have influenced how they are interpreted and commemorated today. In particular, we found that two ideas central to Vygotsky's conceptions of social memory have been marginalized in the Soviet tradition since the Stalin era – namely, the notion of semiotic mediation and the specific distinction between 'the cultural' and 'the natural' which follows from it. I have tried to tell a story which restores these ideas to the centre of discussion. Such a strategy does not, I believe, compromise the integrity of the Soviet Marxist tradition, despite the way it has perceived itself since the 1930s. It does, however, have some radical consequences. The account of social memory we have constructed is no self-contained theory but follows from a general conception of the social constitution of the thinking individual. This idea, which will seem wild and unscientific from the perspective of contemporary cognitive science, remains enigmatic and undeveloped. It is to be hoped that a greater understanding of this idea's Soviet past will lead to its fruitful elaboration in the future.[4]

Notes

1. It is notable that the scholars who offer the most detailed picture of the political setting of Vygotsky's work are the émigrés Alex Kozulin (1984; 1986) and Jaan Valsiner (1988).
2. For accounts of Vygotsky's theory see Bakhurst, 1986; Kozulin, 1986; Leontiev and Luria, 1968; Minnik, 1987; Valsiner, 1988; and Wertsch, 1985. My treatment in this section draws on Vygotsky, 1924; 1925; 1927; and 1934, and those writings which deal explicitly with memory (Vygotsky, 1929; 1931a; 1931b; 1932; and 1978).
3. Both strategies were represented in Russian psychology at the beginning of the century, the first by Chelpanov and other advocates of 'subjective psychology' who formed the psychological orthodoxy prior to 1917, the second by Pavlov, Kornilov, Bekhterev and the 'reflexologists' who sought an account of all psychological phenomena in stimulus–response terms. The latter approach won institutional supremacy immediately after the Revolution as most consonant with the Bolsheviks' call for a Marxist psychology built on scientific materialist foundations.
4. I am grateful to the British Council, the British Academy and the Committee on Research at the University of California, San Diego, for funding research which made this chapter possible. Thanks are also due to Christine Sypnowich and David Middleton for their insightful comments and suggestions on the manuscript.

References

Bakhurst, David (1985) 'Debornism versus mechanism: a clash of two logics in early Soviet philosophy', *Slavonic and East European Review*, June.
Bakhurst, David (1986) 'Thought, speech and the genesis of meaning: on the 50th anniversary of Vygotsky's *Myshlenie i rech''*, *Studies in Soviet Thought*, 31 (January).
Bakhurst, David (1988) 'Activity, consciousness and communication', *Quarterly Newsletter of the Laboratory of Comparative Human Cognition*, 10 (2).

Bakhurst, David (in press) *Consciousness and Revolution in Soviet Philosophy*. Cambridge: Cambridge University Press.

Clark, Katerina and Holquist, Michael (1984) *Mikhail Bakhtin*. Cambridge, MA: Harvard University Press.

Emerson, Caryl (1983) 'Bakhtin and Vygotsky on the internalisation of language', *Quarterly Newsletter of the Laboratory of Comparative Human Cognition*, 5 (1).

Holquist, Michael (1983) 'The politics of representation', *Quarterly Newsletter of the Laboratory of Comparative Human Cognition*, 5 (1).

Ilyenkov, E.V. (1962) 'Ideal' noe' ['The ideal'], in *Filosofskaya entsikolopediya, tom. 2 [Philosophical Encyclopaedia, volume 2]*. Moscow: Sovetskaya entsiklopediya.

Ilyenkov, E.V. (1977) 'The concept of the ideal', in *Philosophy in the USSR: Problems of Dialectical Materialism*, tr. by Robert Daglish. Moscow: Progress.

Joravsky, David (1961) *Soviet Marxism and Natural Science*. London: Routledge & Kegan Paul.

Joravsky, David (1978) 'The construction of the Stalinist psyche', in Sheila Fitzpatrick (ed.), *Cultural Revolution in Russia, 1928–1931*. Bloomington: Indiana University Press.

Kozulin, Alex (1984) *Psychology in Utopia*. Cambridge, MA: MIT Press.

Kozulin, Alex (1986) 'Vygotsky in context' in L.S. Vygotsky, *Thought and Language*, tr., rev. and ed. by Alex Kozulin. Cambridge, MA: MIT Press.

Leontiev, A.N. (1931) 'The development of the higher forms of memory', in his *Problems of the Development of Mind*. Moscow: Progress, 1981.

Leontiev, A.N. (1935) 'Ovladenie uchashchimisya nauchnymi ponyatiyami kak problema pedagogicheskoi psikhologii' ['The acquisition of scientific concepts by school pupils as a problem of pedagogical psychology'], in *Khrestomatiya po vozrastnoi i pedagogicheskoi psikhologii [Handbook of Developmental and Pedagogical Psychology]*, vol. 1. Moscow: MGU, 1980.

Leontiev, A.N. (1975) *Activity, Consciousness, and Personality*. Englewood Cliffs, NJ: Prentice Hall, translation, 1978.

Leontiev, A.N. and Luria, A.R. (1968) 'The psychological ideas of L.S. Vygotsky', in Benjamin B. Wolman (ed.), *Historical Roots of Contemporary Psychology*. New York: Harper & Row.

Levitin, Karl (1982) *One is not Born a Personality*. Moscow: Progress.

Luria, A.R. (1979) *The Making of Mind*. Cambridge, MA: Harvard University Press.

Minnik, Norris (1987) 'The development of Vygotsky's thought: an introduction', in Vygotsky (1987).

Todorov, Tzvetan (1984) *Mikhail Bakhtin: the Dialogical Principle*, tr. by Wlad Godzich. Manchester: Manchester University Press.

Valsiner, Jaan (1988) *Developmental Psychology in the Soviet Union*. Bloomington: Indiana University Press.

Voloshinov, V.N. (1926) 'Discourse in life and discourse in art', in Voloshinov (1927).

Voloshinov, V.N. (1927) *Freudism: a Critical Sketch*, tr. by I.R. Titunik and ed. in collab. with Neal H. Bruss. Bloomington: Indiana University Press, 1987.

Voloshinov, V.N. (1929) *Marxism and the Philosophy of Language*, tr. by Ladislav Matejka and I.R. Titunik. Cambridge, MA: Harvard University Press, 1986.

Vygotsky, L.S. (1924) 'Metodologiya refleksologicheskogo i psikhicheskogo issledovanie' ['The methodology of reflexological and psychological research'], in Vygotsky (1982a).

226   *Collective remembering*

Vygotsky, L.S. (1925) 'Soznanie kak problema psikhologii povedeniya' ['Consciousness as a problem in the psychology of behaviour'], in Vygotsky (1982a).

Vygotsky, L.S. (1927) 'Istoricheskii smysl psikhologicheskogo krizisa' ['The historical meaning of the crisis in psychology'], in Vygotsky (1982a).

Vygotsky, L.S. (1929) 'The problem of the cultural development of the child', *Journal of Genetic Psychology*, 36.

Vygotsky, L.S. (1931a) *Istoriya razvitiya vysshchykh psikhicheskikh funktsii [The history of the development of the higher mental functions]*, in Vygotsky (1983).

Vygotsky, L.S. (1931b) 'Predislovie k knige A.N. Leont'ieva *Razvitie pamyati*' ['Preface to A.N. Leontiev's *The Development of Memory*'], in Vygotsky (1982a).

Vygotsky, L.S. (1932) 'Lektsii po psikhologii' ['Lectures on Psychology'], in Vygotsky (1982b); tr. in Vygotsky (1987).

Vygotsky, L.S. (1934) *Myshlenie i rech' [Thinking and Speech]*, in Vygotsky (1982b); tr. in Vygotsky (1987).

Vygotsky, L.S. (1978) *Mind in Society*, ed. by Michael Cole, Vera John-Steiner, Sylvia Scribner and Elen Souberman. Cambridge, MA: Harvard University Press.

Vygotsky, L.S. (1982a) *Sobranie sochinenii, tom. 1: Voprosy teorii i istorii psikhologii [Collected Works, Vol. 1: Questions of the theory and history of psychology]*. Moscow: Pedagogika.

Vygotsky, L.S. (1982b) *Sobranie sochinenii, tom. 2: Problemy obshchei psikhologii [Collected Works, Vol. 2: Problems of General Psychology]*. Moscow: Pedagogika; tr. as Vygotsky (1987).

Vygotsky, L.S. (1983) *Sobranie sochinenii, tom. 3: Problemy pazvitiya psikhiki [Collected Works, Vol. 3: Problems of the Development of Mind]*. Moscow: Pedagogika.

Vygotsky, L.S. (1987) *The Collected Works of L.S. Vygotsky, Vol. 1: Problems of General Psychology*, tr. by Norris Minnik. New York: Plenum.

Wertsch, James V. (1985) *Vygotsky and the Social Formation of Mind*. Cambridge, MA: Harvard University Press.

Zalkind, Aron (1931) 'Psikhonevrologicheskii front i psikhologicheskaya diskussiya' ['The psychoneurological front and psychological discussion'], *Psikhologiya*, 4 (1).

Zinchenko, P.I. (1936) 'Problema neproizvol'nogo zapominaniya' ['The problem of involuntary memory'], in *Nauchnye zapiski khar'khovskogo gosudarstvennogo pedagogicheskogo instituta inostrannykh yazykov [The scientific record of the Khar'kov State Pedagogical Institute of Foreign Languages]*, vol. 1; tr. in *Soviet Psychology*, 22 (2) (1983–84).

Zinchenko, V.P. (1985) 'Vygotsky's ideas about units for the analysis of mind', in James V. Wertsch, *Culture, Communication and Cognition: Vygotskian Perspectives*. Cambridge: Cambridge University Press.

Index

oppositions, 12–13, 52, 60–78, 94–5, 102; and ideology, 52, 213, 217–18; nationalism, 91–3; reconstruction vs continuity, 81–3; in Soviet society and psychology, 204–5, 213–24
memory and individual cognition, 1, 6, 11, 15, 19, 23–4, 29, 33–5, 41–3, 47–8, 55–6, 72, 120–4, 126–8, 130, 135–6, 141, 143, 203; as accounts vs representations, 121–4, 134; development of in children, 38–41, 209–12; and emotion, 31–3, 39, 122, 129–33, 135–6; and higher mental functions, 207; rote memory, 131–2, 210; social origins, 203–4, 207, 209, 219; symbolic mediation, 36, 207–8, 210–11, 218–20; and volition, 139–40, 209–10
Mercer, N.M., 24, 26, 28, 37, 43
Merton, R., 5
metacognition, 11, 28–9, 30–1
Middleton, D.J., 8, 9, 23–43, 46, 56, 62, 134
Miles, D., 198
Miller, D., 58
Mills, C.W., 123, 126
Moscovici, S., 2, 61–2
Mulkay, M., 36, 37
Myerhoff, B., 187
myths, 52, 73, 99, 117, 195

Nagel, P.C., 93
Nairn, T., 64, 74
Neisser, U., 2, 36–7, 120, 121
Nerone, J., 4
Newman, E.S., 50
Nietzsche, F., 124
Norman, D.A., 6, 141–3

Ong, W.J., 33, 124
Orr, D., 16, 169–88, 203

Padden, C., 17, 190–201
Paletz, D.L., 118
Passerini, L., 3, 20
Peterson, M.D., 82
Plato, 136
Polanyi, M., 170
Potter, J., 36, 43, 62, 78
Powell, L., 95

Pratt, G., 51
Protagoras, 125

Radley, A., 9, 12, 46–58
Reagan, Ronald, 14, 108–18; popularity as media construction, 111–13; popularity in oral tradition, 113–18; popularity in polls vs media, 108–11
rhetoric and argumentation, 9, 11, 12, 14, 15, 19, 28–31, 38, 40, 61, 66–70, 120, 124–8, 131, 134, 159–67; and consensus, 26, 30–3, 66–7, 74
Robinson, M., 113
Rochberg-Halton, E., 47
Roosevelt, Theodore, 81, 91, 94, 96, 101
Rosaldo, R., 175, 180
Ryle, G., 135

Schmidt, A., 190–1
Schrager, S., 3
Schudson, M., 14, 108–18
Schwartz, B., 3, 8, 12, 13, 62, 81–105
Scribner, S., 6, 33
Shanks, M., 57
Sheehan, M., 113
Sherman, E., 50
Shils, E., 64, 82–3, 103
Shotter, J., 14–15, 46, 120–37
Smith, B.H., 176, 179
Smith, H., 115
social class, 49–50, 195, 199
Soviet socio-historical psychology, 2, 15, 18–19, 36, 139, 141, 203–24; Activity Theory, 16, 139–67, 214–16, 221
Starn, R., 3
Stokes, R., 66
Stokoe, W., 197
Stone, Rev. A.L., 84
Suchman, L., 6, 140, 172, 175, 176
Sullivan, W.M., 5
Sutton, D., 3
Swidler, A., 5

Taylor, L., 47
Thelen, D., 3
Thompson, K., 61
Tilley, C., 57
Tipton, S.M., 5
Todorov, T., 217
Turner, V., 175